Praise for *The Olive Farm*

"Rich with wonderful descriptions, adventures and prose that flows along with dreamy, floating ease, *The Olive Farm* is an exceptional addition to literature on living and loving France."
— *Telluride Watch*

"*The Olive Farm* enchants."
— *The Arizona Daily Star*

"Following [Drinkwater's] engaging story is like driving the hairpin turns that climb the hills above the French Riviera; the views are breathtaking, the blind corners frightening, and the safe arrival to the top a joyous relief. And the olives? After much work, an astonishing success."
— *Library Journal*

"Good-humored and well-written."
— *The Washington Post*

"Beautifully written with a great sense of humor, it captures perfectly the dreamy atmosphere of the south of France and its people, as we share her struggle to turn a dream into a reality."
— *Woman and Home Magazine* (London)

PENGUIN BOOKS

THE OLIVE FARM

Carol Drinkwater is a critically acclaimed actress. Among her numerous stage and screen performances she is probably most widely known for her portrayal of Helen Herriot in the BBC adaptation of James Herriot's *All Creatures Great and Small*. She divides her time between London and the south of France.

THE

A MEMOIR OF LIFE, LOVE AND OLIVE OIL

OLIVE FARM

IN THE SOUTH OF FRANCE

CAROL DRINKWATER

PENGUIN BOOKS

PENGUIN BOOKS

Published by the Penguin Group

Penguin Group (USA) Inc., 375 Hudson Street, New York, New York 10014, U.S.A.
Penguin Group (Canada), 90 Eglinton Avenue East, Suite 700, Toronto,
Ontario, Canada M4P 2Y3 (a division of Pearson Penguin Canada Inc.)
Penguin Books Ltd, 80 Strand, London WC2R 0RL, England
Penguin Ireland, 25 St Stephen's Green, Dublin 2, Ireland (a division of Penguin Books Ltd)
Penguin Group (Australia), 250 Camberwell Road, Camberwell,
Victoria 3124, Australia (a division of Pearson Australia Group Pty Ltd)
Penguin Books India Pvt Ltd, 11 Community Centre, Panchsheel Park, New Delhi – 110 017, India
Penguin Group (NZ), cnr Airborne and Rosedale Roads,
Albany, Auckland 1310, New Zealand (a division of Pearson New Zealand Ltd)
Penguin Books (South Africa) (Pty) Ltd, 24 Sturdee Avenue,
Rosebank, Johannesburg 2196, South Africa

Penguin Books Ltd, Registered Offices: 80 Strand, London WC2R 0RL, England

First published in the United States of America by the Overlook Press 2001
Published by arrangement with the with the Overlook Press,
Peter Mayer Publishers, Inc.
Published in Penguin Books 2002

19 20

THE LIBRARY OF CONGRESS HAS CATALOGED
THE HARDCOVER EDITION AS FOLLOWS:
Drinkwater, Carol.
The olive farm : a memoir of life, love, and olive oil
in the south of France / Carol Drinkwater.
p.   cm.
ISBN 1-58567-106-1 (hc.)
ISBN 0 14 20.0130 9 (pbk.)
1. Provence (France)—Social life and customs.
2. Drinkwater, Carol—Homes and haunts—France—Provence.   I. Title.
DC611.P961 D75   2001
944'.9—dc21   2001021096

Printed in the United States of America
Set in Adobe Garamond
Designed by Yellowstone Ltd.

For Michel, who lives life through colors richly,
A private story told out loud:
Je t'aime

ACKNOWLEDGMENTS

This book would have never existed without Michel. So it is to him that I first say thank you; for his encouragement, generosity and expansive love. Special thanks also to our families and friends who inhabit these pages.

At Ed Victor Ltd. I give enormous thanks to my agent and friend, Sophie Hicks, to Maggie Phillips, Hitesh Shah and Grainne Fox, all of whom help smooth the bumps in the running of my professional life, and to old pals, Chris Brown and Bridget Anderson, who are always there in hours of need.

My profound gratitude to a great team at The Overlook Press; especially to Tracy Carns for buying the book and for publishing it with such style and enthusiasm.

CONTENTS

Too much of a good thing can be wonderful.

—Mae West

Southwards into a sunburned otherwhere . . .

—W. H. Auden

PREFACE

The girls stare in dusty dismay.

"Is this the wonderful surprise, Papa?" asks Vanessa.

Michel nods.

Papa had promised them a villa with a swimming pool. Unfortunately, in his enthusiasm, Michel has omitted to mention that the pool is dry as a bone. Worse, not only is the pool's interior cracked, chipping and devoid of one drop of water, its faded blue walls and a fair portion of the base are overgrown with thickly entwined skeins of ivy.

"I need a swim!" wails Clarisse.

"We'll cut back the ivy tomorrow and fill it on Sunday, I promise."

I overhear this pledge as I stagger past with armfuls of cardboard boxes laden with ancient and practically useless kitchenware exhumed from cluttered cupboards in my London flat. Michel's promise is given casually but not without good intention, yet a doubt whispering in my ear tells me he may live to regret it—suppose we discover the pool leaks—but I choose not to voice this within earshot. In any case, my doubts are probably nothing more than the negativity born of a sleepless night.

We drove through most of the night to avoid the worst of the holi-daymakers who throughout yesterday had jammed the main arterial roads to a standstill. At around eight-thirty in the evening we approached the outskirts of Lyon only to discover that the *péage* had become a holiday resort in itself. The delay to pass through it was announced as two hours. So the French, in true French fashion, were grabbing the opportunity to attack a spot of dinner, which, of course, delayed matters further.

It was a colorful and fascinating spectacle. A line of traffic many miles long was peppered with families and pets seated on camping stools along-side their cars (the less organized spread picnic blankets out on the motorway surface). All were eating three-course meals and drinking copious amounts of booze. Aside from our general frustration, I found it highly entertaining. Strolling several miles away, I witnessed vehicle own-ers offering *dégustations* of their regional wine to fellow travelers, morsels of succulent dishes whipped up at the roadside, wobbling and brightly colored desserts passed on spoons up and down the traffic line, snippets of advice on the fine-tuning of an otherwise well-known recipe and, to round it all off, hands of cards accompanied by after-dinner coffee fol-lowed, in one or two instances, by a glass of calvados. What a knack the French have for turning any event into an opportunity to relish the finer points of eating!

By the time the jam was unjammed, I observed families, who had become the firmest of buddies with other roadside families, exchanging addresses in the way some folks do when they've passed a week or two at the same resort.

Once through the city of Lyon, we kept traveling, stopping only for a brief nap in a roadside parking lot, where poor Michel had to grab some sleep with the girls' dog, Pamela, attached to his ankle by her lead, to keep her from attempting an escape. And then on again before dawn, break-fasting outside Fréjus where half the local population was already gathered in bars, enjoying their first cognac of the day.

Now, having safely arrived after sixteen hours of such traveling, Pamela finally has been released from her confined space and is huffing at my side. Why has this infernal creature taken such a shine to me? "The dog needs a drink," I call. No one pays me heed.

"So, we'll have a pool in two days?" Again Vanessa, always the more exacting of the two girls. Michel nods and embraces both daughters, an arm wrapped around each. "Well, do you like it here? The house and all the grounds? I know it needs a lot of work, but the sun is shining, and it's very hot . . ." The final phrase of his sentence melts away in the midday swelter while the girls stare up at him as though he had single-handedly created a galaxy of suns. After their initial disappointment, they seem happy enough, and I am relieved about that.

I find an outdoor tap alongside the garage and cast about for a saucer or bowl, anything in which to give this dribbling mutt liquid. I spy a bright yellow plastic utensil—it looks like the cup from an ancient thermos—encrusted with dirt, lying among the weeds at the foot of one of the cedar trees, and I hurry to fetch it. Pamela puffs and waddles along beside me. She seems about ready to collapse. I return to the tap.

By now, Michel and the girls are dragging the mattresses, twisted out of all recognition, from the trunk of the VW. Two single mattresses for four of us. In this heat. Were we insane?

"Where shall we put these?" he shouts across to me.

"You decide." I am busily battling with the wretched tap, which is locked rigid. "Must be a while since anyone used this." But no one is listening to me, not even Pamela. She has thrown herself at the mercy of shade. At the foot of twelve tall cedars which surround the parking area, there is cool loose earth. There, Pamela is lying on her side; a beached whale snoring contentedly.

I turn the tap so hard it almost comes away from the wall. A small green lizard darts out from a fissure in the facade and, sensing unwelcome visitors, slithers off into an otherwhere. Perspiration breaks out all over my face. I can feel my flush. I am giddy with the effort, and now I need the drink. Pamela, all but braying now, has long since forgotten her thirst.

Eventually, the tap begins to turn, making horrendous squeaking noises. "A drop of oil," I mutter, beginning a mental to-do list which is destined to become longer than life. The ancient faucet turns and turns, but still no water flows. "This tap is not functioning properly, or . . ." But there is no one in sight to hear my concern. I decide to try another tap.

Upstairs, the villa is cool and insect-infested. The blinding, dry heat outside emphasizes the musty and crepuscular damp within. The odor reminds me of when I was a child: compulsory visits to elderly relatives living alone in unaired spaces.

The mosquito netting, curling away from the windows as though fighting to get out into the light, creates blocks of shadows and gives a somber, prisonlike feel to the main living room. Shafts of sunlight cut angular patterns on the floor's terra-cotta tiles, spotlighting the years of gathering dust and moldering, miniature reptile life. Michel is standing with *les filles*, who are looking about them in horror and disgust.

"*C'est dégueulasse, Papa!*" I cannot avoid noticing Vanessa's battle to keep her tears at bay.

"We'll clean it up," he encourages with dwindling enthusiasm.

"Before or after we've attacked the pool?" snaps one of them and stomps outside in a sulk.

"*Chérie!*"

"Michel?" I hardly dare begin, knowing this is a rotten moment to impart such drastic news.

"*Oui?* Go after your sister," he instructs the remaining daughter.

"I've got a sneaking suspicion . . ."

"What?" He looks frazzled and ready to give up. The drive from Paris has been interminable, in a baking car packed to the gills with luggage and livestock (Pamela!), on roads frying with exhaust fumes and August weather. None of us has slept properly. Nerves are frayed. Even the insistent chirring of the cicadas, a sound I usually find romantic and exotic, is enough to make me want to scream.

Suddenly, I see all of this from the children's point of view. This is their summer holiday. I am not their mother. They barely know me. It has been a while since they have spent time with their father, and the location he has brought them to belongs (or will belong) to him and this other woman who is not even fluent in their mother tongue. On top of which, the villa is uninhabitable and looks beyond repair.

"The girls are disappointed," he confides, and I hear the weariness and regret in his voice as I force myself not to feel like the outsider.

"Michel, I know this is not a good moment, but . . ."

"Perhaps it was a mistake to bring them here. It was our dream, after all."

Was, I find myself thinking, but I refrain—just about—from voicing it.

"There's no water."

"What?"

"No water."

"Well, you haven't turned on the main!" he snaps and, calling after his daughters, follows them out onto the terrace.

WHEN THE GIRLS are less upset and Michel is less harassed, he goes to switch on the main water supply, but there is no still no water. He wanders off in silence to pour a glass of wine and figure it out. I leave him to it and continue unloading the car.

"The water must be fed from an external tank that has dried up," he says, returning after a while.

"Fed from where?"

"Not sure. Once I find the tank, I'll be able to tell you. Madame B. said something about a well. I thought she was referring to a secondary source, but perhaps not. Girls all right?"

I nod. "They've gone investigating."

"Good."

We take a moment to look into each other. These last couple of days have been hectic, leaving no room for us. Then I bustle about the living room with a broom, trying to lift at least the top layers of dirt off the earthenware *tommette* tiles, fearing he'll read my hurt. I don't want to discuss it, knowing it will pass because it's too stupid. We are all tired and unsettled. But he comes after me, reminds me he loves me and hurries away.

ALL MY LIFE, I HAVE dreamed of acquiring a crumbling, shabby-chic house overlooking the sea, and renovating it. In my mind's eye, I have pictured a corner of paradise where friends can gather to swim, relax, debate, talk business if they care to, eat fresh fruits picked directly from the garden, prepare great steaming plates of food served from an *al fresco* kitchen and dished up onto candlelit tables the length of railway sleepers. In this land of liquor and honey, guests would eat heartily, drink gallons of home-produced wine, chill out to great jazz and while away star-spangled hours till dawn. I envisage a haven where city manners and constraints can be cast off, where artists, travelers, children, lovers and extended family can intermingle and find contentment. Among all of these altruistically gregarious and bohemian activities, I'd slip away unnoticed to a cool stone room of my own, lined head to foot with books, sprawling maps and dictionaries, switch on my computer and settle down peacefully to write.

But who has not idled away a wet winter afternoon or two with such a dream?

THE

OLIVE

FARM

CHAPTER ONE

WITH PASSION

four months earlier

"**S**hall we look inside?" suggests Michel, climbing the stairway to the main entrance, which is situated on the northwest side of the upper terrace. The estate agent, Monsieur Charpy (pronounced "Sharpee"), confesses that he does not have a key.

"*No key?*"

It is only now that he owns up to the fact that he is not actually representing the property. But, he swiftly assures us, if we are genuinely interested, he will be able to "*faire le nécessaire.*"

I am in the south of France, gazing at the not-so-distant Mediterranean, falling in love with an abandoned olive farm. The property, once stylish and now little better than a ruin, is for sale with ten acres of land.

Once upon a time, Charpy tell us, it was a residence of *haut standing*, which owned land as far as the eye could see in every direction. He swings his arms this way and that. I stare at him incredulously. He shrugs. Well,

certainly that valley in front of us and the woods to the right but, *hélas*—
he shrugs again—most of the terrain was sold off.

"When?"

"Years ago."

I wonder why nothing else has been constructed. The villa still stands
alone on its hillside, and the magnificent terraced olive groves Charpy
promised us have become a jungle of hungry weeds.

"An olive farm with vineyard and swimming pool," he insists.

We stare at the pool. It looks like an oversize, discarded sink. Dotted
here and there are various blossoming fruit trees and some very fine Italian
cedars, but there's no sign of any vineyard. There are two cottages included in the purchase price: the gatekeeper's house, at the very foot of the hill,
is firmly locked and shuttered, but even from the outside, it is plain that
it needs major restoration; the other, where the gardener or vine tender
would have resided, has been swallowed up beneath rampant growth. As
far as we can tell, for we cannot get within two hundred meters of it, all
that remains is one jagged stone wall.

"The villa was built in 1904 and was used as a summer residence by a
wealthy Italian family. They called it *Appassionata*." I smile. *Appassionata*
is a musical term, meaning with passion.

"*Pied dans l'eau*," continues Charpy.

Yes, it is ten minutes by car to the sea. From the numerous terraces,
the bay of Cannes is within tantalizingly easy reach, while the two islands
of Lérins lie in the water like lizards sleeping in the sun.

To the rear of the house is a pine forest. Most of the other shrubs and
trees are unknown to me—those that are not dead, that is. Michel asks
whether it was drought that killed off the little orange grove and the
almond tree, now an inverted broomstick of dead twigs in front of a tum-
bledown garage.

"*Je crois pas*," says Monsieur Charpy. "They caught cold. Our last winter was harsh. It broke records." He stares glumly at four bougainvillea

bushes which once straddled the front pillars of the house. Now they are lying across the veranda like drunks in a stupor. "*Aussi*, the place has been empty for four years. Before that, it was rented to a foreign woman who bred dogs. *Évidemment*, she cared nothing for her surroundings."

The years of neglect aided by the recent freak weather have certainly put pay to Appassionata's former glory. Still, I am drawn to its faded elegance. It remains graceful. There is beauty here. And history. Even the gnarled olive trees look as though they have stood witness on this hillside for a thousand years.

"The *propriétaire* will be glad to get rid of the place. I can arrange a good price." Charpy makes the offer disdainfully. To his way of thinking, paying any sum for such dereliction would be scandalous.

I close my eyes and picture us in future summers strolling paths we discover beneath this jungle of vegetation. Michel, at my side, is surveying the facade. The baked vanilla-colored paint flakes at the touch. "Why don't we try to find a way in?" he says, and disappears on a lap of the house, tapping at windows, rattling doors.

Charpy, ruffled, sets off after him. I hang back, smiling. Michel and I have known each other only a few months, but already I have learned that he is not one to be defeated by such a minor detail as the lack of a key.

The land is not fenced. There is no gate; the boundaries are not staked. There is nothing to secure the property, to keep hunters or trespassers at bay. There are broken windows everywhere.

"Come and look here," Michel calls from around the back. He, with his more practiced eye, points out the remains of a makeshift vegetable garden. "Squatters. Been and gone in the not too distant past. The locks on all three doors have been forced. It should be relatively easy to get in. Monsieur Charpy, *s'il vous plaît*."

Once inside, we are moving through a sea of cobwebs. A deep musty stench takes our breath away. Walls hang with perished wiring. The rooms are high-ceilinged, sonorous spaces. Strips of wallpaper curl to the floor like weeping silhouettes. Tiny shriveled reptiles crunch underfoot. Such decay. We tread slowly, pausing, turning this way and that, drinking the place in. Rip away all the curling, rusted mosquito netting fixed across the windows, and the rooms would be blissfully light. They are well proportioned, nothing elaborate. Corridors, hidden corners, huge rust-stained baths in cavernous bathrooms. In the main salon, there is a generous oak-beamed fireplace. There is an ambience. *Chaleur.*

Our voices and footsteps reverberate, and I feel the rumble of lives lived here. Tugging aside the netting, grazing a finger in the process, I gaze out at eloquent views over land and sea, and mountains to the west. Sun-drenched summers by the Mediterranean. Appassionata. Yes. I am seized.

Charpy watches impatiently, fussing at the sleeves and shoulders of his jacket, while we open doors, shove at long-forgotten cupboards, run our fingers through layers of dust and disintegrating insects and flick or turn switches and taps, none of which work. He does not comprehend our enthusiasm. "*Beaucoup de travail,*" he pronounces.

Back outside, the late-morning sun is warm and inviting. I glance at Michel, and without a word spoken, his eyes tell me he sees what I see: a wild yet enticing site. Still, even if we could scrape together the asking price, the funds needed to restore it make it an act of insanity.

WE HEAD FOR A bar Michel frequents in the old port of Cannes. The patron strolls over to greet him. They shake hands. "*Bon festival?*" he enquires. Michel nods, and the patron nods in response. The conversation seems complete until Michel takes me by the arm and introduces me. My future wife, he says. *Mais, félicitations! Félicitations!* The patron shakes our hands vigorously and invites us to a drink on the house. We install ourselves at one of the tables on the street, and I feel the heat of the midday sun beat against my face.

Although it is only late April, there are many foreigners bustling to and fro laden with shopping bags. Several wave to Michel, calling out the same enquiry. "*Bon festival?*" He nods. Occasionally, he rises to shake hands or, in French fashion, lightly kiss another's cheeks. Mostly, these fleeting encounters are with executive types in sharply cut blazers, light-weight slacks, Italian soft leather loafers. They talk of business. It is the closing day of the spring television festival which precedes the Cannes Film Festival. Both festivals are dominated by the markets that run along-side them. The world of television, the filming of it rather than the selling of it, seems to me a million miles removed from these markets. I marvel at how Michel can survive in such a milieu.

A lithe waiter zips by with our glasses of *Côte de Provence* rosé. These are accompanied by porcelain saucers filled with olives, slices of deep pink *saucisson* and potato chips. He deposits the dishes on our table and departs without a word to us. We clink glasses and sip our wine, silent, lost in our morning's visit. Both musing upon our find, buried aloft in the pine-scent-ed hills way above this strip with its glitzy hotels.

"I wish we could afford it," I say eventually.

"I think we should go for it. They want to get rid of the place, so let's make an offer."

"But how could we ever . . .?"

Michel pulls out his fountain pen, takes his napkin and we start scrib-bling figures and exchange rates; the ink bleeds into the soft tissue. The answer is clear. It is way beyond our price range. There are Vanessa and Clarisse to consider, daughters from his previous marriage.

"The pound is strong," I say. "That will work in our favor. But it's still way more than we can afford." I glance at the clock on the church tower up in the old town. It is after one. Charpy's *immobilier* office on the Croisette has closed for the weekend. It is just as well. We will have left by Monday. I am returning to London, where it is raining, Michel to Paris. I turn, peer up the lane that leads to the old fish market and tilt my head skyward. Only rounded summits of green hills are visible above the blocks of crab-colored buildings. I cannot tell which of them harbors Appassionata.

"Let me talk to Charpy on Monday," says Michel. "I have an idea."

"What?"

"Perhaps they'll sell it in stages."

"Of course they won't!"

OUR PENSION OVERLOOKS the old port. I pass the afternoon watching the to-ing and fro-ing of yachts and the ferries plying a path to the islands. Michel has disappeared for a final, postfestival business meeting. He will not return before evening. I am seized by a desire to slip back up to the hills, but I know that, alone in the car, I would never find my way. Instead, I idle away the afternoon reading and jotting in a notebook.

I didn't come to Cannes to look for a house. Michel was flying down for the festival and invited me to come along and spend the week with him. It's true I have always been drawn to "my house by the sea," and whenever I am at the coast, whether it be Finland, Australia, Africa or Devon, I browse the estate agents' windows, visiting occasional properties, hungry to discover something unexpected, to walk into a space where I belong. No other property I have ever visited has felt this close to belonging. Even so, to buy Appassionata would be an act of madness.

Every bean I have ever earned, I have spent traveling, crossing borders, roaming the world. I have been intensely restless, hungry to live a hundred lives in one lifetime. I have never settled anywhere. I have no capital to speak of. I am not fluent in the language; schoolgirl French is my limit. And as for farming? My mother's family owns a farm in Ireland where I spent childhood holidays, and I played a country vet's wife in a television series: hardly an agricultural pedigree. Still, to restore this old olive farm, with views overlooking the sea—to create roots, and with this man, who proposed the day after I met him. A *coup de foudre*, he said . . . an act of insanity, but since we met, life has been giddy. We've been spinning like tumbleweed. It may be illogical, but it feels *right*.

I begin to scribble several to-do lists, which is out of character, simply an attempt to contain my excitement, to comprehend the enormity of the venture. I'm drawing the possibility of ownership closer to me, to quieten the fever.

Finally, about six in the evening, as the church bells chime the first of the Sunday masses celebrated on Saturday evening and after I have exhausted all avenues to make-believe ownership, I stroll the beach to swim. The water is bracing. I am alone in it, which pleases me. I savor the salty taste on my lips. I flip over on my back and scan the waterfront, the coastline which stretches as far as the cap of Antibes, and the hills behind. I drink in its foreignness. The cream and salmon tones of the buildings, the softly evocative light that has drawn so many painters here. I notice the observatory on a hill to the right of me for the first time. I begin to put myself in the role of habitant. Could I really live here? Yes. Yes!

SUNDAY, WE DRIVE out of town. We head inland, up into the hills, making for the pretty old town of Vence, perched atop a hill at the end of a long winding road. Michel wants to show me the chapel the Dominicans commissioned Matisse to redesign when he was living at Cimiez, an elegant quarter in the hills above Nice, but when we arrive, it is closed. How disappointing! I had expected a discreet mass to be in progress, with monks and incense. We shove our faces through the fencing, clamoring for views of the garden and building, and Michel directs my eyeline toward the chapel roof. The tiles are a brilliant azure blue. So simple, so unlikely and so pure.

And then, drawn like nails to a magnet, we head for the villa.

There is no gate or fencing to prevent us from entering the land, so we do. Without Charpy at our side, we can explore the site more thoroughly. On the tarmac driveway, I find several dead shells from hunters' rifles and look around, wondering what they were shooting. Rabbits?

"Wild boar," suggests Michel.

I laugh. "This close to the coast? No way."

Once up on the top terrace, we decide against going inside. Charpy forcing the door is one thing, but alone, we will not contemplate it. Instead, we press our faces against filthy, sticky, cracked panes of glass and peer in through the windows. The sludge-brown shutters are bleached and peeling.

"We'll paint the shutters the color of Matisse's chapel," says Michel. Azure blue. *Côte d'Azur.* The blue coast. I lift my eyes heavenward. Blue sky. Cobalt blue. Vanilla walls and blue shutters. I try to picture it. A cool yet vibrant combination. "Yes, let's," I murmur.

Many of the slats are splintered and broken, forced by squatters or robbers. "They will need to be replaced," says Michel.

"Everything will need to be replaced. Nothing is intact."

A curious feature we hadn't noticed yesterday is a bread oven that looks like a monstrous beehive. It has been added, stuck on, to the main chimney breast at upper terrace level. "That will have to go!"

"Definitely!"

"We haven't seen inside the garage."

"I bet it's locked." And yes, it is. Alongside it are two stables with the upper and lower doors hanging loose on heavy rusted hinges. I expect them to reek of hay, but they are stacked with misshapen cardboard boxes crammed with disintegrating papers and files. On the ground are a few broken bits of gardening tools, rusting and useless, a cracked cup with no handle and a row of dusty dark green bottles lining the walls. I wonder whose life those objects belonged to. And what became of that person, those people.

A HOUSE IS SO MUCH more than a house. And a house in a foreign country pushes the learning experience that much further. It expands, promises to expand, the psyche; the inner journey. We are two embarking on this path together. Newly in love. Thrilled by each other. The house that Monsieur

Charpy saw with us yesterday and the potential farm, the regeneration we are picturing, are two different properties. We are purchasing a dream. We will nurture it through the pruning of trees and the harvesting of fruit. We will celebrate our union by extending invitations to friends and family worldwide . . .

WE SIT OUT IN THE afternoon sunshine at the pool's edge, side by side, fingertips touching, and dangle our feet in the vast, empty basin. We walk down the steps, enter, stand within it, calling loudly, hooting and singing. Our voices echo. We run around its perimeter until we are out of breath. Swallows wheel and swoop high in the sky above us. We close our eyes and listen to the stillness. I have never walked in an empty swimming pool before. With the soles of our shoes, we shove thick plaits of ivy out of our path and find puddles of sludgy muddy rainwater seeping into the deepest crevices of the basin. Drowned black insects float among speckled ivy leaves. The walls are so much taller than we are. I press my back against the bleached blue cement and feel as though I have fallen into the very heart—no, we will be the heart—the watery womb of the property. We linger and kiss, our pulses racing. We look deep into each other, smiling, overwhelmed. Two tiny excited people in this vast expanse of space. I think of Jules Verne's *Journey to the Center of the Earth*. I feel as big as Tom Thumb. Rather, as tiny. I am Alice in Wonderland. Like Alice, the adventure, the challenge, has shrunk us in preparation for our journey. We will grow bigger and taller as we inhabit this space, as we reach into it and learn from it; learn to farm it and to know its myriad secrets. And in its restoration, we will discover each other.

I love this place already. I love this man at my side who has tumbled into this crazy dream with me. He seems to want to make it work as much as I do. He appears to be as energized and bowled over by the prospects as I am.

Although we have known each other only a few months I feel safe with Michel. I trust him. He loves abundantly, with risk, and is tender.

I needed that. I was losing faith. After a series of short-lived affairs, one rather public relationship—I lead a life in the public eye, albeit at a modest level—I had become isolated. I was losing myself. I was hurt and growing brash. I was independent, driven and alone.

THE SUN IS MOVING to the right, preparing to slip behind the hills. The sky is changing color, augmenting its palette to include tawny orange, pastel red and soft purple. "Where is that?" I ask. "There, where the sun is setting?"

"Mougins."

We are back on the upper terrace. Michel is smoking a cigarette—I wish he wouldn't—and it is time to go.

"We'll follow the sun to Mougins and have dinner there, it's too soon to return to Cannes."

Yes, too soon to return to Cannes and its gaudy lights, its meretricious festival nightlife.

We descend the drive slowly, pootling past the olive terraces to the right and left of us. My attention is drawn to flowers on the olive branches, tiny white specks, little crocheted blossoms, delicate as finger lace. We build the future by enlarging upon our past, Goethe wrote.

AT THE ENTRY to the hilltop village of Mougins, where cars are banned, we find an inviting *petit* hotel restaurant. It has a terrace with extensive views which nosedive into the deep valley and sweep toward the sea. We take our places on the terrace.

Michel orders us *deux coupes*. Our *patron* nods approvingly and disappears. We notice a hand-painted sign that reads *140ff la chambre, parking inclus.* "It's a good price," says Michel. Less than fourteen pounds. "We must remember this place for our next visit. It's closer to the house, quieter than Cannes and cheaper." The monsieur returns with our two glasses of champagne, and says, "I am the only one, *le seul,* in the village with my own parking."

We nod encouragingly.

We eat ravenously. Our meal is delicious and an excellent value as the set menu at 70f. I begin with warmed goat cheese melted on toasts of baguette and dressed with an arugula salad, while Michel chooses *une petite omelette au briccio*, omelette with goat cheese and mint. I follow with *gigot d'agneau*, succulently pink, with *tian de pommes de terre*, a dish of potatoes and tomatoes cooked beneath the roast leg of lamb. Michel orders *veau aux olives noires à la sauge*, veal casserole with black olives and sage. The owner recommends a Bandol *rouge* to accompany; a wine from the neighboring Var region. Michel, although a faithful Bordeaux man, decides we should go for it. It is fuller-bodied than I would have expected, but it complements the meal and our mood of discovery. Michel accepts a slither of *brie de Meaux* to follow and then the *tarte au citron et aux amandes*. I decline the cheese but am tempted by a dessert I have never come across before: *lavender crème brûlée*. It is heaven, one of the most sensuous foods I have ever eaten. We set off into the night replete and happy. The *patron* has wooed our stomachs and won our hearts. To my amazement, as we are leaving, he introduces us to his very glamorous wife. She, he announces proudly, is the chef!

ON MONDAY, AFTER several phone calls to and from Brussels—where the vendors, Monsieur and Madame B., reside—a deal is struck. We will buy the house and the first half of its *terrain* immediately and will sign a *promesse de vente* for the second five acres, to be paid within four years of the completion date of the purchase of the villa. On top of this, Michel has beaten down the original asking price by almost a quarter.

Now we must leave the south of France. We have stayed over a day longer than we had planned, in order to set the purchase of the house rolling. Although we are leaving the sun and the sea, the bustle of Mediterranean life and, tonight in Paris, I must say *au revoir* to Michel for several weeks, my heart is sailing like a kite. A house in the south of France. More than a house: the restoration of a disused farm, a canvas to paint on, a new life to forge and someone to share it with. In my mind's eye, I can already picture the pouring and bottling of liters of olive oil, lashings of nature's liquid gold.

BACK IN ENGLAND, I am barely able to contain my excitement until a friend takes me to lunch and invites me to ponder some well-meant advice. I am warned about the horrors of the French tax laws, property laws, by-laws and the black holes of the Napoleonic system. Should I decide the whole affair has been an aberration and choose to sell, I am told that the French will hold on to my money for five years. I leave the restaurant shocked and weak at the knees.

This is followed by an encounter with another longstanding chum who flummoxes me entirely by telling me for my own good that all these difficulties come of having been too secretive. Next, my family wants to warn me against being hasty. "Have you considered the pitfalls?" my father asks, and begins to list scenarios of corruption and deception, summing up with "You're too impetuous. You don't want to get landed with a pig in a poke, now do you?"

I am still trying to catch my breath when my mother phones, confiding that while out shopping with my sister in Bond Street, she broke down and cried. "I had to been taken into Fenwick's coffee shop. I couldn't stand up."

"What's wrong?" I ask.

"You."

"Me?"

"How could you? We are Irish Catholics," she wails.

I say nothing. What can I say?

"And he's a foreigner. You've always been the same. You've got no common sense!"

I replace the receiver. Slumping into uncertainty, I begin to stew. Yes, I am impetuous, I probably lack common sense, I hadn't been aware that I am particularly secretive and I certainly have not troubled to investigate the pitfalls of the French system. On top of which, we cannot afford the farm. It is an unachievable fantasy fed by a whirlwind romance which is probably destined to go the route of all others. I should pull out. So, my frame of mind when Michel telephones from Paris to say that he has received a call from Brussels is one of mounting hysteria.

"*What?*" is my amorous greeting.

"Madame is insisting on ten percent of the selling price up front, in cash."

"Absolutely not. It's illegal."

That kind of request is quite common, I am hearing, in French property transactions. It is known as the "deposit." The buyer pays a percentage of the agreed asking price in cash, and the vendor declares a sale price lower than the property's true total. It helps to alleviate the astronomical *frais* levied against both purchaser and vendor.

"It's black-market money," I shout insanely. "She can't do that."

"I'm afraid it is a generally accepted practice."

I refuse to discuss it. In fact, I refuse to discuss anything and replace the receiver rather too abruptly. I know, though, that if we don't agree, we will lose the olive farm. A decision that felt organic a month ago is now driving me over the edge with doubts. Virtually everything I own, including the cashing in of my one and only insurance policy—much against my accountant's advice—is going to be sunk into this enterprise. What if it all goes wrong? What if everything my friends and family are telling me is true? I am woken by appalling dreams. I pace the nights away, jabbering to myself. Terror is taking hold.

NOW IT IS HIGH SUMMER. Due to French bureaucratic nightmares, our hope that the sale would be completed before the holidays is receding fast. And while complications of the contract—such as the division of the land—are being wrangled over and ironed out, the pound is falling. Our calculations are out the window. Due to the devaluing exchange rate, the property price has already risen by twenty percent. If matters get any worse, we will have to pull out. I am tearing my hair out. Michel keeps his cool. Bastille Day arrives. We motor down through a celebrating France to visit the abandoned property one more time, mainly to appease my stewing financial fears, before signing any commitment.

Our arrival is greeted by a magnificent tree alongside the top terrace which is in full and glorious bloom. Exhausted, after twelve hours' solid driving, taking turns to catnap in the car because we have too little cash for hotelrooms, we cast ourselves like weary shipwreckers on the upstairs terrace, adjacent to this majestic tree. Its blossoms are the color of ivory, its petals thickly textured with a fragrance so redolent it envelops the whole hillside. Collapsed before the dawning day, my head on Michel's chest, I know that this perfume is imprinting upon me. It will forever remind me of the south of France, and of being recklessly in love.

As the day unfolds, the perfumes, the views, the hot, clear weather seduce me once more and I am calmed by Michel and his quiet strength. I see my doubts for what they are; I am stepping off into the unknown, moving out of one life to inhabit another. Fears, real or illogical, excitements are part of that transition. Misgivings laid to rest, we make for the beach where we steep our weary limbs in the Med, doze the afternoon away and shower off salt and sand in fresh cold water before going in search of dinner and a bed at the little hilltop hotel-restaurant.

As evening falls and we dine by candlelight on the hotel's terrace, a diorama of fireworks explodes across the Mediterranean sky, lighting up the entire bay. Their purpose is the honoring of the French declaration of independence—here, in France, *Quatorze Juillet*, the anniversary of the storming of the Bastille, is the greatest of all national holidays—but in my heart, soothed for the present, I pretend they are for us.

BRIGHT AND EARLY the next morning, Michel puts through a call to the vendors in Belgium. He confirms that we will pay the cash advance

Madame has requested if, in return, she and her husband allow us to move into the the villa before the final contracts are signed. "Ah, you are eager to begin restoration works while the weather is hot and dry, *n'est-ce pas?*"

Yes, well, that would be true if the cash advance wasn't about to eat up almost every penny we can lay our hands on. The fact is, Michel has invited Vanessa and Clarisse, his thirteen-year-old twin daughters, to spend their summer with us. He wants them get to know me a little better and to share with us the thrill of installing ourselves at the property. They are dying to see the place, he tells me. Besides, we haven't a bean left to take them elsewhere.

Madame B. agrees, *en principe*, but insists that we discuss all negotiations over lunch in Brussels. Before hanging up, she offers him the choice of either swift-transferring the money to an account in Switzerland in advance of our Brussels rendezvous or bringing the agreed sum in cash with us on the day.

I am ready to hit the ceiling. I will not hear of one *sou* from my one and only insurance policy, plus savings, disappearing into unknown black-market accounts in Switzerland before anything is signed and settled. Why can't we take a check made out to their wretched Swiss account and hand it to them on the day?

"I suppose she fears it might not be honored."

"*Typical!* At that level, no one trusts anybody!"

I rant and fume until I exhaust myself and Michel's laughter and those gentle blue eyes temper my hysteria.

And so it is arranged.

Two weeks later, the beginning of the French mass exodus from north to south—for a nation of individualists, they certainly behave like lemmings when it comes to late July and the holiday season is upon them—we pack my little black VW convertible with old mattresses, bedding and a surplus of kitchenware from my flat in London and set off for Brussels.

Our plan is to introduce ourselves to the Belgian owners, create the "right impression" (i.e., that we are able to afford the place), sign the *promesse de vente*, hand over our hard-earned money secreted in brown envelopes in Michel's briefcase (unless he can sweet-talk them into holding off this part of the arrangement until later) and, directly after "business," drive to Paris, where *les filles* eagerly await us.

Michel feels that to turn up outside the vendors' home in a car bursting at the seams with sticks of old furniture might appear a trifle presumptuous. It might prejudice negotiations. So when we arrive in the city, we deposit the laden vehicle in the underground garage at the Hilton and make our way on foot to the address we have been given by Madame's secretary. I barely register the city streets and almost don't notice our arrival at the wide leafy avenue that bears the name we are looking for. My head is whirring with what-ifs. What if these people fall upon us and rob us or they try by other less violent means to cheat us out of our money; how can we be sure they are not crooks? Even given we escape such fates, there are the documents we are about to sign . . .

ALMOST BEFORE I realize it, we have arrived and are standing, no, we are frozen, outside imposingly ornate iron gates which rise to the height of an average oak tree. "Thank heavens we didn't bring the car," I whisper, clutching Michel's hand. For a good three minutes, we regard the exterior of what looks to us like a miniature Versailles.

"Here goes," he replies, squeezing my hand tighter before ringing the bell.

The gates slide apart and we crunch across gravel and tiles, climb a marble stairway and approach baronial doors. These are opened by a butler in full uniform. Michel, appearing unflustered, gives our names.

Nodding a dehumanized greeting, the butler tells us in a thick Belgian accent, "Madame will be with you shortly." I, with my already imperfect French, have difficulty understanding even that simple sentence. I sigh at the prospect of the impending negotiations. Then, with a polite but indifferent nod, he leads us across a fabulous black-and-white marble hallway ablaze with sprays of livid red gladioli and into a capacious salon which he describes as "Madame's writing room."

"I'm in the wrong film, wearing the wrong costume," I mutter as we perch in two ornate gilt Louis-something chairs.

As soon as the door closes and we are alone, I rise and cross to the floor-to-ceiling windows which look out upon substantial, perfectly manicured gardens. I count half a dozen gardeners digging and planting a crisscross arrangement of magnificent flowerbeds. An antique Italian marble fountain stands in the center of a crossroads of graveled walkways, a *chef d'oeuvre* of gushing crystal-clear water. I gaze contentedly upon this spectacle until the door opens behind me and a terrifying, tightly coiffured, tight-lipped woman wearing a thick coating of orange face powder enters: Madame B. She is accompanied by another, marginally younger woman, twitching like a nervous bird, whom she introduces as Yvette Pastor, her private secretary. Madame B. apologizes for the absence of her husband, who, she explains, is *malade*. She strides briskly into the hall, requesting us to follow. My heart sinks. I picture our carefree summer plans disappearing faster than Belgian chocolates.

We are seated around an oval walnut table large enough to seat twenty guests with ease. A magnum of Cristal champagne arrives on a silver platter. A message is sent from Madame via the butler to Monsieur, bidding him, in no uncertain terms, to get up and come downstairs instantly; there are papers to be signed. I resist my desire to protest.

Business commences. I barely comprehend a phrase and stare in blind panic as six pages filled with dense legal French are shoved across the table for my perusal—a copy of the binding documents I am about to put my name to.

A little while later, the door opens and a frail old man appears, trembling and pale. He is dressed in elegant sportswear and wears heavy, expensive jewelry on his, mottled hands and wrists which are delicate as parchment. He apologizes profusely for his malady. We shake our heads sympathetically, at a loss for words. He looks as though he might drop to the marble floor at any second. Madame commands the butler to pour Monsieur a glass of champagne. Monsieur declines. Madame insists. *Le pauvre Monsieur* assents and toasts our good health and the prosperity of our future lives at Appassionata. "You have much work to do in the garden," he says.

"Foolish to discuss the growth of the land," she reprimands. Monsieur demures, accepts Madame's fountain pen and signs his shaky, illegible autograph.

Then it is my turn. I down the last mouthful from my crystal flute and, with sticky hands and beating heart, obediently scribble my initials or name wherever Madame points her manicured fingers. I glance at Michel and smile weakly. I am praying to God he knows what he is doing, because I don't, and he is handing over our envelopes.

Business completed, Michel rises. He leans to offer a *bisou* to Madame B., who proffers her cheek, clearly enchanted by his charm and thrilled by his astute business acumen. Watching the pair of them negotiate has been rather like watching two fencing champions in combat. Monsieur and I did not utter a word. In fact, at the very first opportunity, he offered his apologies and retired back upstairs to his room.

"*Mais, non,* you cannot leave now! We must lunch!" Madame says to us.

We have already consumed almost a magnum of champagne among the five of us—Yvette, always present, seated in a chair to the rear of Madame, has tippled immoderately on our future happiness—and we have a three-hour drive ahead of us, but without a word between us, we sense that to refuse would be judged a rebuff and might cloud future business relations.

We nod, attempting enthusiasm. "*Pourquoi pas?*"

"*Très bien.* I suggest zee 'ilton." She excuses herself and orders us to wait out front.

"Well?" I ask Michel in a fraught whisper when Madame has left the room.

"Well, what?"

"Did we get the permission or not?"

"*Chérie,* did you not understand what was being said?"

"Not every word," I reply weakly.

Michel grins. "We have signed and sealed permission to occupy the villa for the summer, in fact from this moment on until it is officially ours."

"Really!"

"Yes, well, at a price."

"What price?"

"Sssh. *Chérie,* don't yell. If we fail to complete, no matter for whatever reason, they keep everything."

"What! Every penny we have given them today—?"

"And anything, everything, we spend on the place. We can't claim a franc back."

"Oh my God! Whatever made you agree to that?"

"*Chérie,* the deadline for completion is next April. So there's nothing to worry about."

"Next April. That's almost a year. Yes, we'll have bought the place long before then." I sigh, relieved.

Outside in the gardens, Madame inquires after our car. For a second we are both flummoxed, recalling guiltily my little Golf packed to the rafters with furniture for "our" house, awaiting us in the underground garage of "zee 'ilton." Michel, sanguine as always in such moments, comes to the rescue. "We parked a little distance from here, *chère Madame,* for fear of losing our way in the city."

Madame nods comprehendingly and then examines me from head to foot as though she is measuring me, which is precisely what she is doing. "*C'est bon,*" she decides, commanding a passing gardener to fetch her car from its garage. "It is a sports car, but you can squeeze in the back. It's not far; you are slim." Moments later, to our speechless amazement, as the garage doors unfold, a gleaming lipstick-red 500SL Mercedes creeps toward us. I had been expecting something a trifle more sedate.

"My weakness," she confesses like a child. "You see, I was born very poor."

We pile into the car, which, with Madame at the wheel, shoots off like a rocket.

During lunch at the Hilton, we learn that she is the richest woman in Belgium. "Poor Pierre," she tells us, "does not care for money or material possessions. All he wants is to potter about in the garden. He adores flowers and plants. It is very difficult for me. I do not know what to do with him. We have known each other since we were twelve. We began a business and have worked very hard, and now we are rich, but he prefers to stay in bed. He cannot handle all the responsibilities our money has brought us. I travel everywhere with Yvette, my secretary. Pierre does not want to go anywhere other than our summer house. It is *très tragique.*" As I watch her, Madame B. begins to resemble a bloodhound. Her expression is drooping, her eyes look lost and uncomprehending. The terrifying woman we first encountered has disappeared. But the mood does not last long. Soon she is beckoning for the bill, which she insists on paying— thank heavens!—and then offers to walk us to our car.

Michel and I exchange complicitous glances.

At this late stage, we cannot possibly own up to the fact that our little buggy packed with two moth-eaten mattresses is parked not a hundred meters from her Mercedes in the garage right beneath our feet. Instead, we roam around a few back streets feeling stupid and dishonest and seeing our ridiculous charade for the time waster that it is, but insisting that we just cannot recall where we parked.

Eventually, Madame B. gives up, hails a cab to deliver her the three streets back to the Hilton and wishes us *bonne chance!* Our parting is good-natured, almost affectionate. "See you at the *notaire*'s office. I will fax you the address," she says. "I look forward to it." And she flutters her eyes at Michel like Betty Boop.

By the time we arrive in Paris, it is late. Michel's daughters are disgruntled. They have been awaiting the arrival of Papa all afternoon. The girls and I have met only a few times, and I am probably more affected by their mood than Michel, who, oblivious to any whining, runs to and from the car cramming bags into any space he can lodge them, telling everyone to get a move on or we won't reach the south before the holidays are over. "What about Pamela?" asks Clarisse.

I turn my head in surprise. Who is Pamela?

Clarisse points to the gate, and there, panting and waddling toward us, is a startlingly obese German shepherd. The addition of Pamela unbalances the carefully considered equilibrium of my already dangerously overloaded Golf, and worse, *elle fait les petits pets* all the way from Paris to Cannes. And they are lethal! Embracing a new family is one thing, but by the time we reach Aix-en-Provence, I am seriously asking myself, can I love this smelly dog?

CHAPTER TWO

WATER MUSIC

The heat is brutal. The search for water and its source occupies Michel's first few days here.

Vanessa and I have set about cutting back the ivy in the swimming pool. We have one pair of garden shears between us. This means one of us clips until aching arms defeat her, while the other tugs, untangles and gathers up the dead foliage. Then we swap. We seem to have a good rhythm going. She is a hardworking, bright girl and I thoroughly enjoy her company. Neither of the girls speaks English, which forces me to use my rather rusty French. Our conversations don't amount to much: the odd polite exchange or earnest requests on my part to know the French word for this or that. From time to time, particularly given the temperature, the arid conditions and strenuous activity, it proves difficult, and we end up working in companionable silence.

Meanwhile, Michel is scouring the hill, up and down, back and forth like a two-legged goat over our ten acres of Provençal jungle for waterpipes or signs of a well. His legs are latticed with grazes from the brambles and from tripping over hidden rocks, but he remains determined. Madame B. mentioned to him that somewhere on the property there is a natural spring, but for the moment, its whereabouts eludes him.

"We may have to cut back the entire acreage before we find it!" he announces on one of his stopovers at the villa, in search of refreshment.

"Where's Clarisse?"

Vanessa and I shake our heads and wipe our sticky brows. "Don't know, haven't seen her for hours. You need Wellingtons and a hip flask, Michel," I say.

He shrugs and disappears in his shorts and supermarket espadrilles—fraying already—ascending yet another barely visible track. I read his concern. The installation of an entire water system at this stage would mean we would be obliged to close up the property and abandon it for the foreseeable future. Neither of us have voiced this sorry prospect as yet.

Each evening, one or both of us drives to the village to fill several twenty-liter plastic containers with water for the day ahead. I learn that in France every village and town has its public supply of *eau potable*. It is considered a basic right in this country that, no matter how poor a person may be, he has access to free drinking water wherever in the land. *Vive la France!* I laugh when Michel explains this national kindness. I am very grateful to the Republic of France for such forethought, because our funds are diminishing rapidly.

Still, funds or no funds, due to the lack of facilities at the villa, we are obliged to install the girls in a hotel. Naturally, we choose the hilltop hotel, where the *patron* offers Michel a generous deal. Each morning, we drive to Mougins to collect them; they order *le petit déjeuner*, which is the usual: rolls, croissants, *confiture* and *café au lait* (*chocolat* for Vanessa, who cannot abide tea or coffee yet frets constantly about her pretty, svelte figure). The girls' breakfasts are included in the price of the room (any rolls not eaten we stuff into my bag and take with us for our lunch), and Michel and I order a pot of coffee for two. This we consume as a family on the *patron's* terrace and, while he and his wife are occupied with the bills of departing guests, one at a time, Michel and I tiptoe up the twisting, narrow stairway to the girls' room and take an illicit hot-water shower. Hot water never felt this delicious or wicked! By day three, Monsieur's flamboyant bonhomie is beginning to diminish, and he is eyeing us with suspicion. I dread to think how he will greet us toward the end of the month!

Michel pays a visit to *la mairie,* the local town hall, requesting plans of Appassionata's water system. But it is August, and there is nobody to search through the files. Everyone is *en vacances,* and even if they were not, he learns, it is unlikely that the information has been registered. The house is too old, the land has been divided, it is a private residence. Water systems, septic tanks, do not have to be listed. We must continue our search unaided. In desperation, he stops at a local phone booth and puts in a call to Brussels, to Madame B.

"I've found a *bassin* at the top of the hill, but the pipes that lead to it disappear into the undergrowth and I can't trace or get at them. Where is the water coming from to feed that basin?"

Madame has no idea. The property was bought as a gift for one of her two daughters who loved horses, but the inclines and terraces made it impossible for her to breed there. She never lived on the property.

"*Hélas,* I cannot remember, *Monsieur,* it was almost fifteen years ago."

"And the woman who rented it from you, who bred dogs?"

"I have no idea where she is. She left owing us thousands, including the water bills."

"Ah, so you do have water bills?"

"*Mais, bien sûr!* At least I think so. She never paid whatever bills were outstanding. Of that I am very certain."

"It's just that . . . you'd mentioned a well?"

"Ah, *la source!* Yes, yes, I think there is a well. Perhaps my daughter has kept everything, but she is away until mid-September. We will try to supply all these details when the sale goes through. Pierre and I are off on holiday tomorrow, so *bonne chance.*"

IT IS EARLY EVENING. The sun is glinting through the olive trees and laying shadows across the weedy terraces. We are sitting alone in an expansive dust patch—once a lawn—alongside the top terrace, in two supermarket deck chairs, sharing a bottle of local *vin de Provence rosé.* Our conversation is about water, of course, and I am discovering how Michel hates to be defeated.

"If squatters lived here and grew vegetables, there has to be a water main. They wouldn't have known about the well. I am going to *Lyonnaise des eaux,* the local water board, in the morning, and pray to God they haven't also shut down for the month of August."

"They might have done what we are doing," I suggest, pouring us both another glass of wine.

"What's that?"

"Taken advantage of French hospitality. Collected their daily water supply from the village."

While he considers this possibility, I tell him that I have driven the girls back to the hotel and that I have promised we would take them into Cannes later for a pizza. Money shortage or not, they are ready for an evening out. I sense they are growing bored and impatient with our lack of facilities and the slim choice of meals we and our temporary cooking arrangements can provide—a couple of old saucepans from London, a two-hundred-franc barbecue, a plastic salad dish, servers, knives and forks bought locally along with paper plates and some form of camping thing belonging to Michel which looks like a Bunsen burner but succeeds in boiling water for potatoes and coffee.

"The girls are fine. It's you who wants to get out," he teases. It is about now that I am recognizing a fundamental difference between us. If I, in my old life, my real life, am faced with something that does not work, I leave it, move on, buy another. "No kitchen, fine, let's eat out" is my idea of the perfect solution. Michel, on the other hand, has patience and an ability to knock up something practical out of what looks to me like nothing more than a useless piece of wire or wood. I concede, "Perhaps you are right," and he hoots with laughter when I confess sheepishly that this is the closest I have ever come to camping.

"Still, you're right. The girls will be happier once I get that pool filled."

He continues to reassure them that once we have discovered the water source and how to pump it to our water basin, a circular cement tank at the very summit of the hill, and ensured its freefall passage back downhill to the house unimpeded by clogged pipes, the very first thing we will do is fill the swimming pool. I turn my head and look back across two terraces to its empty, bleached-out blueness and fantasize about cool, crystalline swimming water. Yes, the days will be more languid then.

"What about the neighbors?" I ask him. "Have you talked to them?"

"Everyone is away. Or at the beach."

The beach! We haven't visited the beach yet. "Hang the water problem. Let's go to the beach tomorrow!"

"Too many tourists," Michel says, as though we had lived on this hill for a hundred years.

WE RISE EARLY. I am delighted to have found a man who loves the early mornings as much as I do. Our days begin when the sun peeps through the towering pines and shines down upon us and our dreadful mattress on the floor to light our bronzed faces.

"I'm off to the sea," I whisper sleepily, throwing on old clothes. I drive to the coast, falling into combat on the way with great orange dust carts and the first of the day's horn addicts. Down in the town, the air is rich with traffic fumes and freshly baked bread. A solitary hour spent swimming followed by a fresh cold-water shower on the beach and I am perky and raring to go. Back at the house I grab a coffee before we drive over to collect the girls from the hotel. This is so much better. I can no longer face beginning each day with the *patron*'s glower. Michel laughs and tells me I am too sensitive. But judging by the look on the *patron*'s face every time we mount the stairs to the girls' room, I feel sure his nights are spent plotting our deaths.

Over breakfast, I relate the delights of the beach at seven A.M., eulogizing about the tranquility, the lack of tourists who are all still slumbering, not a footprint written on the golden sand and the sunrise. Ah, the sunrise! It lifts in majestic silence from a secret heaven beyond the hills, bringing warmth and a honey-ripe light which spreads across the water to meet the horizon, coloring the limpid Med a shimmering gold. At the center of this miracle is me, rippling through the salty stillness.

Having shared my moments of bliss, Vanessa expresses a fervent desire to come with me. Tomorrow, she begs, *s'il te plaît*, Carol, *chère* Carol?

I don't answer. She and her sister would sleep till noon if we left them to it.

S'il te plaît, Carol. She is so solicitous, requesting with pouting and passion. How can I possibly refuse? It is agreed.

After breakfast, back at the villa, the view is a heat haze. It gives an opium-smoked softness to the contours of the surrounding hills. Michel sets off on a visit to the water board while Vanessa and I clear the last of the ivy still clinging like death to the pool's walls and base. When this backbreaking chore has finally been accomplished, we stand back to admire the results of our labors.

"It's so cracked and old," she pronounces.

"It needs water," I encourage, but it does look strangely desolate.

In blistering heat, we hike the mountains of dead vegetation across the terraces and pile it all up as a bonfire, ready for burning at some later stage in the year. We dare not put a match to it for many months to come. In the south of France, it is against the law to light fires during the summer months. There is a high risk of bush incidents here. With our wild acres of growth and acute lack of water, in this temperature, we risk igniting the entire coastline and turning it to charcoal.

I look about for Clarisse. She is nowhere to be seen.

Baguettes for lunch under arm, Michel returns from the town looking fried and frazzled. It was noisy, dusty, packed with tourists and cars, he says, and he encountered a deeply unhelpful female *fonctionnaire* who informed him that they are unable to disclose the whereabouts of our water source without a legal document showing proof of purchase of the property or a recent bill, neither of which we have. Nor would the water board be willing to trace any location details without the name of the last account holder. The most likely person is the dog lady who ran off without paying any bills. He offered Madame B.'s name, but the assistant merely shook her head and then, with furrowed brow, informed him that the board had received a letter some eighteen months earlier from Madame B., requesting the water be cut off.

"Why would she have done that?" I ask.

"In France, if the electricity and water are officially switched off, the proprietors are not responsible for paying the land and habitation taxes," Michel says.

"So now what?"

"I am going back tomorrow with our passports and our *promesse de vente*. It is signed by Monsieur and Madame B. With those to hand I'll insist that they revert the instruction."

"Coo-coo, Papa!"

"Ah, you finished the pool. Well done." And with that Michel hurries inside for his camera to takes photos of Vanessa, waving and calling, alongside Pamela. They are investigating the deserted pool. At its deepest point, it measures three meters and makes even fat Pamela seem minute. I ponder the rushing gallons of water it will require, as well as Michel's tenacity through all of this.

AS EACH DAY PASSES, the land around the house grows more like a dust-bowl. When the wind is up, it settles everywhere—in our clothes, on kitchenware, on our skin, as grit around our teeth. Whatever we attempt, it is hot, dusty work, but the girls remain cheerful most of the time, and in their different ways, they offer their assistance with the task we have taken on. Although they are twins—fraternal—I am enjoying the discovery of their separate natures. Clarisse, possibly the less practical of the pair, spends hours picking wildflowers—her tiny frame is lost among the jungle growth—which she delivers in discarded wine bottles or jam jars to our rigged-up dining table, a wooden plank supported by bricks, broken tiles and other debris dug out of the garden. Vanessa, on the other hand, takes pleasure in the discovery of language and information. She has now owned up to a knowledge of English but adamantly refuses to speak a syllable of it with me. Why, I inquire, but she merely shakes her head and goes away. Is it some deep-rooted resistance to me, I ask myself, or is it that we are in her country and so, in her exacting mind, must speak her language?

Returning from the *boulangerie,* she and I drive by a house named *Mas de Soleil.* Back at the villa, she comes searching for me to borrow my dictionary to look up the meaning of *mas.* I wonder that she is French and hasn't come across the noun before, but then we learn that it is particular to this region, meaning a farmhouse or traditional Provençal house. She suggests we might like to rechristen our villa *Mas des Oliviers.*

"Do you like this house?" I probe, but she merely stares at me, shrugs and goes off about her own affairs. I'd like to detain her, engage her in conversation, ask her about her life in Paris, but only when we are at work together do I feel a bond. Still, whatever their opinions on the purchase of our dilapidated property—and perhaps they have none; after all, they are only thirteen—they appear neutral. I love them for not judging their father's choices. I have no children of my own; I have never married before. This will be my first go at it, and I suppose I am as nervous and inept as anyone in my position. I wrongfoot on a daily basis, but so far, nothing that cannot be redeemed. We are living in combustible conditions in broiling heat, but we make allowances for that, and for one another. In spite of the frustrations, I believe we are a happy band.

WHILE MICHEL BATTLES on with the water crisis, Vanessa, Clarisse and I attack the grounds, cutting them back to take stock of what is there. It is a time of discoveries: empty bottles, slabs of thick ancient floor tiles painted Tuscan earth colors. Were they transported here by the original owner of the house, whose name, I have learned from the reams of history documented in our *promesse de vente,* was Signor Spinotti? Signor Spinotti, a merchant from Milan, the creator of Appassionata. Yes, I like the sound of it and close my eyes to picture him: portly, exuberant, generous.

And Clarisse has unearthed a pond. "Carol! Papa! Come and look!" Who would have thought it? In this arid paradise, a kidney-shaped pond is revealed, about two meters long. It has survived, buried beneath jungles of streaky iris and wild lilies and heaven knows what other thick-stemmed weeds and, astoundingly, has not dried up, but the water is so dank and muddy that we cannot tell how deep it goes.

"Could it be fed from our elusive well?"

Michel kneels and considers its silty blackness. "It's very still; I doubt it, but who can know?" He rises, reminded of our lack of water, and turns around in the hot cloudless day, trying to figure out the puzzle.

I stare at the murky bath, longing to trickle my fingers through, to feel its liquidy velvet sensation and watch the drops dribble and drip back into the pond, but I am hesitant. I don't know what might lurk beneath its surface. Something sinister might rise up and bite me.

"Oh my God, look!" The water shivers and stills again.

Michel bends to survey what I am staring at but can see nothing. Neither can I.

"Something moved. I definitely saw it. I think it was a fish."

He laughs. "A frog, perhaps, but not a fish, *chérie*. The house has been empty for years."

"Well, when we have water, I'll clean it up, and then we really can have fish."

"Mmm. When we have water . . ." He glances at his watch. "I must get going."

HE TRACKS DOWN Monsieur Charpy, the estate agent, and persuades him to write an accompanying letter of attestation which, along with photocopies of our passports and a copy of the *promesse de vente*, the water board agrees to accept as proof that we are entitled to receive water. Late in the afternoon, Michel motors up the driveway honking, triumphant with his news. He rushes to the garage, and we switch on the main tap one more time, but there is still no water.

We exchange a silent, rather desperate look. Is this why Madame B. accepted such a drastic reduction in the price? Have we bought a farm without a water supply? The pig in a poke my father had warned me against.

"What now?" I ask.

"The EDF are coming to switch on the electricity tomorrow. The water supply shouldn't be affected, but maybe it is. Let's wait till then, *chérie*. If there's still no water, then . . . well, we'll see."

THE QUIETUDE OF MY morning swims on the beach alongside the Palm Beach Casino have been supplanted by the hectic itinerary of a family outing à la Monsieur Hulot. Even Pamela accompanies us now. Gone are the languorous laps that acted as my physical meditation, necessary to face the hurdles of house renovation on a shoestring. They have been replaced by a car trunk full of soggy towels, wet bathing suits and leaking shampoo bottles. Not to mention Pamela, who carries another twenty kilos of sand in her damp fur. Now, instead of swimming and quitting the beach in rejuvenated isolation, returning to the house to collect Michel by eight, by the time the troops are out of bed and rallied and we are on our way down the Boulevard Carnot, it is rush hour and I am grumpy.

"I don't want to do this anymore!" I scream. "These were *my* morning swims!" The erstwhile lunatic energy in the car recedes into awkward silence. Our outing is funereal in mood, and neither of the girls answers when I speak to them. Both have retreated into a serious sulk.

Later, over a cup of reheated coffee, because we have run out of water and didn't have time to refill one of the plastic canisters since an electrician and a representative from the EDF are arriving at ten-thirty, Michel chides me. Lovingly, he tells me that I am not behaving like a member of a family. "You are not used to it, *chérie*. The girls understand." And he brushes my nose with a kiss. But obviously they don't. They judge me demented, and I am ready to hurl myself in the bracken or the black viscose pond.

While I am elsewhere, feeling inadequate, the electricity is connected. A painless affair, certainly compared to the escalating water saga. In the presence of Mr. Dolfo, the electrician, Michel gives our water tap another try, but the pipes do not respond. Not one throaty gurgle.

"I don't suppose you know anything about this?" he asks Dolfo, who shakes his head and shrugs.

Still, to keep our spirits up, we celebrate our first step toward modern living by dashing out to the largest supermarket I have ever visited and purchasing a modest little fridge.

On our way back, Clarisse points out a series of brightly colored posters pasted to the lampposts all around the village. They are advertising a fireworks display to be held on the beach at Cannes. She pleads with Michel to take the girls down to the coast for the evening. He attempts to dissuade her, warning of the thousands who will be there, assuring her that we will see much more from our own terraces, but she, and now Vanessa, are insistent. So, along with Pamela, whom we dare not leave in case she has a heart attack from fright or waddles away in terror never to find her way back, we join the lines of descending traffic and head for the beach, which is teeming with holidaymakers. Every parking lot and garage is bursting; there is nowhere closer to Cannes than our own home to leave my VW.

By this stage, I am more than ready to dump the car and walk away, but Michel suggests we drive on a mile or two out of town and find ourselves a deserted stretch of sand to watch the display. This is what we do. Car parked, I wander over to a small stone jetty and sit. The girls are engaged in a rather earnest converstion with Papa, so I remain at a discreet distance, regarding the sea. In any case, I cannot follow what is being discussed, and since my earlier outburst, I have been feeling rather like an exposed nerve. Before me the waves are glinting silver in the moonlight. The water lapping at my feet is tranquil and soothing, but does not reach the confusions churning about inside me. Way along the coast, the pyrotechnics have begun. Great globes of blue, white and red—the colors of the French flag—explode into sprays that fall away silently. I am a foreigner here, an outsider. I travel frequently and regularly have found myself alone in the most outlandish of situations, but this time there is another nuance. I have given every penny I possess, which, granted, is not a whole heap, and thrown in my lot with a man I barely know; steamed off into the rosy sunset without a clue about where I was heading. Now we have an olive farm which we cannot begin to afford, no water, no prospects for any, two girls who are tolerating me . . .

Clarisse's arm presses up against me as she plops down beside me. It takes me by surprise.

"*Tu es très pensive*, Carol. Are you and Papa going to have a baby?" she inquires without preamble.

"I don't know. Maybe. Why, would that trouble you?"

She thinks hard for a minute and then shakes her head. "No, it's just that Vanessa and I have been talking about it."

"Have you? What have you been saying?"

She thinks again. I await her response with trepidation.

"It would be better if it were a girl."

"Why?"

"You both have such a lot of curly hair. It might look silly on a boy."

Innocent as this comment might be, by God, it heartens me.

Later, as we undress for bed, I ask Michel, "Were the girls talking to you about us having a baby?" He looks at me, amused. "No, why ever would you think that? They were wanting to know about the pool. They think we need advice on how to maintain it."

"Shouldn't we wait till we have water in it?" I suggest a mite testily.

"I promised them that one treat. I want to keep my promise, if I possibly can, and give them something to look forward to."

"So that's what you were so deeply engaged in conversation about, the swimming pool?"

He stares in surprise, a tired smile on his nut-brown face, placing his shirt on the cardboard box acting as dressing table. "What's the matter?"

I scramble into bed, and a spring needles me in the back, at which I curse profanely and drag the sheet over my head.

Michel approaches and lifts the bedding from my face. "Hey, what's up?"

"Nothing. I just hate this mattress and I want a bath."

THE FOLLOWING MORNING, even without my daily swim, promising amounts of my good humor have returned, and I kiss Michel lovingly as he sets off down the hill for the hot cramped office set alongside the motorway and occupied by the rather grandly named *Piscines Azurèenes - Construction et filtration - Produits - Accessoires - Contrats d'entretien - Dépannage - Robots de nettoyage* to buy a bucket of chlorine tablets and pick up a useful leaflet or two. The woman recommends that, because our pool has been empty for some time, we have an expert pay us a visit.

Within the hour, a swimming pool–blue van trundles up the drive, honking frequently. I run to take a look.

"Tie up that blasted dog or I'm not staying!" is our introduction to its driver. Poor dear Pamela, who was snoring happily and quietly enjoying her day, is dragged to one of the stables, where I attach her with a piece of string to one of the iron rings. It is only now she begins to bark.

Satisfied, out of the van comes *l'expert*. He is a burly fellow in very baggy trousers, with bloodshot eyes and a big dark drooping mustache, and he reeks of alcohol. (It is a little after eleven A.M.) He takes one look at the pool, throws his arms in the air and scoffs loudly. "This pool was constructed in the late twenties."

"Is that a problem?" I snap crossly.

He screws up his face, eyeing me beadily, then sets off on a slow plod around the pool's perimeter, bending and lifting like an ostrich, appraising it theatrically. "It is a capacious and sturdy piece of workmanship, *but* it has no filtering system."

Fortunately, both girls are elsewhere, because I know that bad news is about to be imparted. And it is. Within three days of its being filled, *même pas* three days, the water—if we ever locate any—will breed galloping algae and turn a brilliant green which, in this heat, would be a serious health hazard. I reluctantly admit to myself that he knows what he's talking about. The long and the short of it is that we cannot simply fill it as we had envisaged; we must construct a cleaning system. His estimate nearly sends me tumbling backward over the terraces.

The girls' disappointment when Michel breaks the news over lunch is heartbreaking, to say nothing of my own. We return to our land clearing in a despondent mood.

In an attempt to cheer us all up, Michel calls us, beckoning us down the hill. "*J'ai une bonne idée!*" he cries.

"No more stupid ideas, please, Papa!" returns Vanessa, refusing to even glance in his direction. "This whole place is a stupid idea," she mutters to her sister. I feel sinewy knots tighten in my stomach.

"A stroke of genius, *mes chéries*," he coaxes. "To put the empty pool to use."

But they will not even turn their heads. I watch him walk away, saddened for his defeat. Then curiously, he gathers up our old radio/cassette player, takes it to the swimming pool and descends the steps with it. I am intrigued. "Look at your father," I encourage, but the girls will not relent. When he has satisfied himself that he is standing in the center of the empty space, he places the machine, a rather clapped-out ghetto blaster, on the ground and slips a cassette into it. The voice of Sting bounces off the walls, reverberating bass and acoustic guitar, and reaches up the hill to the terraces where we three girls are at hot, sticky work. Their cross expressions break in delight. We drop our tools and race toward the music. There we are, covered in earth and bits of scythed weeds, alongside Michel, who is clapping to the beat. "Every problem has a good side," he says, laughing and winking blue eyes in my direction, while Pamela growls uncomprehendingly as we dance and hoot like crazed Indian squaws.

Into this bizarre scene arrives a small white Renault van. It is the electrician, Mr. Dolfo. He looks at us askance, trying not to notice the radio sitting in the center of a huge empty pool and the fat German shepherd going bananas barking at us, not at him.

He takes Michel aside as though there is no sense to be had anywhere near three such hysterical females and begins a conversation that appears to be serious and highly secret.

The evening before, over a glass, Mr. Dolfo tells Michel, he was in conversation with a fellow workman, a plumber and chimney sweep. By chance, he was relating the woes of the new waterless house owners on the hill. *Quelle surprise!* His colleague, who was born and bred in the village and used to hunt on our land as a lad, knows the exact whereabouts of our water house. Mr. Dolfo offers to drop by at the end of the day with Mr. Di Fazio. There is great excitement. I dash to the village to buy beer, cases and cases of it, to chill in our new little fridge and offer our rescuers, though the prospect of water at long last has become almost too improbable to count on, so I try very hard not to allow excitement to get the better of me. When did I ever think that water running from a tap would send me into paroxysms of joy!

THE VISCOSITY IN THE light caused by the day's heat is evaporating. Dolfo arrives up the hilly driveway late in the afternoon in his Renault van—which I later discover he cannot reverse!—followed by the chugging of what looks like an old bus. This is Mr. Di Fazio. The fellow emerges from his van in filthy blue overalls, and in this brilliant clear sunshine, we meet a man covered from head to toe in soot. Cleaning chimneys, he explains with a roar of laughter. I immediately take to him and his thick Provençal accent which twangs like country music and offer him a cold beer. This he accepts like a naughty boy, looking this way and that in pantomimic fashion as though he were about to be chased with a rolling pin. He pats his robust stomach, downs the beer in several thirsty gulps and mutters mischievously about disobeying his wife and the strict diet she administers.

Michel and the two men set off on foot. As he tells me later, they cross the lane bordering our land and disappear into the valley that sits between us and a narrow track winding to the village and on to the sea. There in that valley, they come upon a small stone house about the size of a cote.

"Your water shed!" declares Di Fazio.

Unbeknownst to us, this *petit* cabin was built by our splendid Italian ancestor, Signor Spinotti, in the same year as Appassionata and remains a part of the estate. When Appassionata was first constructed, its domain included this valley and the hills beyond. Nowadays, this particular parcel of land is owned by a syndicate in Marseille. Still, the small stone house, which has electricity, a water meter and an electric pump, remains the property of the villa owners, and they have water rights as well as rights of passage. Because its thick wooden door is jammed closed, Di Fazio wastes no time in breaking in; to reassure Michel, he points out the main pipe, situated aboveground outside and running alongside a small stream back toward the town.

First the three men switch on the water. It gushes forth instantly and splashes into the water house, filling up a cement dugout about a meter deep.

"Now we switch on the electric pump," continues Di Fazio, who makes a gesture toward Mr. Dolfo to do the honors. The pump begins to shimmy like a plump belly dancer.

"From here the water will be pumped to the *bassin* at the top of the hill, and from there it will flow back down to the main house." Michel and the two artisans watch on, satisfied, then they pull fast the door and make their way back up to the villa for a second, much deserved cold beer.

Di Fazio takes a deep slug from his bottle, squinting at the hill's brow. Behind him, we stand like extras in a film, following his gaze, waiting expectantly. A remarkably large black and white butterfly flutters by me.

"*Deux heures,*" our new plumber pronounces with the expertise and wisdom of God.

Two hours. The words are repeated like a Chinese whisper as though the miracle is too incredible to articulate out loud. In two hours we will have water!

"*Quelle heure est-il?*" demands Vanessa, needing as always to be precise. Clarisse shrugs. She has lost her watch somewhere between wild-flower picking and selecting branches for flower arrangements from the scythed broome Vanessa and I have decimated.

"Half past six."

"So, half past eight, then? Yippee!"

HALF PAST EIGHT comes, and half past eight goes. The water does not arrive. Every thirty minutes, one of us is given the thirst-inducing duty of pounding up the hill in the falling evening light to confirm whether or not the water has begun to arrive. Each one of us returns half dead with a shake of the head. *Pas encore*. Five hours later, when we prepare for bed, there is still no sign of water.

The next morning Di Fazio returns. He and Michel, who by now is acquainted with every overgrown square centimeter of this land, set off with shears and a scythe to walk the hills and terraces in search of burst pipes and leaks. They find none. So, *en principe*, there is no reason why the water should not be arriving up in the basin. Eventually, a return visit to the stone house shows them that the electric pump which burst into life at the flick of a switch has died. Clearly the effort, after so many years of idleness, was simply too much for it. We will need a new pump. After a lunchtime consultation with Mr. Dolfo, we learn that the new pump will cost, including labor, approximately ten thousand francs, or about fifteen hundred dollars. This news is bad. Ten thousand francs is more than we have left, and we have not yet settled our bill with the hotel owner. We thank both Mr. Dolfo and Mr. Di Fazio for their assistance and tell them we will be in touch when we next return to the coast. Shaking hands with us, they slip away discreetly. Their disappointment on our behalf is evident.

FRIENDS ARRIVE IN A two-car convoy from England, bringing with them bits of furniture and two large terra-cotta pots I purchased in Crete which will look splendid on either side of the pool steps, as well as other offerings of one sort or another, including, most importantly, my mail. We cannot hide our dismay about the water. A lunch salad is made, and Michel recounts our ongoing water saga over an aperitif while I disappear to our bedroom to read through the stack of letters. Most are junk, a few are from long-distant friends who have heard via the grapevine about my new life—sounds divine, darling!—and want to come and visit, and one is from my agent. A letter from my agent usually contains one of two things: the occasional forwarded fan letter or two, in which case the envelope is usually thicker, or a check. This envelope is slender. My hopes are high. I open it with trembling fingers praying that the check will not be for some ridiculous sum, such as 47 pence from the BBC for a foreign program sale to some remote cable channel in the middle of Botswana. The letter is notification of a check which has been paid directly into my London account for a series of sales and repeat fees on *All Creatures Great and Small.* The check more than covers the price of the water pump. In fact, it will stretch to the first installment on the required cleaning system for the pool. Our day, no, our summer is made.

I run crazily out onto the upper terrace waving the statement like a flag of victory. Friends and family, seated around the table on the level below me, cheer and raise glasses as I deliver the news.

Michel hurtles off in the car to telephone Mr. Dolfo while the rest of us lay the table for lunch and change the cassette in the swimming pool. Funky music echoes around the hillside. Our water problem is at an end.

Ah, how much we take for granted in city life! The simple rituals of brushing our teeth, getting clean, soaping our flesh recklessly, frothing our hair into sudsy turbans of shampoo, make us jubilant. Vanessa discovers a leak on the land in one of the pipes where the water is spraying out as though it were a geiser. She jumps about over it and leaps on the muddied earth, splashing and washing, laughing and whooping. Her exuberant cries cut through the still heat, silencing even the cicadas.

"SEE, THE HOUSE faces southwest. It looks out over the bay of Cannes, the promontory of Fréjus and the sweeping gulf of Napoule and, if we stand on tiptoe or take a ladder and scale the back wall onto our flat, graveled roof, you can clearly see the two islands sleeping off the coast of Cannes, west of Antibes, known as the Îles des Lérins."

From our top terrace, after sundown, when the streetlamps light up along the coastal road that snakes around the promontory of Fréjus, it looks as though someone has dropped a priceless diamond necklace, leaving it to glitter across the westerly half of the horizon. Sometimes the Esterel Mountains turn a dusky blue and resemble a Japanese painting. Alongside, the pink sunset puts me in mind of flamingoes flitting across a mirage. Our friends are falling for this ramshackle villa as much as we have. So we are not alone, not so dizzy.

THANKS TO THE rooms taken by our guests, the *patron* now has a full hotel. He puts up the sign—*Complet*—and the small affair of illicit showers is dismissed with a shrug and a glass of wine. We settle our account with him while the girls pack their bags, and then we drive them home to be with us at the villa. And what is more, they seem excited at the prospect.

"PAPA! PAPA, *viens içi!*" It is Clarisse calling. Everyone downs tools and runs to the terrace where she is standing and waving. Vanessa is at her side. They are now kneeling and staring into our pond. "*Il y a des poissons!*"

I knew it! Ever since that hot midge-biting afternoon when we first discovered the pond, I have been returning there to try to penetrate the living mystery of its smoked-glass surface. Clarisse, with her usual fascination for the minutiae of wildlife, has passed the last hour filling jugs of water from the luxury of our water supply—a running tap!—and pouring them into the pond. The fresh water has stirred the silt and life beneath. There, swimming close to the brimming surface of the diluted, bracken-toned water, are three huge fish. Each is a good foot long.

"*C'est incroyable!*"

The four of us are on all fours like thirsty mogs bent close over the water to examine the fish. They are carp, or monstrous goldfish. Then another appears. And another! In all, we count five or six, possibly even seven, it is difficult to be precise as they dart and dive. But the first three are the largest.

"How have they lived all this time?" I ask.

"On the plankton, the natural vegetation. Still, it is rather miraculous," says Michel.

Another discovery of Appassionata's life—its resilience. Each day, we are thrilled by new wonders.

AND THEN OUT OF the blue, a rather disagreeable guest turns up, an elderly gentleman searching for Michel. He is a writer who has come in the hope of selling a screenplay. How did he find us, we ask ourselves, but can find no satisfactory explanation. Fortunately, our living circumstances are so manifestly primitive that we have no need to apologize for the lack of a bed, but politeness and Michel's endless generosity dictate that we invite him to stay for dinner. Our little gathering has now reached eleven. Dinner is prepared on the barbecue. It is a communal affair and great fun. Running water from the tap in the temporary kitchen facilitates the washing of vegetables and salads.

We dine beneath the magnolia grandiflora. From there we have views to the sea and the mountains. Golden, lambent light from the antique oil lamp I brought from England illuminates our late-evening gathering. Water trickling into the pool threatens to drown out Billie Holiday's "Easy Living." We hardly care. The flow itself is music to our ears. Still, at this rate, we calculate it will take three weeks to fill! Chris, one of my oldest friends, offers to purchase us several hoses as a housewarming gift. We drink to that and assure him that he has guaranteed himself a welcome return.

We recount our search for water to the unexpected new arrival. In response, rather like an embittered old Cassandra, he predicts, "Once a water problem, always a water problem. In my house in Spain . . ." and tells with relish his woeful story as though he were wishing us an equal measure of ill luck. The table goes silent, nothing more than water spluttering into the pool, distant chirring of sleepless crickets and strains of "Good Morning Heartache" can be heard.

"But the problem is solved. Now we have water," I chip in cheerily.

"And there is always wine," rejoins Michel, replenishing glasses all around.

LATER, WINED AND REPLETE, our numerous guests set off down the drive, heading over the hills to the cozy amiability of the little hotel and perhaps a last nightcap at the bar. There is much kissing and embracing; much drunken teasing, a dozen repeated "good nights," bonhomie and promises of outings to the beach and the various flea markets over the course of the next few days. Then, with the receding hum of the last of the cars, we are left alone. *En famille.*

For a short while before turning in, we sit together gazing at the canopy of stars, arms slung loosely around one another; a man, his two adoring daughters and the new woman. An actress. Another breed of woman, nothing like Maman. Little is said. I occasionally read perplexity or guilt in the girls' behavior, particularly today, when a thick letter arrived from Maman and they snatched it like small squirrels and hiked it off to read in the privacy of their bedroom. I am aware that to like me might well be seen as an act of infidelity to their mother or their parents' past life, but still I sense we are creeping toward one another. Shattered after work-filled days, in the hot sticky evenings, in the silence or the lack of language, mosquitoes buzzing like dive bombers, slowly, I dare to believe we are growing to accept one another.

After an embrace, we all drift off to bed.

Michel's back is acting up. I think it is the result of scaling the hills and spending our nights on the lumpy old mattress, but it doesn't seem to stop him from sleeping while I lie awake thinking a million different thoughts, such as how I wish we could afford a proper bed. Yet, I am happy. I love the man breathing peacefully at my side. I love this old house, although I am beginning to comprehend the enormity of our task. But we are not in any hurry. This is our first summer. Officially, the property is not yet ours. That hurdle—oh Lord!—has yet to be faced. For the moment, we have achieved electricity and water. With these two precious commodities, we can live here in a basic sort of fashion. Tomorrow, work on the pool-cleaning system will begin. We have a barbecue for summer, plenty of fresh salad from the colorful market in Cannes, a choice of fine cheeses, oven-warm bread and many bottles of local wine. How better fed could we be? Michel says that when we return at Christmas, he will teach me how to cook on the open fire.

I reshuffle myself, trying to avoid the springs, and cuddle into the arc of his soft back, preparing to dream of our first winter here: log fires, barbecued turkey and outings in search of woodland *cèpes*, when I hear a pitter-pattering above me. I lift my head into the warm starry darkness, trying to locate the sound. The roof is flat. Is it a small animal running to and fro? Then, as the sound grows faster and more furious, I realize that it is rain. Yes, it is raining. The first I have seen here. I drag the flimsy summer sheet fast around me and listen to its falling. Summer rain, after so many parched and waterless days. With it will come a whole host of new perfumes. Drenched nature. We have our own thin stream of water trickling into the pool, and as if to assist it, the heavens have opened. What a cloudburst. I fall asleep to streams of it drumming fast overhead.

The next morning, the rain has stopped. The ground is damp and earthy-smelling and the air is clear, washed of its heavy, thick heat.

Unusually, I am the first out of bed, and I creep sleepy-eyed to the kitchen to brew coffee. Imagine my surprise when I suddenly find it is wet underfoot and look down to discover three puddles sitting like rain clouds on the tommette-tiled kitchen floor. At first, I am ready to blame poor

Pamela for slinking into the kitchen in the dead of night in search of food and piddling there. Then the horror awakens me. I lift my head ceiling-ward and realize that in among all the flaking strips of plaster there are three holes. Tiny holes, barely bigger than pencils, but they are lethal for they are letting in rainwater.

"Michel! We have a leaking roof!"

CHAPTER THREE

HOLIDAY BOARS AND HENRI

We haven't a centime left to plow into the leaking roof, or the kitchen or the replastering, not any of the rest of the *projets* that await us. On top of which, the house still has to be purchased—I wake nightly, soaked in perspiration, haunted by Madame B.'s proviso: if anything should go wrong, you lose everything. We have certainly invested more than we had bargained for at this stage. However, our first major hurdle— the water—has finally been resolved, so in the company of the girls, Michel and I decide to ignore the rest and take it easy. We allow ourselves to be *en vacances*.

We sleep with the French doors open, ready to greet the next dawn. Our room looks out onto a scruffy rear terrace, partially shaded by two fragrant eucalyptus trees and a Portuguese oak, an evergreen whose silvery-hued leaves rather resemble those of the olive tree. This terrace is where we spend time alone. We breakfast here while the girls sleep late: toast, fresh fruit, coffee. Although it is the only terrace that doesn't look out over the Mediterranean, I love it; tucked away at the back of the house, it feels like ours. The rising sun filtering through the treetops embraces us, promising another warm day.

While I put the coffee on, Michel drives down the hill, a kilometer or so, to the village baker who has been up baking since three A.M. There he purchases fresh warm baguettes and *pain au chocolat* so light they practically melt at the touch and, usually, a *sablé*, a large round biscuit flavoured with almonds, which, in spite of my perennial weight-watching, I devour with a greed that would put Pamela to shame.

By now, my morning trips to the beach have been abandoned. Instead, I head for the pool, entering by the steps because there is still insufficient water to dive in. The level in the shallow end has now reached my thighs. I tumble in and doggy-paddle to the deeper end, where I can swim a decent width or two. I try not to splash noisily, so as not to wake the girls, who sleep till noon, then throw open their shutters to blinding, hot light.

After the frenzy of the past two weeks, a more languorous pace is taking hold, and we give ourselves up to it readily. I am beginning work on a novel, my first—having already completed its storyline and treatment—which Michel has found the financing to produce as a television series in Australia at the end of the year. Michel is never without his camera now. Photography is his passion. There are the obvious "before and after" house snapshots for future albums, but mostly he shoots plants, usually flowers. He spends hours gazing through a lens into the stamen of this yellow flower, that wild rose. It is quite staggering how many varieties of flowers have survived among the brambled chaos of this garden and manage somehow or other to find the light, to hold their heads up toward the sun and blossom richly.

I begin to notice the similarities between Clarisse and Michel as I watch them discussing the intricacies of a bud, the feather-thin line drawings on a leaf, the shape of a frond, even a blade of grass. Together, they disappear down unseen tracks for hours on end in their search for ever more layers of nature. They are true children of the earth. In our different ways, we all are. All four of us are Taureans!

In the quietness of a heat-infested afternoon, while they explore and Vanessa, munching one crispy apple after another, sunbathes or studies or washes her long hair and myriad bees busy themselves collecting honey, I decide to take an inventory. For starters, I count fifty-four olive trees growing along the front terraces and to either side of the house. There may be others farther up the hill, but at this stage, it is impossible to reach them. I try to recall tales and myths I have read or heard about the olive tree. Surely the most ancient of all trees? The Greeks brought it to Provence, I believe, two or more thousand years ago while trading in the Mediterranean.

I intend to farm ours. The olive is a bitter fruit and cannot be eaten directly from the tree. The four ways I know to serve it are pressed for oil; bottled or marinated in salted water to be offered with aperitifs or tossed in with salad; cooked; or as a paste known as *tapénade*, created by a Monsieur Meynier in Marseilles toward the end of the nineteenth century. It is made by pulping the fruit and mixing it with anchovies (best fresh, particularly those from the Camargue) and capers. It can be spread on warm toast and served with crisply chilled wine, and is delicious. The name comes from *tapéno*, which is the Provençal word for capers.

But perhaps these ancient trees have other offerings that I have yet to discover. Since being here, I have learned that the timber burns on an open fire better than almost any other wood, and we will find ourselves with plenty of spare timber; every tree needs pruning. They are far too bushy and tall. A perfectly pruned olive tree is one through which a swallow can fly without its wings brushing the branches.

Slowly, I am gleaning such snippets of information. As I stroll the land, making a list, I promise myself that the next time I am in Cannes, I will find a manual on olive farming. No matter how much I study, we will need to find a hands-on person who can perform this highly specialized task; down here, it is a much respected occupation. I have no idea how to go about this, but I feel confident that, in the fullness of time, the right individual for the job will come along.

We have four almond trees, the largest of which is at swimming-pool level to the right of the house, beyond the frostbitten orange grove. It leans forward at a rather precarious angle and will need cutting back and shoring up before a *mistral* rips it from the ground, taking roots and a drystone wall with it. I should hate to lose it. Its position is perfect for its powder-pink blossoms to be in full view from all sea-facing terraces. Almonds flower earlier than most fruit trees, so I expect that we will see the first of the blossoms sometime in February, and later, the nuts, removed from green shells that resemble soft furry caterpillars, can be roasted on our open fire.

Our tiny orange grove is a sorry spectacle. All six trees are dead. Before we close up the house, I will cut them down.

Over to the left, facing the sea, I can make out two cherry trees in need of pruning. They will probably be fruiting around the time of the Cannes Film Festival—we could munch them instead of popcorn during the screenings!

On the opposite side, there is a tall bay tree which, due to the growth, I cannot get near, but I can almost taste the many soups and roasts to come, all seasoned with rosemary, olive oil from our own pressed crop and freshly picked bay leaves.

So far I have counted eight fig trees, one of which must be the largest fruit tree I have ever set eyes on. It reminds me of a prehistoric beast, its trunk thick and gnarled. It shades a segment of our steep driveway and hides a very ugly EDF (Électricité de France) cement pylon which, as soon as funds allow, we will do away with by cabling the electricity under-ground from lane to house.

Several of the fig's branches reach across the drive and hang down over the pool: temptation itself. I imagine relaxing in between laps, stretching for a ripe fruit and devouring it while idling in the water. In the past, I have never been particularly fond of fresh figs, and I wonder if living with them will reeducate my tastes. Gorging on freshly picked figs strikes me as hedonistic. It conjures up images of Roman baths with slaves serving bowls laden with overripe fruit. Even without such a picture, it is a sexual fruit—luscious, rich in seeds with a sticky juice. As I stand in the driveway with my head tilted upward and my fingers pressed against my Panama hat, gazing into its green vastness, it occurs to me that the fig tree has no flowers. I wonder why. And how it pollinates. So much syrupy fodder and the poor bees have no reason to visit.

I TOOK OFF MY WATCH a fortnight ago and have not worn it since. The sun has become my timekeeper. It rises behind us and greets us in the bedroom, breakfasting with us. From there it passes around the cherry-tree side of the house and then, noon-high in the sky, makes its arc around the front, over the glinting sea, until it hovers in the west, where it sinks slowly and graciously behind the hills and leaves a sky of bleeding colors.

Now it is high above the Fréjus promontory. Four o'clock. Time for tea.

I begin a slow meander back up toward the house to face the dratted water heater in our primitive kitchen, still cogitating on my list and wondering where everyone else has gone.

Apples, mandarins, lemons; cut down the dead orange trunks and plant new trees, pears . . . No, there is a pear. I caught sight of it on the level below the pool, next to where we are constructing the pool-cleaning system. A smattering of fruits on it, all misshapen and worm-eaten. It needs treating. I have always fancied an orchard. My parents bought a home with an orchard when I was small, but we never lived in it. Visits there were the few occasions I ever saw my father pottering in the garden.

And what about a modest vineyard? Where did Spinotti order his vines to be planted?

So many dreams. But the stuff of dreams are the food of life, and I marvel at what we have achieved this summer on a shoestring and a bit of graft.

Appassionata is slowly, very slowly, coming back to life. After neglect, the house is waking up. Its essence is reemerging. Shapes, colors, aspects of light are speaking to us.

Michel and I met on a film in Australia, a mass of land we both love profoundly. Its colors, its light, its vast expanses speak to us. Had our lives not been so locked into our careers here in Europe, this house might have been another somewhere on the Australian continent.

It is widely known that the Australian aboriginals go walkabout, but what I did not know until I crossed the world to work there was that one of the purposes of their walkabouts is to sing nature back into existence. I find that such an enchanting image. To walk a land every so often and sing the mountains, the rivers, streams, caves, animals, insects, nature in all its diverse magnificence, back into existence. I equate that image with what we are attempting to achieve here. Appassionata has been abandoned. It—sorry, but I see the house as she, perhaps because the French word, *maison*, is feminine—she, Appassionata, was rented out for many years. Bills were unpaid, the fabric of the building has been left to ruin, its fruits have dropped from the trees and lie rotting. The plants, every bush and shrub, are being strangled. The house has lost its voice. Or rather, its voice has gone unheard.

In my understanding of the aboriginal walkabout—and I am not saying that this is the meaning of the image, it is merely my interpretation of it—nature and its every mountain, hill, waterfall, ant nest and pathway have a voice. To stand at any moment in front of the miracle of any particle of nature and to listen, truly listen, is to hear its song. To hear its song is to allow it to sing. That is how I understand "singing a place back into existence."

Michel and I are rediscovering Appassionata. We are attempting to sing this small holding in the south of France back into blooming existence. We will try to listen to what it has to offer and to celebrate its uniqueness. Of course, all this is subjective, and anyone eavesdropping on my train of thought might very well accuse me of being loco, suffering from a touch of the midday sun.

THE OTHERS ARE nowhere to be found. I abandon the idea of tea, which I am not fond of anyway, and hike a gaudily striped deck chair to the top terrace. There I settle in to gaze upon the sea. It is a very pleasing sensation to spend hour after hour sitting still, simply watching the plays of light on sea and sky. I have not done it for a very long time. Too long. Time passes and I unwind, looking and listening. Even in its silence, it is furiously busy. Ants, lizards, ghekkos, cicadas, they are all going about their day, searching for food, fending off the enemy, screeching their mating calls, thriving on or surviving the heat. They are not on holiday.

But then neither am I, I suddenly remember. In the short term, for a few weeks with Michel and his daughters, but not the long term. I am moving the rudder, shifting the course of my existence. I had not thought of it in those terms before, but that is what I am doing. And there is nothing more sacred or precious in life than that. Choosing a direction, but how often do we miss the signposts?

"What have you been up to all afternoon?"

"Oh, hi there! Counting trees."

Clarisse and Michel are returning. They are dusty and shiny from walking. Clarisse shows me a tiny crayon drawing she has done during the course of the afternoon. It is very impressive, and I tell her so. She beams contentedly. "*C'est la lumière*," she replies modestly, and Michel ruffles her tousled hair.

Yes, there is a quality about the light here—it has seduced so many great painters. It enhances all photos and frames of footage each moment of the day. As I live with it on a daily basis, its subtleties begin to draw me in. On certain days, its purity is blinding; then its colors alter as clouds, winds, hours of heat seep in. Here, light is a living experience. I have known it thus only once before, in Australia. As with Michel and the reproducing of his flowers on film, its contemplation becomes a spiritual experience.

THE CONTEMPLATION OF Pamela, however, is another matter altogether. I watch her with dismay as she heaves herself from one shady spot to the next, continuously hunting out respite from the broiling sun. She has lived all her life on the outskirts of Paris, and I fear that this relentless Riviera heat is going to kill her. "Her heart will give out," I predict. The others tease me and my sense of the dramatic, but I pay no attention to them and announce one morning at breakfast that I am putting the corpulent creature on a strict diet.

"Carol, why must you be so strict? Drink your coffee and leave *la pauvre* Pamela in peace!" chides Vanessa.

"Is it a foolish interference?" I ask Michel, who is not listening. He is kneeling on the ground, like a mutt himself, staring concentratedly at a wall.

"You will live to regret it," Clarisse warns me.

"Come and look at these little chaps!"

A procession of brown furry caterpillars linked to one another causes us all great delight. United, the length of them measures more than a meter.

"They look as though they are bound for somewhere."

They are certainly moving with purpose and visible speed. Are they being led to a conducive hideaway where in tranquility and privacy they can transform themselves into butterflies? All four of us are completely taken with observing them, mesmerized by their single-mindedness. A family of four on all fours, staring at a wall. Must be a curious sight.

Since breakfast on our hidden terrace, which is where Michel first spotted them descending one of the dry stone walls, making their way across the terrace and into the house, they have preoccupied us. They have exited the house now, having crossed the main living room—leaving a clean trail in the dust of untouched rooms—traveled the length of the top terrace down one of the pillars, and are now tramping, at swimming pool level, toward the uncut bracken. Intrepid travelers! Will they get lost in the thicket? Or will they see it for the wilderness that it is, turn around and return to us? The distance they have traveled since this morning—it is now siesta time, baking hot, and I am alone because the others have disappeared to nap—is considerable. They put me in mind of a small train puffing away, heading for the great unknown. A tractor crossing Russia en route for Siberia. I see they have reached the uncut terrain and, without a moment's hesitation, have disappeared into it. *Bonne chance!*

I am very taken with the butterflies here. They are numerous and of many different colors and species. In a few weeks' time, I will look closely into the eye of each circling butterfly and inquire of it: were you one of the visiting caterpillars who left an autograph in our dust?

I HAVE WOUND DOWN to a pace that is almost slow motion. I am watching time elapse. It is a delicious exercise which allows me to focus on details that in my ordinary life, my *real* life, I would not give seconds to.

The bucket that was used to flush the toilets when we had no water is now in the upstairs kitchen. Well, barely a kitchen; it comprises an aluminum sink which is part of a unit containing probably the first dishwasher ever built (now nonfunctional), an electric kettle which must predate the LEB, and a musty, woodworm-riddled cupboard. I have positioned the bucket beneath those three dratted holes which stare at me every time I go in there, the three Cyclops who made thunderbolts. We have been forced to accept that, for this summer at least, this is the most effective solution for the leaking roof. Fortunately, since that monumental downpour, not one drop of rain has fallen. Still, it is amazing to me how much time I can fritter away beneath three minuscule holes, watching them with a malevolent gaze.

Wandering through the dilapidated rooms, basking in the cool generated by the meter-deep stone walls which comprise the husk of the house, I step out onto the upper front terrace and am hit by a blanket of heat and sunshine. I subside into a chair and listen. There are small birds here that flit in and out of the bushes. Occasionally, when they start to sing, I charge indoors, mistakenly thinking the phone is ringing—it's my agent!—and then remind myself we have no phone.

There is so much I should be doing: attacking my novel, washing down walls, scraping encrusted dirt out of wooden window frames, worrying about Madame B. and whether this deal will ever go through or whether I—we—are living a summer's fantasy leading us right into the mouth of financial disaster. Instead I do nothing except sit, listen and contemplate.

Evening comes and I rise to feed Pamela her food. The bowl is kept alongside the garage near the stone-walled stables, well away from our kitchen or food supplies. She woofs down the offering in two gulps, then glowers at me. I have underestimated the force of Pamela's attachment to food—it is her *raison d'être*—but I hearten myself with the fact that she is looking slimmer. Until yesterday evening, she has spent every day lying slumped and panting in the shade as though gasping her last. When Michel descended the drive to put the dustbins out, she actually trudged along after him. Thank heavens, she is growing active.

OUR HOUSE IS NAMED Appassionata, yet there are no passion flowers anywhere to be found. None that we have unearthed, that is. Perhaps we will discover a plant or two languishing beneath all the unruly growth. I drive to a local nursery to purchase one, as well as a twenty-kilo sack of *terreau universel*. My eye is tempted by a small pomegranate tree, meters of curly tumbling geraniums and dozens of richly colored roses, not to mention bananas and lemons and palms. Oh, the list is endless, but I must exercise restraint. I love nurseries, *les pépinières*—which coincidentally is the same noun used to describe a school for young actors—I love the lushness and the damp tropical scents, the splash of sharply colored, exotic blossoms, the regulated coolness. I love, now more than ever, that steady drizzle of hoses discreetly orchestrating the silent, lusty growth. I happily pass the hours I should be spending hacking back the sinuous streams of weeds playing truant at the nursery.

On my way home, I stop in the village to pick up fresh salad. I park, cross the street alongside the square, where half a dozen old men wearing hats and shades and looking like rejects from the mafia are playing boules, and make for the *crémerie fromagerie*. Here I buy two *crottins* of goat cheese, two spit-roasted organic chickens seasoned with herbs and creamy toasted garlic cloves for our supper on the terrace.

As I am leaving, a farmer arrives. He has aroused my curiosity on several previous occasions, because, in the rear of his Citroen van, which looks as though it is held together by elastic bands, is a motley collection of farmyard animals. The animals honk and screech, but even though he leaves the van's rear door swinging open, they never attempt an escape. I hang back to observe him. Always the same routine. He unloads three wooden boxes of small plastic pots brimming with golden olive oil, seasoned with Provençal herbs. Swimming in the center of each pot are generous nuggets of goat cheese. Then come the hams, usually ten, substantial cuts, wrapped in light muslin cloth. Each is carefully weighed as it passes over the counter. The bearded, keen-eyed owner of this modern-day dairy and this farmer do their business in front of waiting customers, including whoever was in the process of being served. Thick wads of cash pass from the till into the pocket of the farmer, and off he goes with his jaunty gait, Wellingtons slapping against the pavement even in this heat. He resembles a living scarecrow.

Why does he travel with his animals? I saw him the first time, with two white goats, four ducks, chickens and honking geese, all wedged tightly together, the fowl shuffling in and around goat legs. I assumed they were on their way to be slaughtered or sold, but obviously not. They are his road companions and seem perfectly content to travel with him squashed up against one another. If the pigs have not become hams, would he be traveling with them? The owner of the *crémerie* is his regular customer, so there must be more pigs back at home, or how would he continue to supply the *jambon*? Later, I learn that the hams are not his. He transports and sells them for a neighboring farmer. The favor covers the cost of his gas. His own lean income is earned from the goat cheese and his traveling circus of fowl.

Back at the house, I deposit the food on the makeshift table in the downstairs kitchen. Alas, in my excitement to get back to the car and unsack the thick dark earth for the planting of my tender climber, I forget to shut the door. When I pass by a mere ten minutes later, I find the two bags which had contained the chickens in tatters on the floor. Even the cheese has disappeared. A brief scout around the garden leads me to Pamela, snoring beneath the cypress trees, surrounded by crunched bones and an army of ants who have already begun to pick dry the skeletal remains. Preferring not to whack an animal, particularly one that is not mine, I take myself back down to the village to buy another pair of chickens and two more of the goat cheese "droppings." The young couple who own the *crémerie* stare at me in wonder as I request precisely what I bought a mere half an hour earlier. "Unexpected guests," I mutter, feeling too foolish to admit that the dog ate our dinner.

THE PALE RAYS OF the late-afternoon sun are lengthening. The hysteric chirring of the cicadas' song grows less strident. The day is slipping into dusky stillness. Evening is falling. Vanessa is lighting anti-mosquito candles as well as my oil lamp. Spaced out on the balustraded terrace, they create golden balls of light. With glasses of chilled Bandol rosé in hand, Michel and I ceremoniously plant the climber on a mezzanine terrace close to the front door. A tender young passionflower; our first purchase for the garden; the perfect offering. Clarisse waters it abundantly. Vanessa takes the shot with Michel's camera.

Our first summer will be at an end soon, but these are the moments that will live on perpetually. I will return to them again and again in the safe harbor of memory. Consummate happiness. I stand back, absorbing the image of Michel with his adolescent girls, and I wonder silently what the unknown future holds for us.

I WAS NOT PREPARED for this. When it comes to the refueling of Pamela's stomach, a revitalized and cunning beast has been awakened. Docile Pamela, who identifies me as the enemy, the appropriator of her food, has declared war. The following morning, I find that the trash cans, ours as well as those belonging to the other two houses situated on the easterly quarter of our hill, have been raided. Half-chewed sticks of stale baguette, empty food packages, and the rest of the mishmash found in any family's trash trail along the lane. I spend twenty minutes gathering up the garbage and chucking it all back into our trash cans. A note from one of the neighbors attached to one of our lids politely requests that we keep the animal chained if it cannot keep its head out of *les poubelles*. Mortified, I admit defeat and write a note of apology to the unknown neighbors, which I slip into their mailbox. It will not happen again, I assure them.

Indeed, the problem will not arise again, for the girls are departing, and with them goes fat Pamela. What a hullabaloo of semi-packed bags, broken zippers, lost combs, whirring hair dryers, newly acquired swimwear, presents for Maman which are *très fragile*, as well as the calming of a most unsettled dog who, poor unsuspecting beast, will be obliged to travel in a miserable airline cage. The frenzied activity keeps my sadness at bay. And when everything is finally arranged, albeit in a chaotic sort of

way, Michel and I drive them to the airport and see them off. This journey to the Nice airport is to be the first of many. From here on, my life
will be governed by trips to and from, welcome kisses and aching *au
revoirs*. Today is the first wrench.

Vanessa and Clarisse. I have grown to love them, and I so long for
them to feel the same. I hope that these weeks, this glorious summer, have
brought us closer. I want them to care for me not as a surrogate mother
but as a friend, as kin. Nothing is said, no parting emotion declared, but
they step forward shyly to hug me, then stagger off with their numerous
bags, trailing towels and sneakers through passport control, waving back
and blowing kisses at their beloved papa and maybe one to his new lady.

This departure is the first nudge that the summer holidays are drawing to a close. In another week, Michel will also return to Paris. I have no
acting job awaiting me, so I have decided to stay on, to get to grips with
my novel and because I cannot bear to tear myself away. Michel will fly
down to spend the weekends with me.

We pass our final week together at our desks, slowly preparing ourselves, for what the French call *la rentrée*—the return after the summer
break. Michel's desk is a wobbly wooden table picked up at one of the
many *brocantes* off the *route national 7*, near Antibes. He has placed it in
the shade beneath the magnolia grandiflora. I have learned that these trees
were originally from the southern states of America. They were discovered
by the French botanist Plumier, who had been commanded by Louis XIV
to seek out exotic plants for the royal gardens. The earliest examples were
brought to France in the first half of the eighteenth century. They were
named after Pierre Magnol, who was director of the botanical gardens in
Montpellier.

Unlike Michel, I cannot concentrate in a blanket of heat and prefer to
bury myself indoors. I choose one of the rooms that we have not yet
touched save for washing the floors and airing. I have secretly bagged it for
my workspace—I hate the word *office*—because it is bright but not too

sunny. It has windows to the front which overlook the driveway and the angle of cypress trees. If I lean to my left, I can even glimpse the shallow end of the pool, now brimming with clear water. And to the rear, its French doors open onto the terrace where we breakfast. Beyond, I see roughly hewn stone steps ascend the pine forest to the brow of the hill and our famous water *bassin*. Here, in this room, I set up a trestle table and store my laptop, reference books, scribbled notes for my story, maps, research literature and all my other papers. After each working bout, to keep dust and falling plaster at bay, I wrap everything in a sheet. When Michel has left, I will strip the walls and whitewash them, rid the room of its hideous pink flowery paper. There is a good feeling about this space; I can lose myself in my own world here. And because it has views in both directions, I don't feel claustrophobic. The only disturbance is an occasional rustling sound which I cannot trace or identify. It seems to be coming from a boxed-in pelmet, which probably once stored a rolling blind above the front windows, but whenever I call Michel in to listen, the noise mysteriously ceases.

DURING AN AFTERNOON break from work, I take a stroll in the valley beyond our land, where I encounter a most extraordinary person who puts me in mind of a minotaur or Goliath. He introduces himself as our neighbor Jean-Claude. Oh, dear. He is the one who wrote the note complaining about Pamela. I smile sweetly. We wouldn't want to get on the wrong side of this fellow. He is built like an ox. He has a wiry black beard and hair tied back in a ponytail which falls to his nonexistent waist. He is wearing nothing except bizarrely cut red poplin shorts and calf-length black Wellingtons, and he carries two empty buckets, one in each hand like a milkmaid. I have barely given our names when he booms at me: "Which water plan are you on?" I have absolutely no idea and refrain from admitting that I was not even aware there was a choice.

"Inquire of your husband, please, and let me know."

This I dutifully promise to do, and content with my reply, he suggests that Michel and I walk over to have an *apéro* with him and his wife, Odile, at seven o'clock. I agree. I am curious.

"Bring your water bill with you," he yells after me as I set off along the honeysuckle-scented track.

Buried away for another hour or two with my work before our *apéro*, I take time out to look up *olive* in the *Oxford English Dictionary* and am amazed to learn how many different varieties of olive trees exist. An evergreen tree, *Olea Europaea*, especially the cultivated variety *O. Sativa*, with narrow entire leaves, green above and hoary beneath, and auxillary clusters of small whitish four-cleft flowers; cultivated in the Mediterranean countries and other warm regions for its fruit and the oil thence obtained.

Extended to the whole genus *Olea*; also applied, with qualifying words, to various trees and shrubs allied to common olive, or resembling it in appearance or in furnishing oil.

American Olive, Bastard or Mock Olive, Black Olive, California Olive, Chinese Olive, Holly-leaved Olive, Negro's Olive, Spurge Olive, Sweet-scented Olive, White Olive, Wild Olive (the wild variety of the common olive).

The fruit or berry of OLEA SATIVA is a small oval drupe and bluish-black when ripe, with a bitter pulp abounding in oil, and hard stone. It is valuable as a source of oil, and also eaten pickled in an unripe state. The dictionary also suggests that the blacker the olive, the more ripe it is. I assume that our trees are of the *O. Sativa* variety, but I will need to confirm this. Where can one seek out the White Olive or Holly-leaved Olive or, indeed, any of the others listed above? If planted, would they survive on our olive farm? What fruit, if any, would they produce? Personally, I find *hoary* too cold an adjective to describe that deliciously sensual, mother-of-pearl tone of the underleaf.

AT THE DESIGNATED hour for drinks, Michel and I stroll along the lane hand in hand. Tall cypress trees guard the route like inscrutable centurion soldiers, while husky-toned insects scratch into the evening calm. Michel is leaving for Paris in the morning, and I am feeling blue. Outside the gate of the stately stone house whose sign reads *Le Verger*, we pull on the bell chain. Inside my bag, I have tucked our best bottle of Bordeaux. It is intended as a peace offering; I feel sure this man will have words about our badly behaved dog. Within seconds, a thickset rottweiler with a head as broad and round as a tire hurls himself against the iron gate. Thud, thud. He growls and barks like a hound at the gates of hell. We retreat a step.

A deep-throated roar sounds from a terrace beyond the swimming pool. Instantly, the dog retreats like a chastised puppy and disappears behind a camper parked in the driveway. The gates open, and we crunch across the graveled parking area, past several rather magnificent agave cacti, one of which has sprouted a gigantic spear with yellow flowers. The camper where the dog is still lurking is equaled in rustiness only by Di Fazio's old bus. Jean-Claude appears and beckons us to the lower level of the house. The monster dog rises and stalks us terrifyingly. Fearing for our safety, we glance back every few steps.

Jean-Claude, shadowed by a pimply adolescent, hails us inside. The young man introduced to us as their son, Marcel, nods and retreats hurriedly as though even this amount of human contact has all but shriveled him. We are now standing in a somber but spacious kitchen all decked out in dark ivy-green wood with rather elaborate metal fixtures.

"Three hundred thousand francs," Jean-Claude announces proudly, following this astronomical figure with the name of the firm responsible for what I can only describe as a monstrosity. No doubt it is meant to impress, but the name means nothing to me. A woman scurries into the room, cigarette in hand.

"*Ma femme, Odile*," he booms. Odile has hair as long and unkempt as Jean-Claude's, but unlike her husband she is dressed in a curious outfit made up of floaty bohemian bits of cloth and masses of expensive, if, to my taste, rather ostentatious gold jewelry. She is exceptionally slender and very effusive.

"*Ah, les jeunes,*" she cries with a throaty laugh and hurries over to kiss us both numerous times. I am surprised by the greeting, because I cannot believe she is a day older than either of us. Jean-Claude tells her that he was showing us the kitchen. She holds up her hands as though profoundly apologetic for having interrupted a scenario of such gravitas.

"Do you have your water bill?"

I tug it from my shoulder bag along with the wine and hand it over to him. "Sorry about the trash cans," I murmur. Jean-Claude, not registering the proffered bottle, takes the bill, studies it with a frown and disappears to ponder it in solitary silence. Odile takes over the displaying of the kitchen. Lights switch on in the most unlikely places, drawers open, vegetable racks swivel, canned food cupboards unfold, bits whirr, every gadget is exposed, does its party piece and slides back automatically to its resting place. We ooh and aah appropriately. Then, from somewhere deep in the belly of the house, we are summoned by Jean-Claude's roar. Odile starts like a nervous squirrel before leading us up a few steps into a very dark winding corridor and through to the *salon*, which, after the kitchen, rather takes us aback. It is an enormous, high-ceilinged room which stretches the entire length of what we are to discover is an eight bedroomed, three-story *mas*. Even though it is a warm late-summer evening, a two-bar electric fire is aglow in the center of a rather magnificent stone chimney hearth. A glance around shows us the room is furnished sparsely, to say the least. It contains four white plastic garden chairs, a matching table—beneath which the rottweiler cowers—and, over in a distant corner, a grand piano.

The telephone rings in a neighboring room. Jean-Claude, barefoot, strides off to answer it. "Zurich!" he bellows, and Odile scoots to the phone, closing folding doors behind her.

"She never stops working. *Asseyez-vous.*" Jean-Claude waves after her, using our water bill as baton. I am beginning to cast him in the role of a rather off-beat wizard, with his crazy hair and no clothing at all except the flimsy poplin shorts. All he lacks is a cloak. We pull out two of the plastic chairs and sit down. No one has so far acknowledged the wine, which I have tried on a couple of occasions to hand over, so I place it on the table where a plastic-wrapped sliced loaf of white bread—the first I have encountered in France —waits with a bottle of port, another of whiskey, an empty ice bucket, four water tumblers and a large pot of paté. Three knives have also been left there.

"Marcel," Jean-Claude yells to his son. From above us, rock music which I had barely registered is switched off. Footsteps on the landing and then the stairs bring Marcel to join us, clearly against his will. He and Jean-Claude take the other two chairs, though Jean-Claude rises the instant he has sat down, seeming incapable of stillness.

"What do you make of that?" he asks Michel, referring to our bill. He opens the bottle of port and pours each of us a more than generous shot. Before Michel has been given the opportunity to comment, Marcel is ordered to take us on a tour of the house. Jean-Claude returns to the water bill, while Odile remains locked beyond the room. The sound of her voice drifts through to us. Whoever has telephoned cannot have spoken a word, for Odile is chattering breathlessly.

Curiosity is bubbling within me. Who, or what, are these quirky, exuberant people? Trailing Marcel, we trek from room to room, each is as sparsely furnished as the last.

"Have you just moved in as well?" I inquire.

"No. Why?"

There are sleeping bags on the floors of each of the eight bedrooms, except in the master room which is decked out with yellow-and-blue-striped curtains, fitted cupboards, swivel lamps, several floor-to-ceiling mirrors and an ornately gilded dressing table. Has to be the firm who built the kitchen.

"Your parents' room," I say, stating the obvious, more to make conversation than anything else.

"Yes, but they don't sleep here."

"Why not?"

"They sleep in the camper with the dogs" is his simple explanation.

Even I am silenced by this response. Having trawled the length and breadth of the house, we are returned to the *salon* just as Odile reappears. She is followed by a second dog, a rottweiler puppy who threatens to grow up looking as mean as his pal.

"Whiskey," she begs. Jean-Claude pours her an exceedingly generous shot and refills our tumblers of port. Given that they were barely touched, we are each cradling about a third of a liter of ruby port. Marcel unwraps the loaf and begins spreading butter on the anemic-looking slices. "*Santé!*" We lift our glasses to the toast and sip the alcohol. The telephone rings. Marcel goes.

"Amsterdam," he calls to his mother. Odile lights a cigarette, sighs wearily, grabs the Camel packet and, scotch in hand, disappears.

"Drink up!" yells a hearty Jean-Claude, which is precisely what I am trying to avoid. We have already been there the better part of an hour—it is our last evening of summer, we want to leave—but it is now announced that we will eat when Odile has finished her call. Michel, charm to the rescue, informs father and son that we have food waiting at home. Jean-Claude will not hear of it. Certainly we can return to our meal later, but first we must share in the paté, which he has shot and prepared himself. *Sanglier.* I enquire where around these parts he might have come across a wild boar to shoot. This little hill may be the last undiscovered corner of rural paradise on the coast of the Alpes-Maritimes, but we are, after all, only ten minutes from Cannes. "There are no wild boar prancing about our garden," I joke.

"*Mais, si, si,* on the far side of your hill," he tells me. "Families of them."

Jean-Claude does not strike me as a joker, though what he does strike me as, I really cannot work out. I peer into his face to see if he is kidding. No hint of humor registers.

"Are there really wild boar here?" I squeak.

"Of course not, *chérie*," Michel says.

"Yes, and snakes and scorpions," Jean-Claude avers.

I slug the port, downing half the glass in one mouthful. During the time it takes Odile to talk at length to Marseille, Paris and finally Geneva, Jean-Claude has forced Marcel to the piano and dragged us to its side as well. We are now engaged in the most squawkingly embarrassing sing-a-long, which eventually includes a radiantly happy Odile. She loves music (music!) she informs us, helping herself to another tumbler of whiskey and another packet of cigarettes. "*Le boulot est fini!*" she ululates. Her work is over for the evening.

The white bread and wild-boar paté are being enjoyed by the dogs, who are up on the chairs, front paws and mouths on the table, licking, slurping and dribbling at a chaotic mess of food. (And these people complained about the antics of poor, gentle—if greedy—Pamela!) No one seems to care. Michel and I are completely plastered. From my point of view, there are six Jean-Claudes in the room, all of them bellowing and trumpeting like a herd of elephants in heat. And when a song is finished, he roars good-heartedly, slapping the piano, filling the capacious space with his monstrous happiness. In my present state, I find myself entirely uplifted by his infectious energy.

And so we stay on.

By the time we stagger back up our driveway, pitching about without a flashlight, the sky is a blanket of midnight navy and the moon and brilliant stars look like a child's cut-outs within it. Too late to eat, too drunk to cook, we linger outside for a while, swimming to clear our heads then spreading out beside each other on a sun lounger, listening to the night which spins and spins before us.

"What was Odile talking so earnestly to you about? Was it the water bill?" I slur but choose not to turn my head from star-gazing. The movement will send my brain reeling.

"No, neither of them explained that. No, she was describing her work," Michel replies.

"Which is?"

"She's a clairvoyant. Clients telephone from all over Europe, pay her by credit card and she gives them a half-hour 'reading.' Curious."

"So, my picture of Jean-Claude as a wizard was not so far off the mark," I drawl.

"Jean-Claude? Oh no! He's an estate agent!"

HUNGOVER, NURSING A raging headache, Michel departs on the early-morning plane for Paris. A strange emptiness descends upon me. The changing of seasons. The first whiffs of autumn in the air. The swallows swooping low, gathering close to the house, anticipating their journey to Africa. Colors are turning, resetting. Tinctures of yellows and russet are appearing. A chunk of time that has been exquisitely winding down is drawing to its inevitable close. All my life I have been ill equipped to cope with such moments of loss, but I remind myelf that this is a temporary shift. We have our lives ahead of us, and the house is barely ours. Challenges await us, and Michel will be back on Friday. My mood rallies.

I work off some of the loneliness by stripping the wallpaper in my workroom. The noise is still there. It has begun to squeak from time to time as well. Has a small unidentified creature just been born? My imagination leaps to trailers I have seen of Hollywood horror movies where small plastic beings begin to move silently in the celler of some unsuspecting, all-American home. They are cute, they squeak, then they grow bigger and by reel six they are threatening world domination! I am tempted to rip the pelmet away from the wall but fear what I might discover. Best to leave well enough alone. It is probably a gecko who has been disturbed by our arrival here. They are timid little chaps and do seem happiest buried in corners away from the harsh sunlight. Once I think it through sanely, I convince myself that it is a gecko and I stop fretting about it.

Some days the heat is so thick, so extreme, that the early-morning dew sops the plants and leaves them drooping. Moistness is everywhere; nature's way of making sure they do not go thirsty, I suppose, which is why I choose to water our recently potted geraniums in the evening.

It is sunset. My first evening alone. I am in the garden with the hose. Circling above me are two buzzards. I tilt my head (still rather the worse for port) and watch them wheel and spin, wondering what they are stalking. I hear one of them screech. It is a haunting echoey cry, reverberating on the still air. Then suddenly there is another sound: heavy footsteps. Someone is moving behind me. I freeze. There is the distinct exhalation of heavy breathing. I go cold. How can I, in this deserted spot, grapple with a burglar? I consider the hose in my hand. I could spray the intruder, drench and confuse him for a few seconds, while I make a getaway. I take a deep breath and turn slowly. There, standing on the terrace a few feet behind me, is a monstrous *sanglier*.

No doubt it is a female, the most lethal of the species. She must be here on a scavenge for food for her young, or she would never have approached habitation. I know by reputation how dangerous wild boars can be if angered or distressed. She might charge me if I move or frighten her. The sheer weight of her could kill or maim me. I stand frozen to the spot, almost wishing that it had been a burglar. With an intruder there is the possibility of prevailing on reason, but not with this great hairy beast. I don't dare to move, but I have no wish to dally. Slowly, imperceptibly, I twist the nozzle of the hose to shut off the water and lower it, half crouching, to the ground. I take my first steps toward the house.

The giant boar holds her ground, watching me. What is she thinking? Jean-Claude with his shotgun may be a match for her, but I am not. I scan the thicket of pine forest to see if I can spot a mate. I see no others. So there is only this female to contend with. I make it to the house, close the door fast and lean against it, listening to the palpitations of my heart. Even dear old Pamela would have scared her off. I have to admit that I am missing that fat dog. I convince myself that I need my own. A guardian, and company, too, for lonesome evenings.

MICHEL ARRIVES. WE drive directly to the local dog pound and choose a lively, wiry fellow named Henri. He looks rather like an overgrown red setter, except that his coat is jet black. I wonder why he has been abandoned. His fur is as glossy as a well-polished limousine; he appears in every way to have been cared for. According to his record sheet, he is only three years old, and the note on the vet's card confirms that he is in excellent health. When I inquire, the lady who looks after the *refuge* begrudgingly admits that he is uncontrollable. In what way, I ask. He runs off. Constantly.

Oh.

"Yes, but you have plenty of land, you say," she reassures us. "He can work off all that excess energy. He is ideally suited to your needs, and you to him."

Michel is not convinced. "Let's think about it, *chérie*. We have no fence yet," he murmurs.

But Henri's expression breaks my heart, that please-don't-leave-me-here look in his eyes, and he's panting with such eager anticipation. I cannot bear to walk away, to condemn the poor brute to that cage again.

"Could we take him out, just for five minutes . . . to be sure?"

She shakes her head. It is against the rules. It raises the animal's hopes, often in vain.

The woman, a true salesperson, plays on my softheartedness. "You have a month. If it does not work out, and you return him within the month, we will accept him back. But I am sure that won't be necessary. He'll settle with you."

Henri pants his eager accord.

We pay, sign the authorization document, buy him a collar and escort him to the car. Or rather, he drags us from the shelter. I can barely hold him. He has the strength of a grizzly bear.

That first evening, Michel insists that we chain Henri, on a generously long lead, to the trunk of the magnolia tree. He can sit with us while we prepare and eat our barbecue dinner, but he will also learn the habit of staying quietly at our side. He must learn a little discipline, explains Michel. That way he will know not to go wandering off. Henri puts his head on his paws and goes into a sulk.

He remains in that position all day Saturday.

"I don't think he's very happy," I say.

"He's adjusting."

His black eyes glower at me with pain and accusation: *You have given me freedom only to take me prisoner*, he seems to be saying. I cannot bear it. I spend hours stroking him and talking to him, but he will not relent. He refuses to eat. Oh, what a contrast to Pamela!

WE HAVE GUESTS FOR dinner, an ebullient Italian artist and his elegant Danish wife. They are a very chic couple who love to party. Paulo is short and plump and passionately adores women. He has on occasion, after a bottle or two, embarrassed me, but in spite of that, I am fond of him. He is a warm, generous man.

I was introduced to them in the early eighties when I was performing in a theater in Copenhagen. Here in the south, they have bought a house in Biot, and we find ourselves relative neighbors. They arrive late, armed with taped copies of the samba music they prefer to listen to during dinner. (Wait till they see our pathetic little cassette player, I am thinking as I accept the tapes with a broad smile.) As always, Paulo is dressed from head to foot in moody black. Olga is tall and slender as a willow and looks sensational. By contrast, her temperament is cool and reserved. This evening she is wearing a floor-length, ice-white linen dress.

Henri, still on his lead, is alerted by their arrival and stands up to greet them. He is animated, bucked up, for the first time in over twenty-four hours and begins to wag his tail and yodel.

"Why is he tied up?" our artist friend asks.

"We only collected him from the *refuge* yesterday and so he doesn't run off . . ." I blather on about the problem of Henri while our handsome suntanned friends pop the bottle of champagne they brought.

Michel, across the dust patch, is fanning the barbecue to prepare it. Smoke ascends into the night air, giving off aromas of Provençal herbs and charcoaled meat. I uncork a bottle of red wine, a St. Joseph from St. Désirat.

"He'll settle only if you leave him free. He has to discover his sense of boundary in a free space." What Olga says makes sense. In any case, I am dying for an excuse to release him. I run to Michel, who is calling for me; while replenishing his glass and laying the various cuts of grilled lamb on a serving plate, I repeat what Olga has said.

"If you think so," he replies, though I sense he doubts his own words.

In one movement, I charge up the steps and release Henri, who is over the moon with glee. In twenty-four hours he has had four pee breaks and one long walk on a lead when he dragged me up and down the hillside. His tail is wagging like a clock.

"Come on, boy," I coax, expecting him to follow me down onto the terrace beneath, to where are guests are poised, sipping champagne and imbibing the view. But he does not budge. The movement of his tail is gaining speed. I fear it bodes no good, but before I can act upon my instincts, Henri takes a gigantic leap and lands on the backs of both our guests. They find themselves splayed out in the dust around our roughly cut grass. Thankfully, the glasses didn't break and cut them, but the couple is drenched. Olga's dress is patched with green stains from the few remaining tufts of grass and champagne.

"What an excessively friendly fellow," whispers Paulo to me as he picks himself up from the ground and dusts himself off. "It's how I encourage my mistresses to greet me!"

THE FOLLOWING FRIDAY, I receive a telegram from the proprietor of Appassionata, Madame B. There has been a mistake in the price of the property. I go cold. I knew it! All summer I have been dreading news such as this, and then I read on. Due to the fact that the second half of the land, known to us now as the "second plot," has measured out at a third of an acre larger than the plot with house—the half we are currently purchasing—we are entitled to a reimbursement of several thousand francs. I whoop and shout in the lane as I watch our postman, who has just handed me the telegram, disappear around the bend. I cannot help remarking that he and his scooter are a precarious marriage of large man and modest machine. By the time he reaches us, his load is almost delivered. How does he negotiate the early rounds of the journey from the sorting office, loaded down with the entire morning's letters and parcels? And how does that little yellow scooter manage to transport his generous frame and his bundles up and down the steep and winding hills?

I hurtle off to the local phone booth to telephone Michel at his office in Paris. What it boils down to, he says, is that we can buy a bed.

YES!

Within the hour I am in Cannes, ordering the largest bed on offer. I leave a deposit; the rest will be paid when the bed arrives in eight weeks. I leave the shop flushed with excitement. We have blown our entire refund on one piece of furniture.

AT THE SOUND OF THE postman's scooter, Henri bounds down the drive, strategically positioning himself to say good morning. As the postman slows to round the corner, Henri leaps into the air in front of him, paws splayed, barking an expansive welcome. Alas, his effusive greeting frightens the life out of Monsieur *le facteur*, who tumbles from his scooter.

I hear shouting and barking and run from my desk to find out what is going on. When I arrive, I find the poor man on all fours. He is grappling with letters and parcels, which have flown in every direction, while Henri, still close at hand, is yapping and panting. I jump forward to lend a hand.

"Oh Monsieur, I am so sorry!" I cry.

"*J'avais presqu'un crise cardiaque!* If he comes near me again, I'll take action!"

I drag away the great hound to more threats from the postman. Henri, wagging his tail, is triumphant.

I TAKE THE COASTAL road, passing by the old town of Antibes, skirting the *Baie des Anges* to visit the antique market in the old town of Nice. I find it situated in the ancient Italian quarter, where the buildings are painted ocher and a deep Siena yellow. There I discover stalls laden with antique linen and lace pillowcases. They are so big and square and cheap, and like new. Some are embroidered in white cotton, white on white, with initials. I wonder who they were so caringly embroidered for and what became of the original owners. What prevented these luxurious pieces from being put to use? A jilted heart, a death? In anticipation of our generously sized new bed, I want to buy them all. I dream of smothering it in freshly starched, lavender-scented crisp linen. Crisp and white and inviting. Sunburned afternoons lying together. Winter nights huddled close, listening to the crackling of the fire.

The stallkeeper, a tiny woman, is hidden behind banks of sheets and tablecloths, eating lunch with a man and a child. I notice that their spread includes a hot chicken dish in a thick tomato sauce, several bottles of red wine, fruit, two baguettes and an assortment of various cheeses. It seems remarkable for a market situation, but I remind myself that this is France. Food comes first. We make a deal that seems to delight us both, and she shoves linen sheets, pillowcases and a tablecloth into several plastic bags, collects her modest sum of money and returns hungrily to her meal. While at the market, I begin to scout the various stalls for large glass jars, carafes or demijohns which I will use later to store our olive oil. I find none, but there is always next week.

When I return, I pick flowers from the garden—most are growing so wild—marguerite daisies, eucalyptus leaves, palm fronds taken from six tiny potted plants I found at the nursery (twenty francs a pot), and gather them together. I place them, decoratively arranged in *confiture* jars, next to our mattress on the floor, and in the hearth.

Michel is coming home tonight. I cannot remember when I last felt this excited by life. In preparation, I am stuffing a chicken. Suddenly, I hear Henri barking like a mad fool. I fear another *sanglier*. I peer out the kitchen window toward the pine forest and, to my amazement, see troupes of people moving in and around the trees, thrashing at the undergrowth. Curious, I hike the hill, thorny brambles ripping at my flesh, and introduce myself. They are mushroom picking, they explain. I, in return, inform them in a friendly manner that they are on private land. They retaliate by advising me that they have gathered mushrooms on this hill all their lives and do not intend to stop now.

Chastised, confused, I descend the hill and leave them to it. Next year, I will know to get up there first and pick the mushrooms myself, but I run the risk of poisoning us because I don't know one variety from another.

Later, in the afternoon, when I go to the village to buy freshly baked bread, I see that the local drugstore has large display cards in the windows with colored pictures naming the different varieties of mushrooms. I learn that it is a local service here. Anyone can bring their baskets brimming with harvested mushrooms, and the *pharmacien* will sift the edible from the inedible or poisonous. So I need not fear. We will be safe to harvest our own *funghi*. I stare at the colored card. Here, among dozens, are drawings of ceps and chanterelles and boleti, which I read later was originally raised by the Italians. Another, birch boletus, grows on the trees and is a fungus as large as a child's head. I am not convinced by how delicious that sounds!

OVER DINNER, BY THE fire, I feel obliged to confess to Michel the tales of Henri's triumphs. He is not pleased. But worse is to come, for the postman is true to his word. On Saturday morning, an official notice arrives warning us that if we do not control our dog we will be taken to court and the animal might well be impounded or, worse, destroyed. I stare in dismay while Henri pants gleefully at my side.

"He'll have to go, *chérie*," says Michel.

"But since Henri, we have had no wild boar prowling the garden, and he keeps me company! Please let's keep him."

Michel frowns. "We need to give the matter serious thought," he replies.

On Saturday afternoon, an officer from the central Cannes police station telephones our neighbor to say that a large black dog known as Henri—the *refuge* has identified him by the name on his collar and put them in touch with us—is terrorizing the guests sunbathing on the private beach at the Majestic Hotel. Michel thanks Jean-Claude for taking the trouble to walk over to us. He is then obliged to drive to Cannes, collect the dog and pay a hefty fine. Henri has been charged with disturbance of the peace!

I walk over to Jean-Claude with a bottle of wine and apologize profusely for the intrusion. His booming laugh reassures me that everything is perfectly fine. In fact, he invites us to come for another *apéro*. Having barely recovered from the previous experience, I fix no date but agree to telephone him, adding that on the next occasion, they should come to us. Over dinner, Michel and I discuss the problem of Henri, and I miserably concede that it would be best for everyone, including the dog, if he were returned.

On Monday morning, the woman at the *refuge* seethes visibly as we sign yet another set of documents, this time relinquishing all responsibility for the poor beast.

I weep copiously as we kiss him good-bye and he, bemused, is led away again to his horrid cage, but I have to admit that I have been hasty. Next year, Henri, I say to myself, when we are better organized, I promise to return for you.

CHAPTER FOUR

TREASURE ISLANDS

It is a crystal-clear, sunny autumn morning. Yesterday it rained for the first time in over two months. Today the air has a nip to it which foretells the changing seasons and reminds me that these long dry summers are not truly endless. Only a few days more, and we must close up the house. Michel and I are flying to Australia to shoot a film based on a story I have written and in which I am to play the main role. The prospects are exciting. Even so, it's going to be a wrench to tear myself away from here. Australia, the other side of the world; there will be no popping home for the weekends.

"If my story had been set here . . ." I mumble, folding away linen which I am storing with lavender bags in a cupboard inside the front hall.

In spite of all that is left to do—I have my work and papers to pack up yet, luggage to prepare and we are still trying to nail down a most elusive *notaire* to a date for the final exchange—Michel announces: "Leave everything, we're going hunting."

"What?" I laugh.

"We're taking a ferry to the islands. To look for treasure."

I agree readily, for the prospect of any boat ride always excites childlike joy in me, and the notion of a mystery tour is too irresistible. Besides, I have never visited the Îles de Lérins. "What kind of treasure are we seeking?"

"You'll see. We will visit the farthest island first, return to the nearer where we can lunch, then cruise home on the late-afternoon boat."

We purchase our tickets from a booth nestled alongside the harbormaster and customs quay in the old port of Cannes. Awaiting our departure, we stroll the length of a neighboring jetty and, from that prominent aspect, peer back toward the lofty *tour du Suquet,* the weathered tower that crowns the very pinnacle of the rock known as the Suquet, upon which the old town of Cannes stands. Here was the original fishing village initially christened Canois, meaning cane harbor, after the canes that grew profusely so many centuries ago along what was then nothing more than a marshy seafront. Cannes as wild nature barely seems conceivable in this day and age.

Returning our gaze seaward along the quay, we are back in the twentieth century; a breeze whispers, and a curved necklace of pearly white yachts stir noiselessly at the water's edge.

"Who owns all these?" I ask. A private musing spoken aloud. I cannot envisage how many millions one has to accrue to be able to cough up for one of these swanky numbers. Several of the cruisers are the length of a train carriage and surely would have cost more than the lifetime's earnings of the average working person.

"There is a lot of foreign money here. And a great deal of corruption. One of the former mayors of Nice, for example, fled to Uruguay."

"Why?"

"If he had stayed in France, he would have been imprisoned for corruption and tax evasion. Apparently, he embezzled considerable sums from the city of Nice and shifted the money to South America, in readiness for his retirement."

"That's right! Jacques Médecin, of course!" I laugh, more out of incredulity than merriment at the breadth and panache of such Riviera skulduggery.

"They got him, though, eventually."

"Yes, they did."

I remember that Graham Greene, who lived in Antibes and whom I met on several occasions, published a book in 1982 entitled *J'accuse*, about corruption in Nice and the close involvement of Monsieur Médecin with the Italian mafia. There was a casino scandal. Greene believed that a worrying percentage of the police force and justice system was engaged in nefarious dealings with the *milieu*, the criminal underworld. Later, Médecin fled the country to avoid charges of corruption.

"Do you suppose," I ask Michel, "all Riviera vice and turpitude ended with his flight and subsequent imprisonment?"

"Somehow I doubt it."

"Might there be zillions of mafia francs, never smuggled out, buried somewhere on these islands?"

"Who knows?"

"So are we going to dig them up and pay off Madame B.?"

"No." He smiles at my joking. "That's not the treasure we're after."

"What, then?"

"You'll see."

I smile, enjoying his game of secrecy. Looking all around us, I notice hosts of bronzed, barefoot young men, clad becomingly in shorts, at work on the string of yachts. Several are shinnying aluminium masts like monkeys climbing for bananas, while others are scrubbing teak decks, washing, hosing or treating the impressive fiberglass hulls.

Varnishing the varnished. All busy as ants, lost in dreams of prospective seafaring adventures.

"We better get moving," says Michel, taking my hand.

The clock tower up in the Suquet strikes ten, and the ferry prepares to depart. Or rather not. A straggle of latecomers is steaming along the jetty, all calling and waving. The captain grins. The boat waits. Everyone shakes his hand amicably and lumbers aboard.

During this short delay, I glance about. I have to admit that there is still great charm in this old port. The Hotel Splendid ahead, for example, with its colorful array of international flags and simple white facade; and then my attention lights on a sign in large black lettering, *Jimmy'z Club*, above the dull beige of the palais block and the plastic blue lettering that reads *Casino*. It is hard to find an uglier sight.

The boat is wheeling, and we are exiting the port. I incline against the rail, allowing a rush of excitement. A water baby by nature, I am at my happiest on or by the sea. Gulls circling overhead, the misty ambrosial hills of the Esterel and the foamy bubbling spray, as white as the yachts, rise up to cool us as the ferry plows through an otherwise calm sea. We pass an anchored five-mast luxury liner with *Club Med 2* painted on its hull and a glass-bottom pleasure boat packed with retirees.

As I look back toward Cannes, the bay gives off an illusion of gentility, but on closer inspection, this luxury resort puts me in mind of a beautiful woman past her prime. Suddenly, I recall a long-forgotten group of transvestites I spent time with while working in Brazil. Even at forty or forty-five, with some kind lighting and some distance, they managed to pull off looking good. I smile recalling their coked-up energy, some of the wild places they dragged me and the outrageous stories they recounted. Silently, I concede that Cannes probably also has many faces.

The Carlton Hotel, situated smack in the center of the Croisette, dominates the bay. It draws the eye instantly to its crisp white elegance.

None of its meretricious marketplace mentality shows from this gathering distance.

Feeling the sun's mounting heat penetrating my flesh, I shade my eyes to pick out the observatory tower high above the town. I scan the *fin de siècle* villas, their windows winking in the light like pirates signaling the all-clear to sailors marking time on the open sea. Splashes of autumnal color—red, yellow, gold—patch the palmy hills, while dozens of umber bodies in richly hued itsy-bitsy swimwear rest on the ever-busy golden beaches.

This boat ride is delicious. There are barely a handful of passengers aboard, and those present appear to be locals who have crossed at dawn to the mainland to shop. Mostly, they are weather-worn old ladies clutching woven shopping bags that bulge with brilliantly colored fruits and vegetables. Two toothless old women, arms wrapped tightly around their trophies, huddle close and gossip contentedly. Their flesh may be creased, tamped olive and leathery by the sun, but their eyes glisten wickedly.

"How many people live on these islands?" I inquire of Michel.

"Île Ste. Marguerite is inhabited. I don't know by how many. Twenty households, maybe. St. Honorat is unoccupied. Well, no it isn't. There is a community of Cistercian monks living there. And one very overpriced restaurant at the water's edge, looking out over the canal that separates the two islands."

"Who frequents it?"

"The restaurant? The yachting fraternity. It's a fashionable weekend haunt. During the season, boats rendezvous here from as far as Monte Carlo or St. Tropez. They drop anchor in between the two islands and motor, by dinghy, from one yacht to another, rounding up their parties, and then disembark for a grilled lobster lunch."

"That doesn't sound too terrible."

Michel laughs. "The canal gets so crowded you can barely move."

We are approaching Ste. Marguerite.

"*Pour St. Honorat, la deuxieme île, vous restez abord,*" hails a voice from a loudspeaker. My eye is drawn to a bastillion atop a cliff at what appears to be the eástern tip of the island. "Is that a fortress?"

Michel grins mischievously. "The Fort Royal. I knew it would fire your imagination. Built by Richelieu to protect the island from the Spanish who invaded anyway, but I'll tell you all about it later."

"There lies our trove? Or there, in that building on the beach? What is that, a deserted hotel?"

"All are for later. After lunch."

Every passenger, apart from ourselves and the crew, prepares to disembark onto the planked-wood jetty which rises out of the shallow crystalline water where shoals of tiny silver fish are darting to and fro. Handfuls of tourists, with their laden bags at their feet, clot the jetty, impatient to come aboard. They must be bound for Cannes. So we have the boat to ourselves. It reverses, heels about and scoots out to sea, nego-tiating the rocky bed beneath us. Dinghies bask like seals in the sun, and a series of small yellow buoys bob like discarded mustard pots. Parasol pine trees and a few lookout bunkers, abandoned since the Second World War, border the island's western beaches.

The air is clear and fragrant.

In between the two islands, a scattering of yachts is moored in the narrow strait. Slender, shark-toothed yachts with equally slender women aboard, lying topless and oiled, soaking up the sun. Paunchy men regard our passing ferry, brandishing goblets of whiskey and ice. I glance at my watch. It is half past ten! We pass the "posh" restaurant. It appears deserted. Perhaps it has already closed for the season or is immersed in preparations for another lunchtime.

The passage to this second island has taken no time at all. We negoti-ate a serious of large, rather dangerously jagged rocks, then land safely at the harbor. Michel takes my hand and leads me ashore. The instant I step foot on the bank I am greeted by—no, swathed in—a pine-scented silence, soft as a human pulse. I breathe deeply and turn about. There is nothing in sight, in any direction, save pine forest, littoral and clear Mediterranean, a patchwork of blue, milky turquoise. Salt water laps the sandy beach, licks the bleached skeletons of driftwood.

Save for the departing ferry, we could be marooned on a desert island. Hard to believe that we are so close to home and that this paradise of eucalyptus and Aleppo pines is visible from our terrace. I spy a statue of the Virgin Mary. Built high among the treetops, she holds her arms outstretched, looking out over and blessing the canal.

"Come on, we'll visit the monastery, the *Abbaye des Lérins*, buy lavender oil at the abbey shop, skirt the island and take the boat back to Ste. Marguerite for lunch."

We turn inland, flanked by vineyards, and walk toward the abbey, the epicenter of the island—five minutes away!—where we will find a church and an arched stone walkway which leads to the shop and gardens. Stone benches have been placed at strategic points along the route to allow for reflection, pause and prayer. I want to dally a second, commune with the natural beauty, imbibe the scents of the pines and eucalyptus, but Michel hurries me along.

As we approach, he delivers me a swift, potted history. The two islands were once the most powerful religious centers in the south of France. This one was first occupied in the fifth century by the hermit Ste. Honorat—hence its name—when the bishop of Fréjus encouraged him here, to create a site for holy retreat. A monastery was built, and under the auspices of St. Honorat, it became a training center for novice priests as well as a school for the study of Christian philosophy. St. Honorat, later bishop of Arles, died in 429A.D., but the traditions of the monastery have been continued even to this day, except for a short period during the late eighteenth and early nineteenth century when the island was snatched by the State, put up for auction and bought by an actress from the Comédie Française.

I chuckle with delight at the notion of ownership by an actress, the exotically named Mademoiselle Alziary de Roquefort, who, according to Michel, was a great friend of the painter Fragonard. I long to learn more. Was she as bewitching as her name suggests?

In 1869—Michel does not know why—the island was returned to the Cistercians, who have occupied, farmed and labored for it and for the renovation of its fortified monastery ever since.

"But see, we've arrived."

The Cistercians are an order of silence. As we approach, we discover discreet signs requesting us to speak in whispers, dress appropriately and respect the ethos of the island's inhabitants. An incongruous spectacle in this historical setting is a public telephone booth situated at a crossroads of dusty paths lined with pine trees.

On the exterior side of the abbey walls, tall palms shade and decorate the approach. During this season, the trees are laden with bunches of dark ruby fruit more reminiscent of fulsome berries than dates. Agapanthas, past their blooming season, line the pathways, as well as *ficus-indica* cacti growing as tall as trees and crowding the flowerbeds. These, too, are fruiting their terra-cotta-colored, ripe prickly pears.

Entrance to the abbey and its church are by iron gates ablaze with lustrous skeins of flowering bougainvillea. I read an engraved cornerstone that tells me St. Patrick studied here under the guidance of St. Honorat before traveling north to Ireland. As an Irish Catholic, I am tickled by this information. Patrick landed up in Ireland, and I here!

The shop is managed by two middle-aged ladies, one of whom sells us lavender oil as well as a kilo jar of rosemary honey which she earnestly recommends. Gregorian chants are playing softly in the background and can be purchased on compact disc.

Situated on the far reach of the island, on the windward shore, is the fortified monastery—dilapidated, solitary, awesome. We approach. A high, austere monument, it has been hewn from hefty chunks of stone.

Constructed on a site at the very tip of a minuscule but windy cap, it faces out across the sea toward, I estimate, Calvi, a town on the northwest coast of Corsica. Everything about its location is windswept, which makes the soft peach tone of the stone even more enrapturing. I notice samphyre sprouting out of the walls flanking the water's edge and unknown purple flowers pushing through like tomboyish daisies. On this open coast, the slap of the waves against the rocks has a relentless, overpowering brutality.

We pay fifteen francs apiece to a lone student girl who sits peacefully on a rusting iron chair close to the water's edge, reading a book whose pages are blowing to and fro. This gives us entry to the ruin.

As we mount the stone stairs, I, compulsively curious, steal a quick glance at the abbey living quarters. There is not a monk in sight. What had I expected, to see them peering out like nosy neighbors? I am taken aback by the filth of their windows, until I realize that the distance has fooled me and their cells are protected by the same mosquito netting we found at our farmhouse. The place exudes stillness, almost a forsaken air. I picture solitary monks on their knees in their cells. I am intrigued by the weight of thought, the depth of spiritual reflection cultivated beyond those walls. These are mysteries forever closed to me. I will never know what such a life, the life of an oblate, claims, nor the courage and sacrifice such a vocation must demand, the unstinting dedication. The Cistercian order was founded at the end of the eleventh century in an attempt to return to a stricter, more disciplined obedience to God. The rule of St. Benedict, the founder of this particular order, is *Ora et Labora,* pray and work. Spoken, it sounds pleasingly achievable.

I return my attention to the fortified monastery. How different the energy on this island must have been when this edifice was built to protect its inhabitants against marauding Saracens. Within—should I say this when the roof is merely a space open to the blue skies?—there is little to see, save for the ancient walls which date back to the eleventh and twelfth centuries and the pockets of restoration work. The *salle du chapitre* is a dark, dank room cluttered with broken wooden chairs and a discarded wooden icon of Madonna and child. There are some fine marble stairs and stone pillars and arches, but all in all, the fort's stately majesty lies in its breathtaking views. Unfortunately, these cannot really be appreciated, because the apertures have been closed, fitted with metal-framed glass like frightful, second-rate double glazing. This addition is so hideously out of keeping with the restored masonry work that it bemuses me. Why have the openings been sealed off? Are they to prevent broken-hearted tourists from leaping to their death on the treacherous rocks? Or to discourage monks who can no longer stand the solitude of their life?

I wander from the *salle du chapitre* to the *cloître du travail.* There, in the center of this work cloister, is what I take to be a baptismal font until I peer into it and discover a deep well. At first, I assume the water lying so far beneath us is seawater, although the building is constructed *pieds dans l'eau,* this seems doubtful because it is too still. From this distance, it looks impenetrable and stagnant. Midges or mosquitoes skate its surface, circumventing a dozen or so jettisoned Coke cans.

I look about for Michel and find him perusing a few historical facts, mainly dates, posted on one of the inner cloister walls. Work began on this fortified monastery in 1073. In 1635, the islands were occupied by the Spanish, and—"Look at this!"—in 1791, the island was sold at public auction to an actress, Marie-Blanche Sainval, who owned it until 1810! So who is Alziary de la Roquefort? Might that exotic creation have been her stage name? I fancy the sound of Alziary better. The deeds of sale might be written in the name of Marie-Blanche Sainval, but I shall continue to think of this actress as Alziary. In my mind's eye, she is a tempestuous, flaming redhead, *une femme d'un certain âge.* Lord knows why.

Nearing the top floor, we enter the prayer cloister, *le cloître de la prière,* where, we are told, the walls date from the twelfth and thirteenth centuries. A hundred years, it took then, to erect another story. Oh, that modern property developers could be so stayed! On the same level, we cross to the Chapelle Saint Croix, which was consecrated in 1088. This confuses my sense of logic.

Here there are wooden benches placed at angles, facing a stone altar where a painting of Christ on the cross hangs. Once again the environment, as well as the strategically positioned seats, invites contemplation. So I settle on one of the benches and, from this elevated tranquility, listen to the waves crashing against the rocks three stories beneath me. I crane my head toward the open sky. The blueness is cool and airy, a visual balm.

Our footsteps echo back at us as we climb one last flight of ever-narrowing, winding marble stairs to the summit of the keep where elegant metal railings girdle the surround—against accident or suicide? There, from that top terrace with its stone bell tower, we behold a 360-degree view which is nothing short of divine.

The Lord often had his prophets climb mountains to converse with him. I often wondered why he did that, and now I know the answer; when we are on high, we can see everything else as small. These are the words of the writer Paulo Coelho, who spent his early years in a seminary and with whom I once had the pleasure of dining in Rio. Everything else as small, yes, including self. How could you not be close to God here?

The light breeze at this altitude is very welcome. I walk to the metal railing and look around me. Far beneath, the clear yet rock-infested water draws me. Although I am not usually afraid of heights, a frisson of fear sends an icy shiver down my spine. Still, I long to plunge the hundreds of feet into the sea and swim and frolic like a carefree porpoise.

A fabulous two-mast cutter plows across the distant horizon, making for where? St. Tropez, Marseilles? Constructed in the monks' vegetable gardens are two large banks of solar paneling.

The abbey clock on the terra-cotta-tiled tower chimes noon. "We should move on," Michel says, and we begin the descent.

Our promenade around the island is crazily romantic. Water licks our feet and soaks our shoes, which we remove. Fish the size of salmon slip beneath rocks, playing hide-and-seek with our shadows. We clamber from eucalyptus-perfumed bay to lavender-scented shade, kicking our toes in the sand, racing miniature crabs, grabbing hands, touching backs, necks, hair, crunching our sodden sandy feet on the spongelike cushion of beached and dehydrated seaweed, dragging our wet swimming towels like lazy kites as salt dries on our pinched, damp flesh. We dally, kiss, linger, taste the salt, lick it clean, then keep pace in blissful silence, or hurry, chattering like euphoric monkeys, toppling over each other. Falling in love: such a free expansive fall. There's no knowing where, if ever, we'll land, but today it's in paradise.

All in all, the circumference of the island is approximately three kilometers and takes us, strolling and with a pause to swim, little less than an hour and a half. We had been intending to swim naked, at least I had. Whenever it's appropriate, we do. Here, even though there has not been a single sighting of a monk, I cannot rid myself of the feeling that they see us wherever we are on the island. Their spiritual presence is omnipresent.

"When we return from Australia, I want to come back here and picnic on that grass bank overlooking the turquoise water," I say.

My thoughts return to our treasure hunt as our chugging ferry delivers us back to Ste. Marguerite in time for lunch. We are famished and don't dawdle along the jetty.

"The restaurant is right over there." Michel points to a white-painted veranda several hundred yards along the coast. Behind it, a half a dozen or so houses with light turquoise or pale lilac shutters, hidden between trees, peer out toward Cannes from their watery aeries. Early clots of autumn-yellow mimosa blossom. Once again, my gaze is drawn up to the hilly incline and the Royal Fort, which I had completely forgotten until now.

"Lunch first." Michel grins.

Approaching the restaurant, we realize that it is closed and pause in the lane while we consider what to do next. "There is another, I've forgotten its name, on the beach down behind the fort. We have to climb and then descend the other side of the cliff. It's not far, but we should hurry. It's getting late. We'll see it from the clifftop, so, if it's closed as well, we won't bother going down there. It tends to be seasonal."

We break into a jog and come abreast of the ramshackle building I spotted from the ferry. A scruffy sign, cobbled out of broken bits of ceramic, reads: *Hôtel du Masque de Fer*. The Iron Mask Hotel. An intriguing name. I approach the tall glass-paned doors and peer in, believing the place to be empty, but then I see a stooped woman with bleached hair tottering across a poorly lit, high-ceilinged dining room.

"There's someone in there."

Michel is intent on getting to the restaurant. He holds out his arm as if to encourage me away. "We can look later."

"I think it's open. Maybe they serve lunch."

He returns to my side and looks in. "Do you really want to eat here?"

"Let's ask." And with that, we open the door and an old man materializes from behind what looks like an exceedingly outdated pizza oven. At first he is reluctant to take us, making the excuse that lunch is over and there is nothing available. We accept his refusal graciously and start to go, but he calls us back with "Still, if you are not in need of anything too fancy, I can offer you—"

The surroundings are deeply shabby, yet the setting is so picturesque and I have such a fanatical attraction to buildings in ruin that we agree to order his suggested pizzas, along with salad and a local rosé wine which, according to our host, has come from the vineyard on the adjacent island of St. Honorat. Perfect. We seat ourselves at a table by the window and stare out at an abandoned landing bay. The water is rippling like corrugated iron across to the bay of Cannes. The view is stupendous. Our wine arrives.

"If we hadn't found Appassionata, this place would set us a challenge. Not a farm, but . . . Why is it called the Iron Mask Hotel?" I ask.

"Because the fort on the clifftop has dungeons dug deep into the rock, and it was in one of those cells that the man in the iron mask was imprisoned."

My eyes widen to the size of our approaching pizzas. "The Alexandre Dumas character?"

"For three hundred years, writers have been inspired by his story."

"He was a real person? I didn't know that!"

Monsieur serves us our plates and retreats.

"He spent eleven years incarcerated here, and never once was his face revealed."

"Tell me about him. *Bon appétit.*"

"Legend has it that he was the twin brother of Louis XIV, or his bastard half brother, but there are many theories. Some have suggested that the masked man was Molière. Others claim that it was a woman disguised as a man. What does seem to be certain is that whomever he was, he was famous."

"Why?"

"It's logical. Why go to such lengths to keep his face hidden if he wasn't easily recognized? Not even his doctor, when he was imprisoned in the Bastille, was allowed to look upon his naked features."

"How did he shave?" I ask. Our carafe of water arrives.

"*Il vous plaît, le déjeuner, Monsieur, Madame?*"

"Delicious, thank you." We nod enthusiastically, although it is so-so. But we don't really care. We are having a wonderful day.

"Has the hotel closed?" I ask our host.

"It is sold, and is to be turned into a new Carlton with a small marina for private yachts," Monsieur tells us, while staring longingly across to the mainland at the outline of the real McCoy. My heart sinks as I picture the vision. "There is only one small problem," he adds.

"What's that?"

"The inhabitants of the island have signed a petition. They intend to block the permit I hope to acquire for the construction of a helicopter landing base."

At that moment, the door opens and a tall, dark-haired gentleman in his early forties enters, dressed in what must be a Cerruti suit and leather Italian shoes polished to a mirrored shine. He is accompanied by eight or nine others, running after his every need. The proprietor abandons us instantly, legs it across the dining room and all but genuflects at the feet of the new arrival. Then comes Madame, welcoming them with the same attention. We are riveted. Tables are dragged together, chairs drawn from here and there. Paper tablecloths are pressed in place and ironed flat by desperate hands. The new arrivals are seated. Bottles of wine begin to arrive. Rosé, red, white, followed, moments later, by heaped saucers of local olives and sliced *saucissons*. Dishes of marinated eggplant swilling in oil and herbs land splashing onto the table. Carafes of water and glasses all but jump of their own accord from the dingy kitchen. Nothing is too much trouble for this bunch, who eat and drink with gusto. We have been entirely forgotten. In fact, we do not exist for anyone in the room save each other. Everything centers on the sleek-haired man.

"Might he be local mafia?" I whisper to Michel, hoping that he is and that I can eavesdrop on hideous tales of local corruption. I watch him vigilantly, attempting to be discreet but failing hopelessly, spellbound by mannerisms that I might put to fruitful use later: he constantly slicks back his immaculately groomed hair or adjusts the cuffs of his shirtsleeves; he never touches his wine, even when a toast is made. He raises his glass, allows the rim to brush his lips, then sets it back on the table. "Always on the alert," I conclude, and as I do, he glances in our direction, allowing a discreet nod. Oh, he is aware that we are watching him and appears to bask in any, all, attention. Michel is ready to leave, keen to begin exploring the fort and visit the dungeons, but I cannot drag myself away from the *commedia* that is playing out before us. In fact, we have no choice in the matter. The guests at the other table have finished lunch and are preparing to depart while we are obliged to sit it out, hoping for our bill.

The proprietor and wife, tea towels in hand—or, in his case, tossed over one shoulder—are poised patiently like dogs awaiting some titbit or expression of what, gratitude? Acknowledgment? A tip? The *padrone* shakes their hands and thanks them. The proprietors bow and thank their esteemed guest for the time and trouble he has taken to visit them. This is followed by every other member of the group shaking hands with the old man and his wife. This extended "*Merci, merci beaucoup. Non, non, merci à vous*" ceremony is followed by the eventual departure of the group. Gratified, our hosts set about clearing away the debris. Michel is now able to attract their attention and requests *l'addition*. Monsieur nods and goes away to calculate it.

"Did you see that?"

"What?"

"Those guys didn't pay for a thing."

Michel grins at me. "You're right. Maybe they have an account here." This makes us giggle. My curiosity cannot resist; when the restaurateur returns, I ask him the identity of the tall, well-groomed gentleman. Our host's rheumy eyes swim with pride as he inform us, "*Mais, c'est Michel Mouillot.*"

In chorus we reply, "*Qui?*"

"He is to be the new mayor of Cannes and has promised us the construction permits we need. We will achieve a far better price for the *hôtel* with permits."

IN THE DISTANCE, the smoky blue hills. Intent on the continuation of our little adventure, we saunter, hand in hand, up the verdant incline in the afternoon sunshine, our minds refocusing on the masked mystery.

"Victor Hugo said of him: 'This prisoner whose name nobody knows, whose face no one has ever seen, remains a living mystery, shadowy, enigmatic and problematic.'"

We reach the walls of the fortress. A rickety wooden sentry box bears a sign—*Billets*—but it is closed up, season over, and we walk on. Cobbled stones, vast spaces and a garrison enclave greet us. Rows of two-story salt-weathered stone buildings, all with identical burgundy shutters, line the cobbled lanes and lead to open squares where nothing more lively than a lizard's retreat is taking place. The site appears to be ours alone. Seagulls and terns wheel overhead. There is nothing of today's world about this settlement, and to all intents and purposes it is deserted, yet there seems to be life here. I sense basic habitation. "What is the place used for now?"

Our footsteps echo all around us. The air is clean and scented, the light sharp. The wind murmurs, carrying sounds of the sea, bird cries. Michel does not know. We come across a painted sign that points us toward an oceanography museum. We make for that. Inside, behind a desk littered with pamphlets, a bespectacled woman sits on a chair knitting. "I am sorry, we are closed."

"A quick peek?" I beg, but she shakes her gray head adamantly.

"Then can you please direct us to the dungeons?"

"They are not open, either. They are very rarely open to the public. Usually only to guests."

"Guests?"

Stony-faced, she returns to her knitting needles and balls of wool, revealing nothing else. I recall that character who is always knitting—in which story, *The Scarlet Pimpernel?* We retreat out into the late-afternoon sun, where we suddenly become aware of music, the drum of distant rock music. I am grateful for its normality.

We decide to go in search of it. This leads us across an immense courtyard where the cobbled cracks at our sandaled feet are sprinkled with yellow-flowering rockery plants and fragrant arrays of mildly sweet herbs.

In this arid environment, they are soft and pleasing; but I sense an unsettling presence here, a hazy, indiscernible danger which is closing in around me and I cannot shake off.

"The music must be coming from a radio or cassette player."

The guitar strumming leads us to an alley, a dusty cul-de-sac, at the end of which is a crumbling stone wall and grassy banks. We turn, confused. The notes waft across the bleating afternoon heat, but from where? Retracing our steps and then branching off, still within the fortress environs, we wander down a widish avenue, parallel to the museum, and come upon an aging wooden door that looks to be as old as the foundations of the fort. I push against it. It is locked. On it, written in tired flaking white paint, we read *Plongée*.

"There must be a diving base here. But where is that music coming from?" It is still audible but remains tantalizingly, inexplicably remote. We plod from one empty space to the next, drawn by the ghostly melody, but without luck. The place is deserted, yet, I have a notion that we are being watched, spied upon in a very different way from the other island. The fort is empty but not tranquil; a troubled nagging power beckons me. Suddenly, clouds of small dark birds, starlings I think, rise up from nowhere and disperse like smoke into the penetrating blue sky. The unexpectedness of their movement has alarmed me, and I find myself trembling.

I mention my discomfort, and Michel squeezes his arm tight around me and smiles. He is growing used to my dramatic interpretations, or my sixth sense, whichever it is.

Somewhere to our left, I see a bronze cannon, a great brute of a weapon. It is trained out over the fortress walls upon the open sea. No doubt in its heyday it would have had the capacity to blow any unwelcome visitors clean out of the water, dissecting limbs from torso with its solid cannon balls the size of modern beach balls. I lean my body way out over the bastille wall and regard glinting wavelets glistening in the axis of the sun.

Where the water breaks against the island, the waves are crashing relent-lessly. It is as though we are in a storm. They smash against the mighty rocks rising up out of the sea upon which this place has been constructed.

"It looks as though there are some very dangerous currents down there."

There are straggly-branched, wind-torn trees and scrub plants grow-ing everywhere on the cliffsides, but the elevated terrain is bleak. Wriggling farther out on my stomach, feeling both the blood and the rosé rush to my head, I notice an opening cut into the rocky wall beneath me. "Look, that must be one of the dungeon windows." Certainly, it is too nar-row for any man or even a child to pass through. It offers no escape. I am feeling giddy and shimmy my body back to cobbled terra firma.

"How many years did you say the mystery man was imprisoned here?"

"Eleven."

I reflect upon it. While an order of monks is freely incarcerated at work and prayer on the neighboring island less than half a mile away, another is forcibly imprisoned here, stripped even of his identity. Locked in a dank underground cell with only a slit of an opening for fresh sea air and a view of the world beyond this fortress. I am wracked with pity for this unknown human being who for three centuries has been an inspira-tion to writers and filmmakers. His existence must have been barbaric. How did he bear the loneliness, keep madness at bay? Might this prisoner have requested his confession to be heard by a monk from the order across the water, the opportunity to unburden his heart to one trained in com-passion? Did he beg the fathers to remember him in their prayers, to help him carry the burden his life must have become to him as he paced his cell, manacled at the feet by ball and chain, masked in iron? And then I remind myself that there are parts of the world even today, where such barbarism exists. Where liberty is snatched for no good reason. Internment against faith, color, political conviction or, as it seems in the case of this pitiable being, birthright.

"It is also possible that the poor fellow was cursed with some hideous affliction. Locked away because he was judged too repulsive to behold, you know, like the Elephant Man."

"Why don't you write a story set here?"

I laugh at Michel's suggestion. "I think many, far more talented than I, have already achieved it."

"No, a modern story. Set it partially here, research locally and you can work from home. Write a role for yourself as well, and then you can work from home twice!"

There is the carrot that draws me. I consider our olive farm and the work and time it is about to demand. One of us will need to remain here on a regular basis once we begin the business of restoration.

"Set the story in Germany, England and France. Thirteen episodes, please."

I smile at him, considering. "So, we have been story hunting?"

"Yes, if you are inspired. But even if you are not, I thought the islands would appeal to you."

They have. But this island in particular has captivated me. And troubled me. And yes, inspired.

THE LAST FERRY DEPARTS from the island at six P.M. We are on it. During the short trip across the bay, the faintly descending light grows opalescent beneath a Wedgwood-blue sky. The clouds are the white patterns on the teacups. The lovely Italian tones of the properties along the coast toward the Cap d'Antibes . . . My musings are interrupted by what I take to be a small girl's scream, followed instantly by an excited male calling from somewhere behind us, "*Regardez, là-bas!*"

"*Où?*"

"*Dans la mer!*"

I fear a child has gone overboard, though I have no memory of any children boarding the vessel. We swing around to find the crew and the handful of passengers leaning over the leeward side of the boat, pointing and squealing.

What is it? We cross swiftly, my stomach clenching with fear at the prospect of a helpless drowning child, and there in the water, not twenty yards from the ferry, is a sleek gray creature leaping in the calm, limpid sea. And then another. *"Dauphins! Oui, ce sont les dauphins. Regardez comme ils jouent!"* A pod of dolphins are leaping and flipping, rising, as they do, four, even five, feet above the water's surface. Stubby-nosed athletes with shiny midnight fins, somersaulting, they change course and stream on ahead of the prow, as though leading us to shore. Then one of them breaks away from his party, circles, tacks and speeds in close alongside us, riding the wave created by our ship cutting through the sea. He spins over playfully, revealing a plump whitish belly, and back over again. I can almost read his mischievous grin. What a sight! What sheer joy!

As I watch these mythical creatures, I recount to Michel the story of an extraordinary American, Charlie Smithline, whom I met years ago in the Caribbean. He trained me for my PADI open-water-diving certificates. On several occasions, we dove together with bottle-nosed dolphins—which I believe is relatively unusual, for they will not often allow humans close—but they knew and trusted Charlie, a regular visitor. I learned from him that dolphins emit and perceive sound at frequencies higher than those at which we humans are able to hear. In fact, the human ear is not equipped to hear in the water.

Our dolphin companion speeds off and turns back, bobbing his head above sea level. He is looking our way, then, almost without any preparation, he soars into the air and arcs back into the water.

"Look at him!"

"You know, they can leap out of the water at a speed of thirty or forty miles an hour!" the captain tells us.

The fading light is playing on Michel's face. He looks animated and relaxed, his head thrown back in laughter. I laugh too. Around us, others are applauding and snapping photographs. Even the crew and our salty old ferry captain, who has a Gitanes glued to his partially parted lips, are transfixed. It is impossible not to be charged by the sight of these creatures. What a finale! What a curtain call nature has provided, to bring to a close the most perfect of days. The most perfect of summers.

CHAPTER FIVE

THE PURCHASE

J et-lagged from Australia, where I have spent the past nine weeks, I land in London. The city is in the grip of shopping fever, and the temperature seems to have settled at around freezing. The bookies are taking bets, short odds, on whether or not it will be a white Christmas. After the blinding white heat of Sydney and a crippling film schedule, I am spinning and want nothing more than to get directly out of the city and on the road again, south to the villa, to spend our first Christmas at home.

For weeks now, staring out at the Pacific Ocean from my hotel terrace, watching one bleached surfer after the next "hang nine," a script forever in front of me, pining for Michel who was back in Paris, or trussed up in corsets and Victorian frocks in an ambient temperature of 100°F, I have been dreaming of barbecued turkey on our open fire. The only cloud on that mental idyll has been that we are still not the legal owners of our olive farm, and we are both growing very apprehensive.

The purchase has not been going smoothly, and while we bite our nails and wait, reflecting on the money we have already invested, the sterling currency against the franc is going through the floor.

As far as we can glean, because no one is exactly keeping us informed, the delays seem to lie within *le bureau des impôts*. Apparently, the French tax authorities are querying Monsieur and Madame B.'s right to dispose of the estate. Investigations are now in progress into both their and their offspring's inheritance deeds. The Belgian owners, through the offices of the French *notaire,* have written to declare their foreign resident status, furnished letters from the daughter to support this fact and relinquished all claims on the estate. As far as we can ascertain, they have filled out and furnished every document the French patrimonial tax system has ever drawn up on the subject. Now, it seems, we are awaiting only this unfathomable body's acceptance of the situation.

Save for the death of poor ailing Monsieur B., which would complicate matters horrendously, Michel and I have been assured that all hiccups have finally been ironed out, all stumbling blocks removed; even the division of land has been satisfactorily registered, without any heart attacks, on the commune survey plans, *le cadastre.* Nothing else can further hinder or delay the sale. All we need is the official thumbs-up on the Belgians' declared status and an agreed date when the three parties—the *notaire,* Monsieur and Madame B. and ourselves—can gather to sign and settle the matter. Given that France and Belgium, unlike Britain, do not close down for two full weeks over Christmas, Michel has telephoned to propose December 28. The *notaire*'s assistant has faxed back to say that she will be in touch. It's a cliff-hanger!

At some pitch-of-night hour, we take a ferry that lands us at Calais before dawn. We drive directly to Paris, where Michel needs to spend some hours at his production office, and then we speed like a rocket to reach the house before the following morning. This self-imposed itinerary, wacky as its seems, actually suits me because I'm still on Sydney time.

A few days earlier, Michel put through a call to an Arab we ran across briefly in the summer who owns a Provençal gardening business—actually, Amar seems to have his finger in a mind-boggling number of pies— requesting him to supply us with a Christmas tree. A blue pine is our preference but not essential. When we arrive well after midnight, we find the tree slumped against one of the villa's exterior walls on the top terrace. Its height and size make it better suited to Rockefeller Plaza, and we are obliged to lop almost three feet off its crown before dragging it like a corpse through the French windows.

Laughing insanely, loony with exhaustion and the pleasure of being together again, dying of hunger because we haven't eaten a thing since an early-evening stop in Beaune, we hack at our tree by moonlight. We have decorations from Bon Marché, the big department store in Paris, which I purchased while Michel rushed from one meeting to the next. I suggest staying up all night to decorate our monster. Michel recommends sleep.

"We have our new bed," he reminds me.

I had forgotten. We stagger exhaustedly to our bedroom to find, staring up at us from the floor, our old lumpy mattress now laced in cobwebs as well as months of settling dust and gecko droppings. What the hell, we fall into it like shot soldiers.

The following morning, Michel sets off for the market while I walk to the phone box to telephone the furniture store in Cannes and am informed by a most disdainful *vendeuse* that their driver kept the rendezvous, cutting a path with his load all the way up the corkscrew hills, but was obliged to take the bed back to the depot because there was no one at the villa to receive it. Jean-Claude and Odile, who had promised to be here for the delivery, have disappeared, gone away, are not contactable even by phone.

I apologize profusely, attempting to explain the problem, but this saleswoman remains unrelenting and *froide*. It is no longer her responsibility, she says. They have honored their side of the agreement. Our delivery, which next time around will cost us four hundred francs, about forty pounds, will have to wait until well into the new year. The date I eventually manage to drag out of her is weeks beyond our planned closure of the house. We will have returned north again.

So, no new bed for Christmas. But we are not too disappointed. It is so rejuvenating to be back. I wander the rooms, reinhabiting them, breathing in the evocative scents of pine and citrus wafting on the warm air. I peer through the glass at vistas cradled in my memory during distant weeks. A fire piled high with pine, oak and olive wood crackles in the hearth. Freshly made soup is bubbling in the makeshift kitchen: a whole free-range chicken in a bouillon spiced with bouquets of Provençal herbs, leeks, onions, carrots and bay leaves picked from our tree in the garden. Randy Crawford croons from the tape deck, high plaintive notes drifting through the near-empty rooms.

Holding hands, trekking from here to there, up stone steps, down rocky tracks, we reencounter our terrain and remain upbeat in spite of the clumps and thickets of weeds, the brush and thorny climbers. All have shot up as tall as sunflowers in the spaces we had cleared. So much summer threshing gone for nothing.

I glance back along the terraces toward the villa. Beyond the open French windows, our towering Christmas tree is garlanded with winking silver lights. On a table, a radiant blue glass vase I bartered for in the old town of Nice, after a visit to the Matisse exhibition at Cimiez, is crammed with long-stemmed yellow gladioli Michel picked up for a song at the market this morning. It glints in the winter sunshine. Gently hued bulbs blink on and off at a sleepy pace alongside the pool.

This *mise en scène*, with its early art deco feel, puts me in mind of a shabby yet elegant liner setting sail for the high winds, the open seas; or the faded glamour of a past era, a Hollywood just beyond my grasp.

My reverie is arrested by a strangled cry coming from somewhere near the parking area. We run to investigate and discover a cat tucked away in a dark corner in one of the stables. As I approach her, she hisses a warning. Michel presses my hand and inches me back. This wary creature is thin as a wisp, a scraggy-coated, white-and-marmalade feral, protecting a very newborn litter of blind pink faces. She could turn vicious, so I step back, pondering her and her young. What should we do? Cats are good ratters, and there are plenty of rats and mice about, or so we presume, though we haven't seen any—only the telltale black pellets left on terraces and steps. Should we try and tame one or two? As if in response, the cat hisses her malevolent disapproval. No, let's leave those furry orange balls to their destiny, to the same wild existence as their mother. Besides, after dear, much-missed Henri, how can I accept responsibility for any animal?

And then I remember our kidney-shaped pond and its prehistoric carp, and I feel sure this feline intruder will have poached them. But when we hasten to look, we count not seven, as we had calculated in the summer, but eleven! We dig out two of the sheets of curled mosquito netting slung in the garage and secure them across our pond. The squatting cats can fend for themselves.

HAVING LIVED ALL MY adult life in a big city, I was never aware of the tradition of calender-giving. Does it exist in villages and small towns in England?

Michel has disappeared to the fish market in Cannes in search of oysters. They are one of the mainstays of the traditional Christmas Eve and New Year's Eve menus here and are deliciously cheap, approximately thirty francs for two dozen. I am at my desk pegging away, trying to get to grips with my ideas for the story I want to set on the islands, when I hear honking in the driveway and look out the window. There beneath is a fire engine. Naturally, this concerns me and I hurry downstairs to find myself greeted by five stunningly fit, handsome young men clad in tight-fitting navy blue uniforms.

"Is there a problem?" I ask, trying to resist the temptation to be flirtatious.

"*Bonjour, nos meilleurs voeux.*" Each shakes my hand before a tender-faced member of the team shoves a bunch of calenders at me and asks me which one I would like. I don't particularly want any of them but guess that this must be a local tradition—donations for a local charity, perhaps?—so I choose one and all five nut-brown faces light up, waiting expectantly while I run back upstairs to find my purse. There is no set price, I am told, so I offer a sum that seems to satisfy because each man shakes my hand one more time. Again they wish me warm felicitations of the season. They depart and I return to my work. But not for long. Now it's the turn of Monsieur *le facteur* who climbs the drive on his yellow scooter. He honks, waves and settles. I descend and am greeted by yet another array of calenders.

I decline, explaining "*Merci,* we have one," genuinely assuming that they are all selling on behalf of the same local charity, but I quickly understand by the scowl that runkles his bearded face that this answer is simply *pas acceptable.* Images of a triumphant Henri confronting the mailman, on his knees, flash before my eyes. Best not make enemies, or he'll have us all in the doghouse. Smiling stupidly, I dutifully choose another calender and race back upstairs to collect my purse. I proffer the last cash I possess, a one-hundred-franc note, which seems to satisfy him, and he now wishes me the best of the season, steadies his overloaded bike and pitches off, skating down the drive at a precarious angle.

The garbage collectors arrive next. We go through the same rigmarole. Unfortunately, I am out of cash, which does not please them at all so I am obliged to hurry to the *salon* upstairs, where I all but wreck our luggage in a harassed search for my French checkbook. I pick my calender, write the check and wave merrily, offering good wishes as they depart. Back upstairs, I toss three calenders, all offering identical aspects of our village, onto the makeshift kitchen table, pour a large drink and begin preparations for lunch.

Michel returns, honking and smiling, laden with salads of every shade of red and green and clementines from Corsica still bearing sprigs of sharply scented leaves. I press my nose into the orange and green nobbly skin and inhale the tangy perfume. "Christmas!" I whoop. I unpack several plastic containers of Provençal olives. Dark, fleshy drupes pickled in brine, others marinated in oil and garlic or pimientos, and then our oysters, still locked within their salty corrugated shells: a dozen chanteclairs from Brittany. We place them, with all the care given to newly laid eggs, in the darkest, coolest spot at the back of our little fridge to await our evening meal.

Christmas Eve is the slot traditionally set aside for the French family Christmas dinner; because the girls are spending their holidays with Maman in Paris, we are looking forward to ours, *à deux*, by candlelight. While we are busy unloading the shopping, I recount the story of our host of visitors. Michel, uncorking a fresh young Chablis, laughs heartily and asks, "So, the police didn't come by yet?"

THESE WINTER EVENINGS are enticingly mild. A new moon, slender as a child's pearly hairslide, appears in our cornflower heaven. I am spinning my thoughts for the television series with Michel as we huddle on the terrace, keeping at bay the chill that descends with the fading light by wrapping ourselves in each other and thick cable-stitched woolies. I am describing my main character as she takes shape in my imagination while enjoying an *al fresco* glass of wine before the silvery shimmer on the water disappears into jet-blue night. Nutty, ambrosial whiffs of woodsmoke waft our way on the still, late-evening air. A neighborly owl hoots a *bonjour*.

Bats swoop low, whizzing directly in front of us before wheeling and soaring like excited birds. We catch the distant call of the *muezzin*. The Arabs are at prayer. I grow silent and listen.

Although our house and its modest olive farm are situated in an area designated as *zone verte,* at the far end of the valley, tucked beyond gangling and bushy pine trees, is a settlement. It has been constructed on land purchased from the proprietors of Appassionata thirty or more years ago. At that time our local council, managing to overlook the small detail of the land status, stamped a permit that assigned to a syndicate of developers operating out of Marseilles the rights to construct upon the green belt site.

Although there were no immediate neighbors at that time, the local community was up in arms—as only the French can be when they feel their rights have been abused—and, we hear, lobbied furiously but lost. One can only speculate on how the permits ever negotiated the system in the first place, when to construct a garden shed or even a very humble lean-to in this zone requires a mountain of forms and months of badgering for planning permission. Such a blatant flaunting of the land codes would, of course, have contributed to the racist sentiments rife in southern France against all foreign workers, but aimed particularly against the Arabs. Southeast France is the heart of Le Pen country. No matter that the firm of developers and the managing agents, therefore the beneficiaries of all profits from the rudimentary housing, are French.

But we have no argument against the Arabs, and we love their tinny summons. It feeds my imagination, my attraction to diversity, and unlocks fantasies of caravans led by camels, treks across mystical Arabia on horseback, the new moon as our guide. Then, as the prayers grow silent, I settle back into life in the south of France and the prospect of our delicious oyster supper.

WE WAKE TO THE DISTANT bray of a donkey—another new sound on our horizon—and flocks of small chattering birds. These winter morns are glorious, gentle and pine-scented. The sun has a warm amber glow, rich as an autumn leaf; viewed from the upper terraces, it streaks across the sea in chilly silver strips. Winter is decked out as I have never known it, but our future home in another season also lays bear ill-considered responsibilities. During our months absent, without anyone to clean and care for it, the water in the swimming pool has turned a rich emerald green. Its floor is carpeted with decaying fig leaves. It cannot be neglected like this for months on end; it needs regular attention—skimmers emptied, pipes unclogged, filter system rinsed out, walls and base vacuumed—or the works we have invested in will have been a waste of precious funds. We add "maintenance of pool" to our growing list of chores.

I, who will swim in the most arctic of conditions and dankest of waters, decide to take a dip anyway. The water is so icy as I plunge into it that I hoot and holler. Blood courses fast through my veins. After, I run and leap about in the garden like a loony, gathering soil on my naked throbbing feet. Michel, passing by, shakes his head and disappears to collect wood and cones for the chimney. He builds monumental fires which thaw my chilled, goose-bumpy flesh and roar in the hearth like winds from Siberia. Their blaze envelops and heats me, roasts and reddens my flushed, damp cheeks.

Our winter existence revolves around the commodious sitting room. For this season, it has become the heart of the house. We sit for hours with our books and laptops, me at work on my prospective script, plumped on cushions at the hearthside. The light leaping from the flames makes shadowplay on our faces and shapes on the peeling walls.

Without resources for a kitchen, we are cooking our Christmas meals, as Michel had promised, on the open fire. When the piled embers have settled into hillocks of simmering scarlet red and blood orange like the sunsets, Michel sets the meat on the makeshift grill to sizzle and spit. Our fare is modest for this festive season: slender *faux-filet* steaks with crispy fresh salad from the fantastic food market in Cannes, accompanied by new potatoes, round and smooth as pebbles, boiled in a copper skillet I bought in Nice on Michel's elementary gas ring, fueled by bottled gas. Instead of Christmas pudding, we have cheese, crumbly Parmesan and creamy St. Marcelin preserved in olive oil with herbs, washed down with glasses of deep red wine.

The heat of the fire, the Bordeaux and the food seduce and inebriate us. No meal has ever tasted this luxurious.

The room is perfumed with cloves I have scattered on the embers and the skins of the consumed Corsican clementines which sizzle and hiss, turn crisply brown and curl like potato chips. They give off a tangy sweet scent and recall memories of childhood Christmases and stuffed stockings ripped open at the foot of the tree. We crawl into bed early to treasure the last joys of the day on our lumpy mattress, which we have dragged from the room we had elected to be our bedroom to the warmth of the jumping flames. Cuddling up close, we count five geckos on the chimney breast.

"I wonder if they are aware of us here," I say to Michel.

"Surely. They are guardians of the house. They are watching over us."

Irrationally, it has a ring of truth. Every cupboard unlocked or door opened reveals a gecko scuttling from the glare of the light and discovery to anonymity and darkness, but here, within our simple festive sitting room, with flames leaping, they have taken up residence on the warm chimney breast to share Christmas with us.

"I doubt we could ever be this happy again," I whisper as we close our eyes and listen to the crackle of olive branches burning. It is a passing comment spoken in a moment of blissful contentment, but better that it should never have been voiced, for it has risen up from a dark, unconscious prescience.

The following morning, Michel finally manages to get hold of Madame Blancot, the assistant at the notary's office. Unfortunately, the paperwork has not arrived from the tax office in central France, and in any case, Monsieur and Madame B. have informed her that they are not available to travel during this period. When Michel replaces the phone, he smiles encouragingly, and I attempt cheeriness. This will be resolved, we reassure each other. But we are growing concerned.

CAUGHT UP IN THE biomass of weeds and herbs, cobwebby trailers and tangled climbers are the fruiting olive trees. Their abundant offerings are dropping from the unpruned trees and disappearing into the soil. Hidden in the overgrowth, they rot secretively. These fruits are returning unused to the earth, leaving only their stone hearts as witnesses. How it pains me to see the source of such a potent elixir go to waste.

It is essential, I suggest to Michel, that as soon as the sale has been concluded, we hire a professional to cut back the entire acreage of land. Amar would be our man, if we can agree on a price. Amar is a Tunisian who has been living in the south of France since he was a teenager. Unlike many of the foreign workers who spend certain periods of the year in France and then return to their families in one of the various North African countries for the remaining months, Amar is married and is raising his family as young French citizens. He is a rogue, but a kindly one who wishes no harm to anyone. He has a full-moon face rather like a newborn baby's. Add to that the darker African tones of his skin, and he puts one in mind of a polished chestnut, but set within that shiny innocence are shrewd, calibrating eyes.

A call from Michel, and Amar pays us a visit that same afternoon. A fact we have yet to learn is that all foreigners buying properties in this part of France are automatically judged *très riche* and therefore easy pickings for the huge labor force—cowboys as well as true artisans—living off the villa trade close to the coast. Amar studies the width and breadth of the terrain, silently calculating the value of the property and then the road-weary, battered vehicle parked in the drive, which does not suggest wealth. To this he weighs how far he dares go and then names his price with due care, testing the water. The figure is astronomical. He reads our shock and instantly retracts. "But that is the market price, *cher monsieur*. Obviously, for you, I would consider a discount."

Michel frowns, studies the ground, shifting dust with his shoe. He appears to be considering the proposition and, after due thought, counters it with a ninety-percent discount. Amar grins like a playful child, appreciating the daring of the counterplay. The ritual has begun. The bartering goes back and forth until a price is warmly agreed: one fifth of the sum originally requested. Everyone shakes hands. Amar accepts a soft drink—as a practicing Muslim, he never touches alcohol—and prepares to wend his way, but just as we reach the parking, he turns, smiling broadly.

"Ah, Monsieur . . ."

"Yes?"

"We have forgotten the Christmas tree." We genuinely have. We apologize profusely.

"Yes, indeed. How much do we owe you?" Michel is digging about in his jeans pockets for cash, for these matters are always dealt with in cash.

Amar, with a smile as broad as a Cheshire cat's, demands "*deux mille francs,*" approximately two hundred and thirty-five pounds!

....

Now we are at the beginning of March. At long last a date has been suggested for us to gather at the *notaire's* panoramic office up in the hills behind the perfume town of Grasse to sign the papers for the purchase of the house. Unfortunately, I am rehearsing a new play which is due to open out of town, run for three weeks and then go straight to London's West End for a three-month minimum season. The date fixed by Madame B. is a Monday toward the end of March, the only date that she has available in the forseeable century. It is the week after the play has opened in the market town where I am currently rehearsing.

"I can't be there," I say via phone to Michel, who is in Paris. "I will have to assign you power of attorney."

"Would you prefer if we wait until the play has opened in London?"

"No. If we do that, it could be another year before we own the house."

"That's probably true," he agrees. "We'll organize the power of attorney. It will involve your going to the French Embassy in Kensington. Will you be able to arrange that with your rehearsal schedule?" Alongside requesting permission to fly to France, an hour in Kensington does not seem such an unrealistic demand, and I reassure Michel that a brief trip to London is entirely feasible.

Two hours later, the *notaire's* assistant, Madame Blancot, telephones Michel to inform him that *le maître* will not agree to this arrangement.

"Whyever not?" I moan when he calls to pass on the news.

"Because we are not married yet, and here in France, with the Napoleonic laws in force, the girls have certain inheritance rights. *Le maître* is insistent that the signing take place when, and only when, you can be here. Madame Blancot assures me that it is your interests he wants to protect."

"I see." I am deliberating long-distance. "Do you think you could charm Madame B. into bringing the date forward? Why not suggest the week before I go into production?"

"I'll try, but *chérie*, there's one other small point the *maître* pointed out which we have overlooked . . ."

"What's that?"

"Our *promesse de vente* runs out at the beginning of April."

The impact of this hits me instantly. The contract we signed in

Brussels bound us to purchasing the property before the fourth of April. If the purchase does not go through by that date, we will forfeit our hefty cash deposit as well as all monies dispensed on improvements to the property. Worse, we lose all preferential rights to the purchase of the property. It will go back on the market. It does not bear thinking about.

"But these delays have not been of our making! French bureaucracy is enough to send anyone to the madhouse."

The fact is, Michel reminds me, that Madame B. had offered us *one* date in mid-February, which we were obliged to refuse because both he and I were back in Australia for a month of postproduction on the series I shot before Christmas, so any grounds we feel we have for complaint will be judged inacceptable. The long and short of it is, we both stand to lose everything.

I am sitting silently at the back of a smoky rehearsal room—in reality, a church hall—weighing up my options over a Styrofoam cup of coffee so disgusting it might have been brewed with water from our bracken pond at Appassionata. If the notary does not accept Michel acting for both of us, then the bottom line is I am forced to find a way to slip off to France. But how?

Where I am, things are not going great. The director is on his fifty-ninth cigarette of the morning. I fear that the leading actor, who is playing a psychopath—the play is a thriller—may be close to crossing the boundaries between acting and life. While the other actor—the cast is a mere trio—is an affable, easygoing fellow, he looks ready to lose his cool with his colleague's uncontrolled outbursts. We are only eight days into rehearsal. Already there are daily confrontations between these two, and the situation shows signs of growing uglier. I am depressed and wish that I had not accepted the job, now, in light of my own predicament, more than ever.

The fact is that, although the date on offer is the Monday after we open, because the play is new, the chances are we will be called to rehearsals every day until after the first night in London, when the critics will have reviewed the piece and all damage to our sensibilities and the box office, if any, will have been achieved. Until then, there will be cuts, rewrites, new plot twists, different stagings, a host of directorial and managerial responses to the reactions of both out-of-town audiences and newspapers. This is all perfectly normal, but it does not help my present dilemma, and there are no scenes without me. The only reason I am not up on the rehearsal stage at this very moment is because the two men are debating the finer details of gun-toting. The tone of the conversation taking place at this very moment goes something like "Don't keep sticking that f—— thing in my eye!"

Timing is of the essence, in real life as in theater. I am going to have to wait my moment and then speak to the producer, who is a charming and reasonable individual. I decide to put the problem out of mind for the moment, wait till matters look a little more sanguine and return to work.

During my lunch break, from a phone booth a discreet distance from the theater, I telephone Michel in Paris. "Confirm the date," I tell him, "and I'll settle it with the management this week."

"Are you sure?"

"Yes" is my reply. The truth is I am not the least bit sure, but the fact is we have no choice.

I am not ready to return to the theater and still have another fifty minutes of lunch break, so I decide, insteading of sitting hunched up in a dressing room learning lines—which is what I would normally do—to browse the suburban shopping street. Coincidentally, I spent many years of my youth, my salad days, in this town of Bromley, so its homogenized modernizations hold a certain fascination for me. I range around, trying to remember how it was and which formative experiences took place where, until, passing one of the pubs, I catch sight of our supporting actor sitting alone on a stool. His head is bent over a glass, and he looks desperately glum. Although we barely know each other, having met only eight days earlier at the read-through, I decide to intrude on his mood.

"Hey," I say as both greeting and to alert him to my presence. I notice that his drink is a tonic and something . . . gin, vodka? He turns to face me, and I realize immediately that he has downed more than one. His bloodshot eyes glare out from a face that looks bemused, hurt and despairing.

"How are you doing?" I ask. The question is redundant. The bartender saunters my way, and I order coffee. "Would you like one?"

My colleague shakes a mute head.

"I can't work with him, he's a f—er." I can see this actor's point, but I won't say so. After all, we are three and have five months of work ahead of us in a piece that is demanding and intimate.

"I guess he's nervous. Probably pinning a lot on it. Big role . . ." My coffee arrives, for which I am grateful because I do not believe a word of what I am saying. My fellow thesp takes the bartender's presence as an opportunity to order another double. I look at him quizzically. He says, "Listen, why don't you do a spot of shopping. I'll catch you back there."

I nod, leaving coffee and coins on the bar and my poor workmate to his angst and alcohol.

When I return, our leading player is sitting with the director in the rehearsal hall where they are sharing anecdotes, firing off one after the other. I find this a common practice among actors in rehearsal, and I have never quite understood why it happens: a performance within a performance. I concentrate on my script. The next time I look up, it is fifteen minutes beyond the allotted lunch hour, and my friend from the pub has not returned. The leading actor has begun to pace. His face reddens; his blood pressure must be mounting. He is growing manic. The director is chain-smoking. A few moments later, the company manager, a caring young woman in her mid-twenties, enters with a note which she hands to the director. He reads it, frowns furiously, screws it up into a ball and tosses it onto the floor.

"Tony has gone home. He's not feeling too good."

The leading actor explodes. We are all knocked backward by the sheer vehemence of his response and the foulness of his language. I turn to the company manager, who returns my duplicitous look. The director rises and announces that probably the best plan is to spend the rest of the day with the wardrobe mistress, who will take measurements for our costumes.

When Michel calls in the evening, I say nothing of the problems I am facing and only assure him that all is well and that I will be in France to sign the documents. I sleep fitfully.

My call for the next morning is slightly later than the others'. When I arrive, I discover the three I left behind the evening before, all wearing long, murderous faces. Before I have the opportunity to say good morning, I am informed that Tony has left the show. A treacherously unprofessional thought then creeps into my mind: we are two left in the cast, only one week to go before we begin technical rehearsals and production days, there is too little time, the management will be obliged to cancel or at least postpone the first night, and *I will be free go to France!* Obviously, I keep such rising delight well in check.

The morning is spent calling agents, casting directors and chums to find a replacement for Tony. I offer no suggestions because I cannot in all conscience recommend any of my pals to what I am beginning to perceive as a sentence rather than a job. Our star is fulminating and cursing, then suddenly rounds on me. "I suppose it'll be you next!" he hisses poisonously out of earshot of the others.

"To do what?" I reply, a little shakily.

"You'll be walking out on me, too."

I refrain from pointing out that the play is not about him but a team effort. "No, I won't," I answer.

I have never walked out on a job, but at this very moment there is nothing I desire more. However, for many reasons, high on the list being the cost of house renovations and land-maintenance equipment, it would be an irrational act. I stay put and go on with the business of learning my lines and worrying about how I am now going to persuade the management to give me the Monday off, less than two weeks hence, to fly to France.

"So you're going to stick it out then, are you?"

"Please," I say, "let's just drop it."

A replacement is found. A jolly chap, resilient and good-humored. I try hard not to feel disappointed that the production has not been canceled. I need this job, and the actor is someone I have worked with before and like. He makes me laugh. He is exactly what we need and, astoundingly, learns the piece in two days. As far as everyone else is concerned, we are back on track. The other poor victim has been written off as unprofessional. Interestingly, our lead has met his match, for every time he grows even vaguely nasty or malevolent, the newcomer bats back with a quip or joke and the star has no brunt for his sadism. Or has he? As the days creep toward the out-of-town opening and he grows jumpier, he settles his attention on me. After one of the early runs of the piece, he accuses me in front of cast, technicians, management and crew of being entirely without talent and timing. Alone in my dressing room, I shed a few tears. Then, like every actress in desperate straits, I call my agent, who cheers me with "Oh darling, he's famous for it. When so-and-so finished working with him, she went to bed for a week." Now he tells me!

The sole high point of my week arrives with the blissful and unexpected news that we will not be rehearsing on the Monday after we open. It has been deemed a much-needed rest day. Our call will be the performance. In the light of this news and all that is going on, I make a precarious and highly unprofessional decision which is to go to France and not mention it. Such a move could lose me my job, but by this stage, I would be almost grateful. Still, it goes against the grain for me to behave with such dishonor, so I decide, for form's sake and to offload a little of my guilt, to confide my plan in the company manager, who, when she hears, stares at me in sheet-white horror. "You have no understudy until we reach London," she yelps. "I'd have to cancel the show."

"I'll be back, don't worry," I reassure her. "The signing is at nine-thirty. It will be over, latest, by eleven. There are two British Airways flights leaving Nice after that. Either would land me at Heathrow in plenty of time, and with a taxi to bring me to the theater, there's no way I'll miss the show." She relents. What choice have I given the poor woman? Her sole request is that, should worse come to worst, I am never, *never* to mention that she had cognizance of my plan, or her career will be in ruins alongside mine. It seems a fair bargain. I agree.

ON SUNDAY, MICHEL, WHOSE plane from Paris landed earlier than mine, is waiting to greet me at the Nice airport. It is a glorious spring morning. In spite of a tense week and a dawn departure from London, the prospect of the following day's trip up into the hills exhilarates me. Added to which, after an interminable wait, we are finally taking legal possession of our home, our farm. When we arrive at the house sitting atop its hill of dusky olive trees, which we have not visited for almost three months, it is unrecognizable. Amar has cut back the entire expanse of land. We are gazing upon new geography.

The bosky acres, the brush and brambles, the jungle have been trimmed, laid bare and raked into hummocks ready for burning. However, this fleecing has left Appassionata looking naked and vulnerable, a deserted, crumbling shell, yet newborn, with much to discover. We count sixty-four overgrown olive trees (ten I had not seen before) as well as space on the upper terraces for dozens more, terraces cut back in their entirety for the first time in many a year. The trees are now free to breathe, to grow anew and produce.

"I thought you had agreed with Amar to wait until after—"

"So did I," says Michel.

It is both a lovely and troubling greeting, for we have no gates, no fencing, no boundary partitions of any kind. This will have to be addressed next. So much will have to be addressed next!

But aside from all future cares, there is a revelation too exquisite for words. The cutting back of the land has exposed a fabulous stone staircase. Unbeknownst to us, it has lain buried beneath the layers of brambles, forgotten and unused. Now, its secret unfolded, it rises like a bird taking flight from the foot of the hillside to the house itself. Michel suggests that it must have been the original entrance to the house before the tarmac drive was put in, before a route for cars was deemed necessary, before the lane between our entrance and the caretaker's cottage was ever thought of. Judging by a series of small rectangular holes cut into the stones, it looks as though a rose bower covered pretty much the entire ascent, a distance of approximately three hundred meters. In full flower, it must have been an impressive sight, and what a perfumed entry!

Our approach also reveals soft pink almond blossoms, past their best, fading now, and all around us, bursting from the branches of the deciduous trees—figs, cherries, plums, pears—fresh shiny bamboo-green shoots, as well as literally hundreds of flowering wild irises, white and violet, bordering the terraces, at every level. Pale pink, bamboo-green, white, inky violet: a palette I have never associated with the south of France. We inch forward in the car taking in these sights, these explosions of unexpected color. What release must this nature be experiencing? When did this earth, the soil of these terraces, last feel the beat of sunlight? I consider the millions of creatures and insects who have been rendered homeless, who have lost their bearings, and alongside them, the plants that have been given back the light.

After lunch on the upper terrace, the sky clouds over.

We make the most of our chilly Sunday afternoon working, keeping

warm through activity. It is such a pleasure to be outdoors, to be physically busy. Invigorating and reassuring. I weed the flowerbeds; Michel
sweeps the steps, which are knee-high in mulchy leaves, then strips and
prepares the garden chairs for painting: lilac and ocher. I discover tiny
spring-green shoots at the base of the chopped trunks of what we had
believed were dead orange trees. Somewhere in the middle distance I hear
gunshots, a hunter out after rabbits or small birds. I feel my skin, which
is tired and tight from being coated in layers of stage makeup, begin to
breathe and glow in the sharp brisk air. As the day draws to its early close,
it starts to rain. I jump in the brilliant green pool and swim for my life in
the freezing water, circling and paddling like an otter in the drizzle while
Michel readies the fire—we have unlimited supplies of firewood now—
for our evening. A propitious moment in time: our last evening as official
squatters, for tomorrow we will become *les propriëtaires*.

Lounging on cushions in front of the fire, we listen to the rain beating hard and fast against the windowpanes and splashing into our well-
used bucket in the makeshift kitchen. And we don't care. Tomorrow, every
leak, every flaking crumb of plaster, will belong to us.

The rain grows tropical in its intensity. All night it beats and slaps
against the roof, and when we awake bright and early, ready for our
excursion into the hills, our driveway is streaming with water. It runs in
rivulets, taking sticks, a dead rabbit and rotting leaves in its wake. Only
in the rainy season in Borneo and in the last throes of a hurricane in Fiji
have I witnessed such a torrential downpour. As we bolt to the car, it
soaks us. The force is so overwhelming that the wipers are barely able
to beat back and forth, and in any case, they achieve little. Fortunately,
Michel knows the route. We arrive on time but dripping like river
rats. Madame B. awaits us, dry as a bone and impeccably turned out.
Pierre is not with her. The *notaire* looks on in operatic horror as we
drip and squelch across his pristine beige carpet to our appointed
leather chairs.

The panoramic views in this area beyond Grasse, about which I have heard so much, are masked by the sheeting rain. "*C'est dommage,*" says the *notaire*, who sports a pince-nez and a well-cut but rather old-fashioned double-breasted navy suit and is as manicured and pointy-faced as a poodle. His elbows are poised on the armrests of his chair and never leave that position. He joins the tips of his fingers together regularly, as though in prayer, and I discover that he has an infuriatingly meticulous attention to detail. Here is a man who puts brackets between verbal brackets and then parenthesizes! Every law, bylaw and clause is thrown open for consideration, then explained at a rattling pace. The history of the estate of Appassionata is not only written into the contract page by page, franc for franc—husband of, wife to, born of—but is now read aloud and commented upon by him.

The villa was constructed in 1904. This was the year the great Provençal poet Frédéric Mistral was awarded the Nobel Prize for literature. Because the process is ponderous and I have aready lost the thread, I search for a quotation of his I learned by heart recently, but it slips beyond recall when the *notaire*'s droning drums me back to consciousness.

I try again to concentrate but find myself completely, hopelessly lost. *Le maître*—all *notaires* in France are addressed as *le maître;* literally translated, it means the master, an acknowledgment of rank and learning equal, I suppose, to our addressing a judge as Your Honor—swivels his leather chair, as his is the only one not fixed, and talks at great length to Michel. Michel nods and interpolates every now and again, and once in a while, I am fired because I have caught a word or phrase, though I am unclear as to why this notary's words are directed exclusively at Michel. Madame B. does not appear to be listening. She is crossing and marking the contract spread out on the desk in front of her as though it were a script in need of drastic and immediate rewrites.

When *le maître* pauses to draw breath, Madame B. interjects, politely but firmly, "*Maître, s'il vous plaît* . . ." I haven't a clue what finer points they are debating, and I cannot possibly ask Michel. I long for the distraction of the view and am struggling not to steal a quick peek at my watch. A tiny worm of concern is wriggling about in my interior monologue: is all this just a teeny bit long-winded, or is it because I am on the outside looking in? Is it going to take all morning? I have to catch that lunchtime flight . . .

The rain is percussionless: no rolls of thunder, no crashes of electric white lightning, nothing but interminable rain.

Suddenly, when I have drifted far away, the *notaire's* chair swivels once more and stops like a roulette wheel to directly face me. "*Madame Drinkwater?*" All eyes turn to me.

"*Oui?*" I reply weakly.

"*Avez-vous compris?*" Have I understood what? I am asking myself. I shoot a glance at Michel, who is gazing at me warmly. He speaks for me, explaining to the *notaire* that I am not familiar with all of this.

"Aaaah," sings the man as though it explained my mute inattention, my lack of delight in dissecting these sacred deeds paragraph by paragraph. And then he launches into a history of my life. Where and when I was born, the name of my parents, which banks I patronize in England and France, my annual income (a figure I must have pulled out of thin air, for I have no guaranteed income), my profession, my mother's maiden name, the sum I have contributed toward the overall price of the estate, the fact that no debts remain unpaid by me. I am stupefied. And then he pauses, throwing his text on the table. "So, you are from Ireland?" I nod, and he removes his glasses and opens up a personal parenthesis about Ireland and the various holidays he has enjoyed there. Green. I understand that word. Yes, I nod, very green. And wet, *malheureusement.* Yes, Ireland is wet, I counter. Everyone laughs and shrugs and throws their hands about the way the southern French do when they are discussing the living habits of those poor unfortunate folk forced to live in climes less blessed than theirs.

"Mais..." He gestures, Shakespearean-fashion, toward the window, which opens onto nothing but the blanket of rain. There is a pause while the rain is considered. I and my history have been forgotten, or so I think. Seconds later, he is back in his role, text in hand, and other details of my private existence are shared with the room. Madame Blancot is taking notes, though heaven knows how anyone could possibly keep pace with this man; silently tucked away in the corner is the estate agent, Monsieur Charpy, who first introduced us to Appassionata.

And so it goes on. And on. I am asked if I have been informed about the existence of Michel's daughters, his ex-wife. The whole business feels like a preposterous interrogation. Then I am gravely warned about the risks I am taking in signing these documents and in part-purchasing a property with a man who has offspring elsewhere. I fear that were my understanding of legal French any better, I would pick up my bag and make for the door without signing a single page of what turns out to be five copies of a twenty-nine-page document. We are all obliged to initial every page and sign our full names at various strategic points after we have handwritten the words *lu et approuvé:* read and approved.

The whole process is really quite comical, a merry-go-round of papers and pens, with only one person doing nothing, the estate agent. He, I realize later, is there to receive his settlement from Madame B., which, she begrudgingly gives him in cash. The thick wad of five-hundred-franc notes is quite literally passed from richly bejeweled fingers to grasping hands under the table, but only after every last *i* has been dotted. I am amused by the *notaire*, who, while this black-market activity is taking place right beneath his desk, pulls out an enormous white handkerchief and busily blows his nose. The size of the handkerchief, little short of a sheet, manages most conveniently to cover his eyes and most of his face; hence he has seen nothing.

But first, the contracts are passed around the table, Michel followed by me, Madame B., the *notaire*, and his assistant Madame Blancot, silently and concentratedly initialing and signing.

It is after midday when we finally get out of there, say our *au revoir*s to Madame B., whom we will meet once more when we go through the whole process again for the purchase of the second five acres of land.

The rain has grown heavier, if possible. The sky is dark and brooding. Madame B. disappears in a chauffeur-driven limousine, and we huddle tight beneath the *notaire's* porch. We had planned an early lunch at the farm: a toast to our new, elevated position, to our home, the hillside, the new bed we found waiting for us the day before, but none of this is possible. We look at each other and smile.

"The airport?" Michel asks, and I nod. The drive is horrendous, the roads silted with mud and rivers of water. Everyone is driving with headlights on full beam, and the corkscrew hills and bends are treacherous. Descending through Grasse, where there are danger signs painted on the roads at the best of times, is a muddle of impatient, bad-tempered motorists. The journey is slow going, but we still have time. I try not to be anxious. We are silent because Michel is concentrating and I am sorry to be leaving, knowing that I won't be returning until the end of June, which feels a lifetime away. There is so much I want to begin.

Upon arrival at the airport, I run ahead to check in for the flight while Michel returns the rental car. When I arrive at the desk, there is no one about, neither staff nor passengers. It is ominously deserted. I look at my watch. The flight is not due to leave for another thirty-five minutes. It is tight, but surely the check-in has not already closed. They should only begin boarding about now. In a frenzy, I spot the British Airways inquiry desk, where there is a worryingly long line and gaggles of troubled or angry passengers. At the desk, I learn that, due to the weather, the flight has been canceled. My stomach feels as though it has just been punched by Muhammad Ali. Everyone, including myself, is scrabbling to book the next flight. While doing this, I upgrade to business class, figuring that should there be any further problems, it will give me an advantage. Michel arrives. I explain what has happened. His flight to Paris is not for another hour and is due to take off from the terminal for national flights. He hurries over to the Air France desk and changes his flight to one that leaves around the same time as my new scheduled departure.

"Well then, let's have lunch and celebrate," he says, and leads me to one of the airport cafés. We decide not to go into Nice because the car has been returned, and in any case, I do not want to stray. I feel I must keep a careful eye on events here, though, after some mental arithmetic, I am reassured. Even traveling on the later plane, there is plenty of time to reach the theater comfortably before curtain. Still, I would have felt calmer if the earlier flight had not been canceled.

After a simple meal, we kiss a passionate, heartfelt good-bye, and Michel waves me off through security toward passport control. As I look back, I see him hurrying for the bus that will carry him away to terminal one. We will not see each other for three weeks. In spite of the events of the day, the securing of the house after almost a year of delays, my heart feels heavy. I am torn between two worlds—the past and present and the present and future—and two countries; my heart and home are in France now, but my work is still in England. It is confusing and unsettling for a child of the earth like me, who needs to know where her roots are. During these musings I have been only vaguely aware of information coming over the loudspeaker. It is repeated in English, and this time I pay attention. Due to the weather, the British Airways flight has been delayed.

"No!" I cry and run to the boarding gate, where a pretty young French woman is switching off the microphone she has just used for the announcement. "How long is the delay?"

She shrugs. "We do not know." We both stare out of the window at a waterlogged runway and a fleet of planes standing idle. Should I telephone the theater? Could I hire a private plane? But if the Boeings cannot take off, what hope has a small jet? I decide to ask anyway. My fears are confirmed. All air traffic has been grounded. I return to the departure lounge. There is nothing to do but sit it out. The delay turns out to be a little over an hour, during which I am going over mental calculations involving arrival times, moving through passport control, finding a taxi. Fortunately, I have no luggage. Should I book a taxi to the theater from here? But I do not know when we will be departing. My brain is beginning to scramble. It is going to take a miracle . . .

Should I telephone the company manager? But if I do, what can she do? I have no understudy . . . I am going to be fired. Throughout a career spanning almost twenty years, I have never yet missed a show, not even due to illness and certainly not because of an act as irresponsible as this one. I am still berating myself when the boarding is announced.

As the fllight attendant directs me to my seat, I mention to her that I have a show, and I ask if there is any possibility of being given priority disembarkation.

"We all have problems. You should have taken an earlier plane."

Chastised, I spend the flight trying to rest. I am exhausted with worry. A plump American woman from Texas tries on several occasions to engage me in conversation, but I am in no mood and close my eyes firmly until I am stirred by a hand resting on mine. "Honey," she says, "I wanna tell you something . . ."

I open my eyes. "What is it?" I snap.

"You sure as hell are worried about something, and I want you to know that I know about it."

"Know about it?" I rejoin weakly, for if she has some secret, I am so desperate I am ready to hear it.

"I see things," she continues. "And you have nothing to worry about. You're gonna make it."

"I am?" I look at her in amazement, then realize that it is only my need trying to take heart from this utterly vague statement. "No," I say, "I can't make it. There is no taxi in the world that can transport me across rush-hour London in time for curtain."

"Oh my God! You're an actress! Have I seen you in anything? Anything on TV that shows in the States?"

I wish I had never been drawn in, but she is well meaning enough, and it is I who am foul-mooded and anxious. I give her the name *All Creatures Great and Small,* for it is usually the key that unlocks the door to my curriculum vitae. She is thrilled and "sooo happy! Let me tell you, honey, you will make that show, I have no doubt about it."

I smile and thank her for her optimism, then close my eyes; whatever she says, it is now a physical impossibility, and I have decided that as soon as we land I must call the theater, which is what I should have done from Nice, and explain to our very dear company manager that she has two choices: to hold the curtain or cancel the show. Either way, I am finished.

We fasten our seatbelts and the plane prepares for landing. As we hit the runway, the flight attendant makes the usual announcements and follows them with: "And would Miss Drinkwater please make herself known to the cabin staff."

I press the overhead button, and she approaches.

"We'll be disembarking you first," she tells me. "Please have your bags ready."

I nod gratefully, even though I know this assistance cannot help me now.

My Texan friend brushes my hand and wishes me well, reassuring me once more that she knows I will make it and beaming with the pleasure of having met me (!) and how she will tell everyone that I am equally charming in real life (!).

As I exit the plane, a member of the British Airways ground staff stands holding a card with my name on it.

"Miss Drinkwater?" he inquires.

I nod. "Follow me, please," he says, and strides on ahead with singular purpose. I follow obediently. "We have a short car ride across the tarmac, won't take more than a couple of minutes. Your pilot is ready and waiting." He smiles with professional reassurance.

"My pilot?" I am completely confused.

I am driven across an area of Heathrow Airport I have never crossed before, and deposited alongside a very capacious helicopter. I step out and the man shakes my hand and says, "Nice to have met you. Good luck." Off he goes. The pilot waves and sees me aboard. I settle into the helicopter, which is equipped to seat ten. We prepare for yet another takeoff. "Sorry it's so large. We had nothing smaller available." I shake my head because I am speechless. "It's fine," I mutter. Have they made a mistake? I am thinking. I dare not ask. "We'll be across London and landing at Biggin Hill Airport in ten minutes. All being well, there should be a taxi waiting to take you to the theater."

This is a miracle!—which I am trying to figure out. That rather uncharming, or perhaps harassed, flight attendant must have thawed during the flight and notified the pilot, who notified ground staff. Or has the Texan woman some miraculous powers she only hinted at?

Finally, I ask, "Did British Airways arrange this?"

"No, your husband booked it."

"My husband?" Thoughts whirl about in a flurry. I am not married. Have I taken someone else's place? But no, my name was written on the arrivals card, and they have a taxi waiting to take me to the theater.

And there it is, a taxi waiting on the tarmac. Into it I fall, gratefully. The traffic is heavy because we are hitting rush hour, but my driver seems to have been briefed and knows that this is an emergency. He shoulders his way in and out of lines of vehicles with a cutthroat purpose usually known only to the French, depositing me fifteen minutes later outside the stage door. We are twenty-five minutes before curtain. My knees are weak, I am soaking with perspiration and feel little better than a damp rag, but I am here. I walk in the door, collect my dressing-room key and stagger along the corridor. The company manager finds me. She looks ashen. Officially, contractually, all actors are due at the theater by what is known as "the half." The half is a theatrical abbreviation for half an hour before curtain up, but curiously, the half is actually announced thirty-five minutes before curtain up. Don't ask me why. All I know is that, right now, it makes me ten minutes late.

"Sorry," I mumble.

"Thank God you're here," she whispers, shoving me into my room and closing the door behind her. "No one knows a thing, but Christ, I have been having kittens."

I nod. I cannot speak. I am trembling like a leaf.

"Are you OK?"

"Fine," I manage.

"Want anything?"

"Rescue Remedy," which is a Bach herb-and-flower homeopathic tincture for shock. I know she keeps a bottle of it in her first-aid kit.

"You got it." She nods and rushes to the door. "By the way," she throws after her as she exits. "He's in the foulest of moods."

I nod again, taking this in: "Make that a double brandy." I never drink before a show, but tonight I doubt my knocking knees would transport me to the stage without it.

Later, once the performance—which has gone surprisingly well—is over, I pour myself a large glass of wine and ring Michel in Paris from my dressing room.

"How did you do it?"

He laughs and recounts his afternoon. He had been sitting in the national terminal waiting for the departure of his Air France flight to

Paris when, by sheer chance, he glanced up from his laptop and noticed a British Airways plane sitting on the sopping tarmac. He inquired and was informed that it was the delayed Heathrow flight. There was no way he could reach me, but what he did know was that every second that ticked by without that plane leaving the ground lessened my chances of reaching the theater in time. With the brilliance and agility of mind of a film producer—a breed who lives by the motto that every catastrophe must be turned to advantage if financial disaster is to be avoided—Michel understood that what he had to buy me was time. He checked himself off his own flight, purchased several phone cards and began ringing helicopter firms operating out of Heathrow. It was the helicopter company that gave him the name of the taxi company who frequently services the private airport to which I was delivered.

And delivered I am! When the bill arrives, the whole exercise costs every penny I am to earn from the out-of-town contract, money that might have purchased us a gate or contributed toward the laurel-bush fencing we have decided upon, but I am no longer counting. My professional reputation has been saved and the show has gone on.

As night falls and I curl up and close my exhausted eyes, the extraordinary catalog of the closing day's adventures (and misadventures) plays out again before me. In all the gut-wrenching and stress, I had almost forgotten that today we bought ourselves an olive farm in the Midi, overlooking the Riviera coast.

Pride and contentment wash over me for the first time, and the reality of our act sinks sweetly home. Then I contemplate the strikingly generous gesture of Michel. Reflecting on this, as my eyes grow heavier and my body slips warmly and safely toward sleep, I am lulled peacefully by the certainty that I have finally secured the shambling house that I have sought during so many years of travel and searching, and what is even more delicious, along the way I have encountered the one person with whom I desire to share that corner of paradise. What remains is for us to find the means to transform that crumbling shell into a home and, later, an olive farm. For the foreseeable future, until my West End run is over, I must set such dreams aside, because there will be no more snatched escapades in France.

CHAPTER SIX

A MELON AND LEATHER BOOTS

The instant I step out of the plane, I feel that whoosh of heat envelop me and the sun beat like a great fan against my tired features. What a welcome relief to be back. To be home. Michel, who flew down from Paris a couple of days ago, is there to greet me. He takes my bag and leads me to the car while I breathe deep the scent of eucalyptus wafting from the towering trees that dominate the airport parking. I take in the distant frantic honking of horns, gently listing palms, pure white buildings, clean blue skies and settle back into my seat to watch the Mediterranean world flash by. And then he breaks the news: the villa has been broken into. It's as though he has just slapped me. "When?"

Michel has known of the burglary for several weeks but chose not to mention it to me because there was nothing I could do about it. Worrying about it at a distance, he argues, would have been both distressing and frustrating. "I would have preferred to know," I state emphatically. I have been looking forward to this day for three months. I cannot deny that the news has clouded the pleasure of my return.

Once at the house, Michel unloads the car—my luggage and the fresh salads he bought before collecting me—while I roam from room to room, assessing the extent of the damage in our dusty foreign home. Little has been stolen, but then there there was precious little to steal. I am very relieved to find that our new bed has not been soiled, not even touched, but our cassettes and tape deck, modest as they were, are gone. Every tune had a place here, a memory. My fusty workspace is bare. My books, my precious books, have all been stolen, every one of them—dictionaries, guides, a history of the islands, manuals on local horticulture, even the dog-eared, beach-stained paperbacks—as has a brand-new espresso machine, a frivolous purchase I made the day before our New Year's departure. I hid and locked it in a cupboard, and due to the brevity of our last stay, we never even found an opportunity to use it. Curiously, the bed linen and tablecloths from the market at Nice have not been snatched though they are surely more valuable and salable than my paltry writing gear. Angry as I feel, I am grateful we have not been denied at least a few souvenirs of our first days here.

Michel finds me standing alone in the *salon*. "How did they get in?" I ask. He points to splintered spaces, where our old peeling shutter slats have been hacked out and replaced, windowpanes that were smashed by the thief when he made his entry as well as to a newly fitted lock on the main door through which he made his escape. Who repaired them and when? Amar, he answers, regarding me. I think he is taken aback by how hurt I am. Though the damage has been made good and the loss is minimal, I want to cry. I take it personally. It is an intrusion, a despoilment and, more crucially, a warning.

Outside the kitchen window, I come across an empty, discarded Marlboro packet. Should I keep it, present it as evidence? I try to picture the character and face of that smoker, but its discovery is five weeks too late. I ditch it in the wastepaper basket. Best to let it go.

Still, the cropping of the land has exposed the property. We are vulnerable now. It forces us to address the need for security. The hill where we are situated may never have been fenced in before, but we cannot afford to remain romantic about these matters. In the beginning, there was nothing else, no other property for miles in any direction. As far as the naked eye could see, it was owned and inhabited by one family, our predecessors—the Spinotti clan. Life was probably less cutthroat then, but more importantly, in the dependencies, the *mazets* of Appassionata, the gardeners and permanent staff lived, a cluster of people who tended the place all year round. We are not as privileged, so another solution will have to be found.

After lunch on the terrace, Michel telephones Amar, who arrives before evening and quotes us for the laurel bushes we have decided to plant to border the grounds. For the time being, we do not have to face the enormous expense of fencing in the entire property, because flanking either side of our terrain is the same overgrown jungle we had here. We have no idea who owns these two plots, but unattractive as the weeds and climbers may be, they are a burglar deterrent.

My behavior toward Amar is antagonistic. This is partly due to my frame of mind, but mostly because he knows we are beginning to count on him and I feel him taking advantage. His estimation of the number of bushes required far exceeds mine, and I tell him so. Eventually, over a fruit juice, aided by Michel's appeasing charm, we settle upon a more reasonable figure and a price. Even after hefty negotiating, he is expensive, added to which the cash we give him to settle for the land clearance, he now informs us, is insufficient.

"A rate has been agreed. Hands were shaken upon the deal!" I bark.

"Allow me to explain, *chère Madame* . . ." And he proceeds to explain in an irritatingly apologetic manner that he has underestimated the total number of man hours required for his two workers to climb up and down the hill and is obliged therefore to add this to the bill.

I am speechless with fury at his audacity and invention. Here, in the Midi, I am discovering, there are always reasons why the valuations change or why the work is not done in the manner or to the standard agreed. In this part of the world, quotations and budgets might as well be used as barbecue kindling.

Michel pays with good grace, and we order the laurel shrubs, for this is urgent and we cannot afford to delay while we look around for another gardener. Better the devil you know . . . Still, before *plein* summer is upon us, with all its distractions and harassments—the onslaught of tourists, lines, traffic congestions, when even the tiniest chore takes twice the time and every factory, *société* and office closes down for the entire month of August—we would do well to find ourselves some able-bodied help. We have a daunting list of tasks to accomplish. Most will be left to me to oversee, because Michel must return to Paris and will only be here on the weekends. I am tired from the run of the play and grateful to have an excuse to stay here and hang out. Besides, I have my writing project, inspired by our day trip to the islands, to complete.

And then there is the leaking roof . . . Yet again, after evening calculations over a bottle of wine, we realize that our funds are desperately insufficient. We will have to choose what we attack now and what gets left until some future date. But we are not downhearted. After my initial bad mood, I grow cheery again.

Last summer we managed and, better still, enjoyed magical months. There is no reason why this year should be any different. Now that the property belongs to us, certain pressures have been lifted. We can create our own pace. Installating a kitchen, rewiring throughout, building a bathroom between two guest bedrooms, replastering and painting upstairs and down, renovating an ancient scullery—*une souillarde*—as a summer kitchen while preserving its magnificent blond stone sink, replacing lengths of piping and cracked tiles, repairing and painting Matisse-blue all shutters and doors, planting palm trees, fruit trees, flowers, more flowers, creating vegetable and herb gardens, purchasing the second five acres, even my precious olive farming—such a never-ending list! But they can all be achieved in the fullness of time. If, during this summer, I can study the basics of olive farming and we can find ways to secure the house against the undesired entry of thieves and rain, we will have accomplished a great deal.

I AM STANDING ON THE roof in the company of Monsieur Di Fazio, our chimney-sweeping plumber. He has agreed to coat this flat, leaking expanse with a layer of asphalt and gravel. Although it is a temporary solution and the work does not carry a damp-proof guarantee, he assures me that it should keep out the rain for up to a year, even two, until we can raise the hefty sum needed to execute the job in a more professional way. (The three quotes we have received have left us reeling.) While pacing to calculate meterage, he spins a kind of lumbering pirouette, a 360-degree turn, scans the length and breadth of our land, then screws up his face and peers south toward the bay. The view from this *hauteur* is breathtaking. In true Midi fashion, Di Fazio grimaces his approval. Coming from him, this is a rare compliment, for until this moment, he has recommended repeatedly that we raze the villa and construct a new one. But today, the early-summer warmth mingled with an agreeable breeze coming off the hills seems to have put him in good humor. He concludes, "*Pas mal, Madame,*" with, as ever, the authority of God.

I nod, gratified.

He turns his regard toward our pine forest. "You have plenty of wood."

"Yes," I agree. Hardly a debatable point, for the felled trunks and branches are lying at angles all over the grounds like pick-up-stix.

"You know, a word of advice . . . if I may be so bold . . ."

I brace myself, expecting to be counseled to build ourselves a cabin and abandon all hope for this once-neglected farmhouse.

"There is enough wood here to pay my bill for the roof work."

"Really?"

"*Mais oui, Madame.* Sell it for cash and then pay me in cash. It will be a *très bonne affaire* for you." His eyes are ablaze with thoughts of a good business proposition, particularly if it is *noir* and therefore tax-free. We saunter toward the roof's edge, preparing to descend the rear wall of the building by a ladder which I have placed there expressly for this purpose.

Di Fazio signals me to go ahead. I twist and lower myself onto the first rung, stepping cautiously because descending backward down ladders always makes me queasy. I leave him to follow. He is a hefty man and, I assume, will wait until I have reached solid ground before climbing aboard, but he doesn't. I am only two rungs beneath him when I feel his weight and the ladder begins to shift. "I have discovered your secret, Madame," he bellows from above. I wish he wouldn't talk now. I try to hurry, concentrating on reaching terra firma.

"I told my wife. But no one else. I'll keep it to myself. You don't want the entire village gossiping."

Whatever this secret of his is, it is amusing him greatly. I stare into the soles of his thick workman's shoes while trying to avoid the not very pretty sight of his blue trousers flapping around extremely hairy legs. He is laughing so loudly that the ladder is now slapping back and forth against the wall. I picture us crashing to the ground, a damaged heap of limbs and metal.

"Tell me in a minute!" I yell, flinging myself to the ground, which seems the preferable alternative. From there, flushed and giddy, I await his revelation. "What secret, Mr. Di Fazio?"

His eyes are twinkling like those of a big kid who has uncovered the whereabouts of stashed sweets. "*Pas un mot.*" One finger is raised and pressed against his pouting mouth.

"But surely—"

"Ssssh. My lips are sealed." How he loves to play-act, to revel in his moment of drama.

I shrug and lead the way to the front terraces. I have no idea what he is talking about. Surely not that *le monsieur* and myself are not yet married? He winks and shakes my hand ferociously, transmitting his soot to me in the process. "You are busy, Madame, I must leave you to your work. Don't worry, your secret is safe with me." And off he goes, clattering down the drive in his rickety bus filled to bursting with old sinks, bits of pipes and blackened chimney brushes.

Frankly, I am baffled. Still, his suggestion about selling the wood appeals to me. Unfortunately, I am not quite sure how to go about finding myself a purchaser, until one morning a few days later, returning by the back roads from a gym I have recently joined, at the wheel of an antiquated Renault 4 I have just purchased for five thousand francs, I pass a fenced field stocked meters high with lengths of tree trunks. I park the car to take a look. Beyond the gate, which is locked, is a small wooden hut. A notice is pinned to its door. I clamber onto the lower of the wrought-iron rails and peer over, searching for a telephone number or the hours of service, but its message is too faint to read. I glance at my watch. Twenty past twelve. No doubt the *patron* has closed up for a hearty two- to three-hour lunch break. It's no problem; this little entreprise tucked away in the woods is barely five minutes' drive along the circular lane that skirts the foot of our hill. I resolve to return later and, in the meantime, dash to the village to buy myself an olive and tomato *fougasse* before the baker closes for his lunch and another bout of baking.

Approaching the village square on foot, I spy Mr. Dolfo, our good-natured electrician. The poor fellow looks hot and flustered, locked in desperate combat with his van, the engine of which is screeching. It whines and starts to overheat, as does he, all in an attempt to reverse into what seems to me to be a perfectly generous parking space. When he claps eyes

on me, he abandons all further shots at parking and simply switches off
the engine. I am a little taken aback, because the vehicle is skewed at a
rather dangerous angle, a fact which concerns him not a bit as he steps out
and greets me heartily, shaking my hand as though I had just informed
him that he has won *le Loto.* "*Bonjour,*" say I, still regarding his atrocious
parking. I am ravenous and fearful of losing out on lunch. I make a move
to leave, but he grips my hand fast and murmurs in a highly confidential
manner: "We had no idea, Madame. *Je suis désolé.*"

"About what?"

"*Et enchanté.*"

This has to be Di Fazio's doing.

On the far side of the place, I regard the automated shutters of the
boulangerie creeping toward the ground. My breakfast consisted of two
cups of black coffee, I have worked out for two hours and I have nothing
edible in the house. "I have to go . . ."

"Mr. Di Fazio said *pas un mot,* so *pas un mot.*" He winks, releases my
hand and wanders off aimlessly with a wave and complicitous nod.

Hurrying across the cobbles to purchase my loaf, I am all but flattened
by a speeding Peugeot 5 which, after missing me, narrowly escapes swiping
the entire hood off our electrician's ill-parked van. In the smoke-filled *tabac,*
alongside the bakers, a village resident I have noticed once or twice presses
his thick speckled nose against the window and, beer and cigarette in hand,
heeds me lasciviously as I hurry back to my car.

I cannot imagine what story our plumber is spreading around!

BEFORE DI FAZIO BEGINS work or guests arrive, I have a few days to organize my summer. I have scripts to write. Gardens I want to create. Books
to buy, a restock after the robbery. I browse in air-conditioned *biblio-
thèques,* hunting the ABCs of olive farming. In my quest for knowledge of
the olive, its history and farming, I buy everything I can lay my hands on.
I learn that there are certain esteemed connoisseurs who hold that the olive

oil produced around Nice has only one rival, the Italian variety from Lucca. Others pronounce that the fruit produced here on this French Riviera coast is second to none. It yields the finest virgin pressed oil in the world, as well as the most expensive. Legend has it that Adam's grave was planted with an olive tree. I cannot think how this could be substantiated, but given the Middle Eastern locales of the Old Testament, it is not implausible. As tales go, I rather prefer the one about the battle between Poseidon, god of the seas, and Athena, goddess of wisdom, for the title of the city of Athens. The gods named the city after her rather than him because she planted the first olive tree within the Acropolis as a symbol of peace and prosperity, and the gods judged her legacy to mankind more fruitful than any of Poseidon's trident-bashing, art-of-war chicaneries. (Women had the ruling vote on this: there were more goddesses than gods.)

Getting back to facts: olive trees thrive best in Mediterranean climes. They will grow and produce in stony as well as well-drained soils and will survive happily at lofty altitudes, where other fruit trees would perish. Once established, they need little attention, minimal water and can with-stand all but the severest of droughts and even frost, if the temperature does not drop beneath 45°F for any length of time. These gnarled and characterful plants survive for centuries but commence production at a tortoiselike pace. They do not produce their first fruits until they are seven or eight years old and will not deliver the full extent of their bounteous crops until fifteen, even twenty, years old. For any farmer who is beginning from scratch, it is a long-term investment. Fortunately, that is not the case at our place, but it might explain why it is illegal in southern France to chop down an olive tree. Any road or building must be constructed around existing trees.

I stroll our dusty tracks flanked with the silvery trees, the sky above me Gauloise blue, digesting the knowledge I am amassing, seeing the cleared land anew. Now that we are rid of the stranglehold of weeds,

I spend delicious time alone examining trunks and roots, the hang of the branches, the fattening drupes. The ancients deemed the olive tree a healer, and I feel its soothing power at work on me, chilling me out, slowing me down.

On my return to the house, to my work, I observe two magpies warning off a russet fox, a battle for territory which the fox loses. The magpies send the rather sleek creature scuttling off into the undergrowth.

I HAVE BEEN AT MY trestle table scribbling notes, lost in the history of the olive, and have left my return visit to the wood store till late in the afternoon, but upon arrival, I find the place still padlocked behind its iron gate. I hang around for a bit, kicking my heels, wondering if I should leave a note and, if so, where best to post it. The early-summer warmth embraces me. Several retired horses are grazing in a neighboring field, and I stroll over to stroke them. I have driven by these creatures on numerous occasions but have never had reason to stop.

It is a pretty uninhabited country lane, and I decide to while away some time examining the hedgerows, in the hope that a woodman might appear. Scraggly clematis vine is climbing everywhere. A flattened milk carton lies in the road. It attracts my attention because its lettering is Arabic. I pass a bay tree as tall as a fully grown cypress. There is a peppery perfume in the air which I cannot identify. Is it wild sage? Yellow broom in full blossom brings a sweet, bright coloring to the roadside brush. Shards of green-tinted glass from bottles thrown carelessly on the tarmac threaten my feet, shod only in rope-soled espadrilles. Around the next corner is a tiny vineyard which I have noticed frequently on my *trajets* to and from the inland village of Mougins. The vines are years old, short and stubby and gnarled. The green fruit hangs like breasts heavy with milk. There are several cherry trees growing among the neat vine rows. Should I seek out this vine tender and ask his advice on preparation of soils, planting seasons, fruit flies, harvests, oh, a million questions? A jeep rattles past, and I am suddenly aware of how perfectly silent it is here, a meditative silence. There is no breeze. The day is still, intense.

I pause by a narrow shady lane, speckled with shoals of pebbles and the crumbling remains of last winter's forgotten leaves. Michel has pointed out this little pathway on several occasions. It leads to the rear side of our hill, he says. I notice, because I am on foot and not beetling by in my battered old car, that a few yards down the lane the route has been barred but is not impassable. There is no red and white *Défense d'entrer* sign; the land probably belongs to the local commune, which has installed the gatepost in an attempt to discourage the infuriating habit some have acquired of jettisoning old sinks, fridges and rusty electrical junk anywhere and everywhere, be it country lanes, gutters or roadsides. The Arabs are normally blamed for it, but I have no idea how sound these accusations are.

I hear a mewling, or is it a bird? It is so unexpected within the silence that, at first, I take it to be one of the horses whinnying, back near the wood store. I hear it again and trace its source to farther along the lane. I had been intending to turn back but decide to take a quick peek. As I walk, slipping beneath the horizontal post, the sound grows more audible. On either side of me, the brush is thick with dozens of misshapen Portuguese oaks. They have repeatedly seeded and now struggle for light and space. In amongst them are many fluffy-fronded mimosas. There is a small clearing ahead, and at the farthest point, half the carcass of a rotting car. The sound is coming from there. As I approach, I see a gorgeous golden-bay animal lying on its side, panting heavily. It is a dog, a large shaggy one, shockingly thin. I bend and kneel, too timorous to reach out in case it snaps at me. One of its rear legs is bleeding badly. It must have ripped its flesh on the jagged, jutting metal. Gingerly, I put out a hand, and the creature bears its teeth in a ferocious grin. For a moment I wonder if I am mistaken. Might it be a wolf? It could very well be. Whichever, it is a magnificent animal, and in distress. I rise, considering what to do for the beast. I am close to home, but I couldn't possibly carry it even if it allowed me to. And because of the barred entry, I cannot bring my old car to the rescue. I decide to hurry home, find the name of a local vet and meet him here. I start to run, and the dog lifts its head and whines miserably. I halt, look back, heart torn, then scoot fast back down the lane.

When I reach my Renault, I discover another, a shooting-brake, parked by the gate of the wood firm. A short silver-haired man is unloading two chainsaws from his trunk. I call to him, and he spins around. His face is flushed and friendly and kind. I tell him about the animal and ask for his help. He reloads the chainsaws and beckons to me. I jump in beside him, and we motor along the lane as far as the post. Together we return for the dog, who is yelping helplessly but grows defensive as we draw near. Eventually, after several fruitless attempts, the wounded animal allows us to approach and carry her—I now see that it is a her—to the trunk of the car, where she is settled on her side, hemmed in by the chainsaws, baskets, a profusion of wicker and dozens of empty wine bottles.

Back at the farm, I run in search of a couple of torn sheets and a pillow, and the dog is installed on our obsolete mattress in one of the stables —where we found the wild cats at Christmas. The man introduces himself as René and offers to take me back for my car. During this short journey, I explain to him that I had been waiting for him, with the intention of selling him recently cut wood. Pine, olive, oak. "Would you be interested?"

"*Pourquoi pas?*" His eyes are blue and creased, and I know instantly that I like him.

While I slip off to telephone the vet René has recommended, he examines the wood and offers me one thousand francs above the sum Di Fazio is charging for the temporary sealing of the roof. More than that, he pulls from a leather pouch in his car a very healthy bankroll of notes and pays me, on the spot, the entire sum in cash.

"Don't you want to wait until—"

"No, no. I'll be back with my son tomorrow. We'll saw it into logs here, if that's all right with you. It will be easier to transport." I agree happily, we arrange a mutually convenient time for his return and off he goes, leaving me staring at a satisfyingly thick wad of five-hundred-franc bills.

The dog has no collar, no name and no tattoo. In France, a tattoo is obligatory. If a dog is found without one, it can be destroyed. Worse, it can be sold and used for experimentation. I am horrified and promptly arrange to spend more than half the cash René has given me on a whole host of treatments for this magnificent hound. Her paw needs a minor operation and stitching. Two teeth have been broken, almost certainly while being thrashed, on top of which, she has a stomach complaint and bleeding lacerations on a mauled hind leg. This animal doctor is hugely tall and equally rotund. He is a good-natured, bearded German from Bavaria, a really delightful fellow whose love of animals exudes from his every pore.

"Leave her with me," he says. "I will call you in a couple of days. You can collect her when she is a little healthier. Do you know her name, by any chance?" We are talking in English because the doctor enjoys the opportunity to test out his skills.

I shake my head. "I don't know her name," I say.

He looks surprised, then chortles and writes something on her card while wishing me a *bonne soirée* and assuring me that I am not to worry.

I return home to my work, thinking about what to do with the dog when she is well again. I have not forgotten Henri and the promise I made to return for him as soon as our circumstances allow. These concerns prompt me to telephone the animal rescue center, *le refuge*.

When I inquire after Henri, I learn that a home was found for him shortly after we returned with him. My heart sinks, and yet I cannot begrudge dear wild Henri a decent bed. "*Il est très, très content,*" the *admin-*

istratrice informs me. I thank her, wish her well and replace the receiver, saying a silent *au revoir* to the big black hound who turned our lives into a spin for a few short weeks.

René does not return the next day for his prepurchased wood, nor the following. I have no telephone number for him. I did not even catch his last name. I am puzzled. Am I in possession of stolen or homemade notes which I am about to pass on to the vet and to Mr. Di Fazio who clunks up the drive, ready and eager to begin the repair on the roof?

I watch as he unloads the most gruesome collection of tools and asphalt-heating equipment, something not unlike a giant Bunsen burner. All the while, he sings and whistles and grins, nodding and bowing every time I am anywhere near him. On one occasion, as I pass by, he slaps his thigh as though he were the principal boy in a pantomime and grins, shining white teeth exposed like an open zipper within his soot-smeared face. "*Pas de bottes, eh!*"

Which means, No boots! It is now July. I am running about everywhere in shorts, a tube top and flat espadrilles. I have no idea what he is talking about, and I don't want to ask, but I am beginning to fear that he might be completely balmy.

UNTIL THE END OF the twentieth century, when dieticians the world over pronounced the Mediterranean diet the healthiest in the world, the olive and its by-products were used almost exclusively in southern cuisines. The hue of the oil is as golden and luxuriant as a summer afternoon spent dozing in a hammock in the Midi. It is as familiar and vital to the kitchens of this region as, say, garlic or *bouillebaisse*. Quintesssentially Mediterranean, it evokes the climate, terrain and character as instantaneously as any wrinkle-faced Niçois playing boules in his dusty village square.

It was the Greeks, some twenty-five hundred years ago, who planted the first olive trees on this southern coast of France, but they spent precious little time cultivating or reaping here, they were not an agricultural people. They were navigators, explorers, seafaring traders. Moving westward, they founded such seaports as Antibes, Nice and, of course, Marseille in 600B.C.—its original Greek name was Massilia—and then they moved on. For the Greeks, the bustling port of Massilia was a watering place and a spa as they headed inland, hell-bent on securing their tin and amber routes. The citizens of Massilia spoke perfect Greek. They dressed and comported themselves like Athenians and kept well away from what they perceived as the contamination of the barbarians living all around them, the tribal Celts.

I GIVE UP ON MY writing and olive studies because Di Fazio is marching to and fro on the roof. His every step is acoustically exaggerated and shudders the house as though a giant were striding the heavens. And how he whistles and sings!

I close up my laptop and go outside for a swim, but almost as I plunge into the pool, he calls down to me, asking for a beer. He is *très soif.* Fair enough. The day is hot, and he is up there with a flame as high as a laurel bush. I ascend the ladder, dripping wet, to take him his beer. The heat and activity have broken him out in a sweat. Perspiration is running down his face and has washed away the soot in stripes. His face looks like a zebra's. I hear the telephone ringing, so I hurry across the semi-surfaced roof—it is as hot as hell up there with the gas flame roaring and spitting—and begin my descent. As I turn, he holds up his bottle: "*À la vôtre!*"

I nod. "Good health to you, too, Monsier Di Fazio." I smile and disappear. His cheeriness is quite extraordinary. I am about to enter the house, hurrying to the phone, when he leans out over the roof again and calls, "*Et votre mari, il porte un melon aussi?*" And he roars with laughter. I am thinking about it. The question he has asked is: And your husband, does he carry a melon as well?

" 'ello?"

It is the vet's young receptionist. "No Name is ready to be collected." No Name! I smile and tell her that I will be by in a short while. I have decided to keep the dog until she is fit, and then . . . I haven't thought that far ahead yet. Michel is arriving later this evening. I intend to discuss the dog with him.

Although the vet's bill is somewhere in the region of five thousand francs, about five hundred pounds, he refuses to accept one centime. "Why?"

"Because No Name was not your responsibility and because you have given us many hours of pleasure. In Germany, the program is called *The Doctor and His Dear Friends*. I will accept a signed photograph of you, and that will be my payment." I am bowled over by his kindness and delighted to set eyes on the dog, who is now answering to No Name. She is bandaged from snout to neck, ears exposed and erect, and has another dressing protecting the wounded hind leg. It does not inhibit her ability to walk, albeit with a limp. She wags her tail at the sight of me, so I cannot have been entirely forgotten. Armed with a dozen boxes of antibiotics, I lead her gingerly to the car, and she follows without a whimper.

"Hard to believe," says the vet who accompanies us, "that anyone would abandon this creature. She's a purebred Belgian shepherd and a particularly splendid example of the race. If you can't keep her, let me know. I'll have no difficulty finding a home for her."

When I return, our chirpy plumber has packed up for the weekend, but the wood has still not been removed. I settle No Name in a makeshift basket and head for the airport.

Michel is tired. Actually, he looks exhausted and speaks only in monosyllables about his production affairs, but I can read in his expression how pleased he is to be here. On the journey home, I am recounting the adventures of my week while he listens, silently stroking my shoulder and hair.

My pride at selling the wood, the vet's kindness . . . oh, yes, there's a dog, and I have understood correctly, haven't I? The word *melon* means melon, doesn't it? As in English. Michel considers, pondering Di Fazio's comment."That was all he said: does your husband carry a melon?"

"I think so."

"Ah, *porter* to wear!"

"Do you wear a melon?" I am giggling. We are now kneeling beside No Name, who is uncertain about the arrival of this unknown male, but she does not bare her teeth.

I take Michel on a swift tour of the garden to show him various shrubs and flowers I have potted and inform him blithely of my purchase from one of the village stallholders of a hundred roses, paid for in advance, to be collected when the market next passes this way. Without a hint of criticism, he tries to point out that I lack symmetry and that I am not necessarily choosing the plants that will withstand the heat. "Where will you plant a hundred roses?" he asks. "If the fellow ever comes back, that is."

"You are cynical. Of course he'll come back." I wave my arm vaguely to the right. "Up there."

"But, *chérie*, the earth is full of stones, and there's no shelter or water source. It will be blazingly hot, which is not ideal for roses."

"Sometimes you are so full of logic!"

"*Überblick*," he replies warmly, which I think is his favorite word. Translated, it means overview. "Are you sure Di Fazio didn't ask you whether your husband is a melon?"

I burst out laughing. "Why would he ask such a thing?"

"A melon is a fool, a simpleton."

"Are you?"

"I hope not." All this is lighthearted banter as Michel prepares the barbecue and I make a salad. We are eating on the upper terrace, looking out over the moonlit sea. The crescent of lights along the promontory of Fréjus string out and camber, winking in the darkness. Standing in the center of our clothed, temporary garden table is my oil lamp. We watch it glow, a warm ball of honeyed light. It is already past nightfall, and the evening, because we have not yet reached full summer, has turned coolish. Clad in slacks and long-sleeved shirts, we pour ourselves glasses of dark red wine. Michel brings the sizzling lamb cutlets spiced with herbs from a small vegetable patch I have been creating as I return from the house carrying the cash paid to me by René. I pour it onto the table for Michel to examine. It has spent the past few days stowed in the bottom drawer of an antique Irish pine chest we found in a junk shop in Paris, buried among our lavender-scented linen. He looks at it, then at me, queryingly.

"Why didn't you bank it?"

I have to think a moment, because I am not exactly clear why I have left the equilavent of a thousand pounds sitting in the chest. "In case it's counterfeit or stolen," I confess.

Michel roars with laughter. "*Chérie,* you are so dramatic. It is black money, no doubt, but surely *tu as déjà compris* that a considerable percentage of all money that changes hands down here is earned on the black market. It is the *modus vivendi.* I am sure this René fellow didn't physically make it!"

"Then why hasn't he returned for his wood?"

"He will. This is the Midi. Everything happens in its own time."

Yet again I have forgotten to remember that time has a different interpretation here. Tomorrow does not necessarily mean tomorrow. It means at some point in the future beyond now. And the only way to know when that might be is to cheerfully wait and see. For a woman as impatient as I am, this has to be a learning curve! I accept his wisdom, and we pass a blissful weekend without sight nor sound of workmen.

As EVER HERE, WE rise at the first call of the sun. Now that the land has been cut back, we like to walk. This morning, we pick our way up the winding narrow track, ascending through the steep pine forest, hiking to the very pinnacle of the hill. Puffing, we drop to the needle-strewn earth, inhale the heaven-sent perfumes, sharp with a twist of early morning dew, and watch the sun rise. Its rays stream through the squiggle of treetops and blank out the crescent moon.

Daybreak. I have watched the sun rise, the breaking of the day, in myriad locations all over the world with companions or past lovers, but nowhere has it felt this blessed. Here it belongs to us and our intimacy. I close my eyes and breathe deep. Sometimes, for a moment, it feels scary to love this much.

Wending our way back down the hill to the house, we take an early-morning dip in the still, cool pool, followed by a warm bath. Together, through the window of the cavernous blue-tiled room, we watch families of rabbits steal out from beneath the stacks of wood. They poke cautious snouts and whiskers into the new day and then scamper freely, hopping about, taking stock of their newly undressed playground.

These early mornings are a treasured time of day. We have snatched them for our own. They are a part of who we are and what we share. Most of our waking hours are given over to work, weekends too, because if we don't create, we won't have a gnat's chance of restoring or even holding on to this ruin of a farm.

"BREAKFAST!" CALLS MICHEL. His curly hair, which he has let grow, is damp from his bath and clings to the nape of his neck. He is tanned from the sun.

The days are growing too hot to breakfast on our hidden terrace, so we shift our wooden table and chairs to the front of the house, where the sun will not hit until after ten. Over eggs and coffee I begin to fill Michel in on some of the olive material I have been reading. "It was like a journeying caravan, like good news or a creed spreading, the way the olive tree and the production of its fruit traveled. The Greeks brought it here to southern France, but it was also exported across northern Africa to Tunisia, Algeria, Morocco. There, right across the northern littoral of that continent, the Arabs began to cultivate it. Oil was produced. Fruits marinated, recipes and methods passed on, adapted to their cooking. It found its way quite naturally into the local cuisines. Later, the olive tree sailed across the waters north to Portugal and Spain, along with Arab traders, perhaps. The two migrations in that direction from Africa were the Arabs and the Sephardic Jews."

"Did you know," Michel chips in, "that the Koran speaks of it as a blessed tree of neither the East nor the West?"

"No, I didn't. I have been wondering, though, if priests, seers, ancient gurus, the family cook, a tribal grandmother, whoever, understood its mythical powers, its curative properties. Facts were handed down until somewhere in the melting pot of a more modern world, the second-millennium migrations, wars, et cetera, this knowledge was lost, and only now are we beginning to rediscover it."

As we natter, we watch a band of bushy-tailed auburn squirrels leap from the cypresses to the lower almond tree. They are stealing the nuts we have not harvested. Their expeditions are surprisingly orderly. Two at a time, they descend upon the tree, where the branches bounce like trampolines as they gracefully land, collect their share of the hoard and then give way for the next pair. The only argument develops when a greedy magpie swoops down and begins to screech and rattle the branches. He is furious that the squirrels have beaten him to it. Several landowners I know shoot magpies; watching the birds on this estate, I am beginning to understand why.

AFTER BREAKFAST, WORK. Buried in my space, my *atelier,* I hear the distant clip-clipping of Michel's busy fingers at his laptop. I open my book on the history of the olive and read that, after the Greeks, the Romans came to the south of France. Unlike the parched topography of Greece, the land-scape of Italy was richer, lusher. It was more verdant and rolling. Because of this, the Romans moved more comfortably by land than sea. During

their trek north and their taking of Provence—it was Caesar who christened the region Il Provincia—they quickly grasped the potential of the
dusky groves growing everywhere on these hills, their recently conquered
territory, and they wasted no time in cultivating the fruit.

Both the Greek and Roman cultures have left profound impressions
on Provence. Both are Mediterranean peoples and both stamped their systems, philosophies and architecture on this more northerly region of what
we now know as Europe. The differences in their natures has had a
deep-rooted effect on Provence. The Greeks introduced the olive to the
Romans, and the Romans, in their own country, husbanded and created
a thriving industry from it, perfecting its storage, and then they began to
do the same here.

IN THE AFTERNOONS, we make love, screened from the relentless heat by
the spill of shadows from closed slatted shutters. The century-old house
creaks and shifts, waking like Rip van Winkle after decades of sleeping.
Then it relaxes into peaceful stillness, as do we. Our sole companion is No
Name, who heals by the hour. After, I read or scribble while Michel dozes.
Beyond the walls of the cool room, our magnolia has flowered. Its blossoms resemble teacups sculpted out of clotted cream.

During an evening stroll on the upper reaches of the land, we find that
many of the drystone walls have sunk into rubbled piles and are slowly
spilling across the terraces. They will need to be rebuilt. The removal of
such a surfeit of vegetation could be the cause. The root systems may well
have been holding the stones in place or, Michel suggests, it could well be
sangliers in search of food. Although no wild boar have been near the
house since my first encounter, it is unlikely that they have deserted our
farmland entirely. We take a little tour and find their footprints everywhere and untidy holes where they have been snouting for grub. I better
take heed! During our stroll back, Michel asks me how my story is getting
on. "Slowly," I reply.

"Might you have it finished by the end of summer?"

I smile and nod, knowing he is inching me toward our agreed-upon deadline. The acceptance and production of these scripts would make a monumental difference to our chances of acquiring the second five acres of land and to holding on to the farm. It would also mean a great deal to me personally, to the fashioning of this new life, the redefining of myself.

Dusk falls, shadows lengthen and we bathe in the pool basked in moonshine, then cook supper on the barbecue. I have taken to preparing the simplest of meals with lashings of olive oil, garlic and herbs. Bliss.

MONDAY ARRIVES AND WE are up at the crack of deepest morn, crawling out of bed before the lark sings. Michel needs to be on the earliest flight to Paris, which means we must leave the villa at five-thirty. At the terminal, huddled in my rather temperamental fossil of a Renault, we kiss good-bye. There is heaven in this relationship, and I try not to allow a sense of abandonment or sadness at the prospect of yet another week apart. In three more weeks we will be together for the rest of the summer.

When I return to the house, having stopped off for a much-needed *croissant* and several *cafés au lait* in Antibes, Di Fazio turns into the lane. He grinds up the drive behind me.

Before we have barely uttered good morning, he announces, "You're an actress, aren't you?"

I nod, feeling at this particular moment more like a bag lady. He roars triumphantly. I am puzzled as to how he has acquired this tidbit but know that it must please him, for he has been regaling me regularly with stories of a highly renowned French pianist and *chanteur* who, according to Di Fazio, lives not too far from us and whose pipes this plumber has replaced. "Plumber to the stars!" he cries exuberantly, and I picture his vision of it, written in bold paint across the beam of that clonking banger.

One of the characteristics I most love about the French is their appreciation of the arts. We are all, even the humblest of entertainers, *les artistes* in the eyes of the French. The very mention of the word *actress*, or even better, *writer*, fills them with apoplexisms of delight and awed respect. Di Fazio is no exception.

"I saw you on television, didn't I?"

I shrug. It is possible, but I cannot think what he might have seen. Little if anything I have ever acted in has been bought by the French networks. I understand that *All Creatures Great and Small* has been shown all over the world except France. Even in Poland, before the fall of communism, when all American and English programs were banned, *All Creatures* slipped through the system and continued to be screened.

"You are very famous. I had no idea."

I head on toward the house because he has overestimated my notoriety, because I fear that our plumbing bills are about to escalate and because I am feeling lonesome. But not for long! Amar arrives with an army of *ouvriers* or *jardiniers* who unload what looks like an entire forestry commission project's worth of shrubs and laurel bushes. Definitely way beyond the number we ordered. And then he departs, leaving his *équipe* to go to work. I steam down the drive. Shovels, rakes, garden utensils of every shape and size are digging, hacking at pine branches, throwing sods of earth every which way, transforming the face of our border land.

"Stop!" I screech.

There is no leader here to take heed. I am the madwoman from atop the hill. Sun-baked faces stare, eyes glare, but they return to the job in hand, the contract they are being paid for, no doubt at a menial rate. I dread to think what Amar will charge for all of this, and I hurtle back to my papers in search of his telephone number. This has to be stopped before I find we have purchased an entire garden center!

While this performance is at play, René arrives, followed by a bevy of cars, all of which have open trailers attached. Our drive is now completely blocked by vehicles. Even if I wanted to escape, I couldn't.

René, who is a little over five feet five tall, leads his party up the hill. Fit and stocky with a wine-tinted face and a shock of gray hair which grows so thick and lustrous it almost doubles his height, he begins organizing his gang, all of whom are wielding chainsaws. No Name begins to bark. Then there is Di Fazio above me on the roof, melting and pouring asphalt, unloading and raking gallons of gravel, singing his socks off, five chainsaws zirring at full whack in the pine forest above while, lower down the terraces, shovels slap against stones, branches crack and hit the earth, voices yell . . . I cannot hear myself think or speak, and I am screaming like a lunatic into the telephone, insisting to Amar that he come over here right now and put a stop to all this planting.

"But the plumbago will be magnificent. Blue creeping up through all those cedar trees. It will be splendid."

"But we didn't order plumbago, and we can't afford it! We don't even have a fence yet."

He sighs and agrees to be there as soon as he can. The prospect of not receiving his money seems to have clarified his sense of reason. I put down the phone and run my fingers through hair that hasn't been combed since I got out of bed, when I barely had time to brush my teeth. I catch a glimpse of myself in the mirror and see how utterly disheveled I look. Somewhere distant, in the village of Le Cannet, where Bonnard painted some of his finest works and Rita Hayworth lived out many of her later years, the midday siren sounds, and as though a switch has been flicked, all work activity stops. Ah, silence. From a dozen quarters, men tramp to the parking area and pull from their various cars, vans, trucks —or, in the case of Amar's Arabs, their satchels—lunch. Each seeks out the shade or a step to perch on. I watch from a window, fascinated. The Arabs each have small plastic lunchboxes similar to those given to schoolchildren. Within, I see sandwiches and a piece of fruit, an apple or a banana. They also have bottles of still water; the Crystal, which is for sale at one franc a liter. They sit on the ground alongside or close by one another, always in the deepest shade.

Elsewhere are the French.

René and his chainsaw gang are unfolding and setting up a portable table. Onto it are placed unlabeled bottles of rosé and red wine, water, paté, salad, plates, saucepans of hot food (how, I ask myself?), while knives and forks are passed out like leaflets. These are followed by glasses which, when filled, are raised while each drinks the health of the rest. Di Fazio, who is alone but French—more precisely Riviera-Mediterranean, because his family hailed from Italy a couple of generations back—hovers close by his fellow citizens, wishing them *bon appétit.*

The Arabs munch in businesslike silence.

The French still have preparations afoot. Di Fazio walks over to his prehistoric bus and pulls out a cooler, from which he extracts chilled water and two bottles of beer. He paces the parking area, slugging back the beers, one directly after the other, in thirsty need. The water is then poured over his head, which now renders him the complexion of an albino. He saunters over to René and his troupe and begins to make conversation. His voice is loud, but his accent is so thick I have no idea what he is talking about; whatever the subject matter is, it calls for a great deal of gesticulating. The others are entranced. So am I, but for different reasons. I find this social spectacle fascinating. Even the Arabs, whom Di Fazio swings to face one or twice to include them in his storytelling, seem hooked. Di Fazio is now acting out with great pizzazz what looks like a bank robbery. Two fingers go up in the style of a child's gunplay. Then he slinks his portly body about, as though imitating a woman, slaps his calves, makes a kick in the air as though booting someone off the face of the earth, before his gaze is reverentially raised in the direction of the house.

It is only then that it dawns on me, as all eyes turn toward the villa and I jump guiltly out of sight, that the female impersonation was meant to be of *me*!

Monsieur le plombier then makes a gesture that I have noticed is very common here in the Midi. It is a shaking of the hand, thumb turned upward, that denotes wealth or power or serious money. Even his French audience has stopped eating, so spellbound are they by his gossip. Is he telling them that we robbed a bank? But he hasn't even been paid yet, and if the cash *noir*, stashed in the linen drawer and burning an illicit hole in our sheets, is stolen, it is René's!

Fortunately, the arrival of Amar breaks up the party. He heads over to his workforce and wishes them *bon appétit*, repeating the same to the French contigent. I exit the house and make my way to him, feeling just a mite self-conscious. As Amar and I approach each other, René calls to me: "*C'est vous qui jouez dans chapeau melon et bottes de cuir?*"

Everyone awaits my response to "Is it you who is playing in a melon hat and leather boots?" Having no idea what this means or what to reply, I take the Midi approach and shrug. This they translate as an exceedingly modest affirmative. René rises to shake my hand, as does one of his companions who already looks the worse for wine and keeps repeating: "*Enchanté, madame. Vous êtes charmante, charmante.*"

Panic drives me to grab Amar by the arm and drag him down the hill. Nothing I say now will convince him we purchased this olive farm and are attempting to renovate it on an already fraying shoestring. Di Fazio has scuppered everything. Still, after persistant nagging, Amar agrees to dig up those shrubs not agreed upon. But he says that because he cannot take back the bags of fertilizer and horse dung that have been laid and shoveled everywhere, they must all be paid for. When I query the astronomical figure charged for horse manure, he tells me that it is a particularly potent mix since these sacks have been collected from a stud farm! The finest stallions. He smiles wickedly.

I can barely credit the sheer ingenuity of his invention. Yet again he has managed to augment his contract fee by a substantial sum. I thank him for his cooperation and resolve that this will be his last, very last, job for us. Thank goodness I ordered the roses elsewhere.

Later, when Michel and I talk on the phone, he agrees that the time has come to look around for someone else. We say good night, sending love through the airwaves, and I almost forget that I haven't told him about Di Fazio's latest pantomime. I narrate it hastily, and Michel is highly amused. "A bowler hat and leather boots," he explains. "Yes, I didn't think of that."

"A bowler hat and leather boots?" I repeat like the simpleton described in French as a melon.

"*Melon* also means bowler hat. Because of its shape. In this instance, it is the French name for a British television program."

"Which is?"

"I can't remember the title in English. I'll think of it and tell you tomorrow."

"Have I acted in it?"

"I don't think so. I'll remember it, don't worry."

The village gossip is spreading with the relentless persistence of the bush telegraph. As a consequence, the entire community now has me identified, I learn, as the actress who played the role of Emma Peel in the hit television series *The Avengers.* It is cult viewing here in France. The French title is *The Bowler Hat* (as worn by Steed) *and Leather Boots* (as worn by Ms. Peel). No amount of negatives will shift their opinion. In fact, it serves only to confirm their conviction. They smile patiently, reading my effusive denials as modesty and a plea for the rights of *les artistes* to live their lives in peace. In the eyes of the locals, I am a glamorous actress. But what most amuses me about this whole affair is my crazy response to it.

I was wild here, scruffy and at ease. Now that I have been found out and labeled, albeit mistakenly, I switch like a programmed puppet into actress mode whenever curious eyes are upon me. Instead of leaping into my battered car and racing down the hill to catch the postman or pick up a forgotten baguette, I now take the trouble to run a brush through my pool-bleached curls. I don lipstick and mascara and trade in my stitch-worn, faded cotton espadrilles for polished toenails and leather sandals with tiny heels which show off my legs. Such vanity! The public perception which so easily ends up defining the boundaries of character. It was part of what I have been running from.

NOT LONG AFTER THE Romans began to press the oil here in France, rather than using the method of the more popular Italian family-run businesses, the cooperative system was established. Small community mills were constructed, and the olives were taken there by the locals to press or cure. Although there were, and still are, many single estates and farms cultivating their own olive groves, very few, if any, own a private mill. It has long been the norm here in France to take the harvest to one of the nearby cooperatives where the fruit is pressed—as a single-estate extra-virgin oil—and sold or used locally. Since Appassionata is modest, Michel and I agree to use this system. The finest olive oil is extremely costly because it is a very labor-intensive process. The trees do not demand heavy watering but they need to be fumigated, pruned regularly—usually biannually on a rota system—and treated once every twenty-one days from around mid-July to early or late October, depending on the weather. Although I am learning all this, it is not until I finally encounter "our man" and we begin to work with him that I understand the challenge we are taking on.

CALM RETURNS. Di Fazio's reparations are complete, and I hand over the agreed sum in cash. René's cash. Di Fazio counts it carefully and requests one last beer for the road, which he drinks in two gulps before trundling off down the hill, a contented man.

The laurel bushes are planted. Begrudgingly, I settle Amar's account with him, the agreed sum plus many hundreds of francs for the manure. I must water the shrubs on a daily basis, he advises. Then, as he takes off, he calls back a parting shot: he cannot be held responsible for their life expectancy, because, due to the escalating heat, nothing should be planted this time of year. "It's too risky!" I want to throw my gardening tools at him.

Fearful that the precious new bushes will begin to wilt before my eyes, I abandon my writing and rush directly to buy several lengths of hose which René very kindly offers to help me knit together. I am grateful for his generosity because the whole business is unnecessarily time-consuming and complicated, with plastic sockets which in my hands simply will not marry. After much frustrated fiddling, we eventually lay the hose, which winds like a yellow serpent, nudged up against the Italian stone staircase, all the way to the bushes at the foot of the land.

While I was at the hardware store, René sawed the last of the trees. The logs have since been carted away in *remorques* by various members of his family. All activity is at an end. Evening is approaching, so as thanks for his much-needed assistance, I invite him to stay for *un petit apéritif,* which he accepts.

Pastis? No, he prefers to join me in a glass of red wine. With the bottle, a *Côte-du-Rhône Villages,* I serve a humble dish of local olives and another of pistachio nuts because I haven't had time to shop. We sit in contemplative silence, listening to the frogs and inhaling the perfumes of dusk.

"Are these from your trees?" He has an olive pinched between his workman's fingers.

I shake my head.

"You know, since I retired, I live my *rêve,*" he tells me. "The wood business is not mine. I am helping a friend who cannot afford an assistant."

He asks me to guess his age. It is a game I always try to avoid, but in this case I decide to not subtract five years and speak my mind. "Early sixties" is my pronouncement.

He sits up straight in his chair and shakes his head, thrilled by my mistake. Seventy-four, he announces with pride. And indeed he has every reason to be proud, for I am genuinely amazed.

His two great pleasures in life, he tells me, now that he has passed seventy and has settled into retirement, *la retraite*, are his boat, which he takes out most fine days to the islands—ah, the islands!—and he spends lazy hours fishing, and the husbanding of olive farms. He oversees and runs four, the largest of which boasts over two hundred trees. That particular estate is owned by a long-standing chum of his. They were boys together. Both were educated here in the village. His school pal, René continues without the slightest hint of jealousy, is a multimillionaire and the proprietor of the largest and most famous chain of hardware stores in southern France. René speaks of his septuagenarian companion with fondness but of himself with pride. "He works too hard, has too many responsibilities. *Mais moi*, I do what I love in life. I have over six hundred and fifty olive trees in my care." And he sweeps up his glass, proposing a toast to doing what one loves in life. I drink to that! Then with a twinkle, and not without a *soupçon* of Provençal wiliness, he adds, "You have the perfect position here. The fruit from your trees must be *excellent*. Tragic to let it go to waste. Why not allow me to care for them for you?"

I am silenced by his proposition. This is so much more than I had hoped for at this stage. My sole regret is that Michel is not here to share this fortuitous moment.

The bottle has grown lighter as evening has fallen. I pour what remains into our glasses, and he gives me the deal. He will prune and treat the trees, gather the olives and deliver them for pressing at the *moulin*. For this service he demands two thirds of everything farmed and pressed. We will receive the remaining third.

I had thought we might share the harvest on a fifty-fifty basis, but he shakes his head firmly. He is adamant. *Ce boulot* requires a great deal of labor, skill and expertise. I nod, knowing this to be true from my books and study, and accept René's proposition without debate. We raise our glasses to the partnership.

The sun is sinking into underbelly tones, gold seeping into tender flesh-pink. I have lived my life through my senses, looked at, experienced it through prisms of light and emotions. Touching, feeling. Now I am attempting to be not less romantic but more practical, particularly about the renovating of this villa and the reestablishing of its olive farm. Michel describes it as honing new muscles. Still, I hope when he meets René he will agree that fate has dropped a nugget of good fortune into our laps; instinct tells me we have chanced upon our man.

CHAPTER SEVEN

OUR DESERT PRINCE

My father spent his war in Africa. He was a corporal in the Royal Air Force during the Second World War, but his remit was never to fly planes, bomb cities or fight. Always a big kid at heart, he happily occupied himself by dressing in high heels and women's clothes, sporting face powder and streaks of carmine-red lipstick. All in the broiling desert heat. This along with sliding out of camp, hitting the hot spots and getting roaring drunk with the likes of such veteran *comédiens* as Peter Sellers and Tony Hancock. This trio was imprisoned together on several occasions when discovered by their commanding officer falling about the streets of Cairo completely plastered, attempting to hitch a ride back to base, instead of being already tucked up in their bunks. Never dejected by a night in the slammer, my father continued to sing his young heart out and play the fool and was applauded enthusiastically for it, for he was a proud and dedicated member of one of the most renowned of the wartime entertainment troupes, the Ralph Reader Gang Shows.

I spent much of my childhood sitting on his knee or on the floor at his feet, listening to his stories of those days in far-off Africa. They were outclassed in brilliance only by my grandfather's tales of big-game hunting, though now, looking back on it, I don't believe my father's father ever set foot in Africa, whereas my own father's tales of high jinx were certainly true, if a little embellished.

I mention this now because, over the years, those stories painted in my mind's eye a scintillating and very colorful picture of the dark continent, of Arabs and bazaars, of South African beaches and Zulus. It was one of my favorite bedtime victories to persuade my father to sit with me a while and speak to me in Zulu. All that clicking on the upper palate, short phrases spoken in deep and resonant tones, used to thrill and excite me. I pictured those seven-foot natives clicking and communicating and banging tall, hand-painted spears, all to ask little more than after your general health! If there had been an Oscar awarded for ham acting, my father would have been a serious contender.

But nothing matched up to his tales of the Arabs. In retrospect, I see that in some ways, his attitudes were shockingly racist: "Never trust an Arab" was a regular piece of wisdom which I took to be the gospel truth. Many times I heard his sorry tale of the day he was sitting on a train outside Cairo, returning to camp after a few days' leave in England only to have the reading glasses snatched off his face as the train was pulling out of the central station, leaving him unable to see, let alone recognize the escaping culprit. His only certainty was that the blasted thief had been an Arab!

France was long the imperialist power in northern Africa. The horrors of Algeria are known to us all. Today, France's second labor force is African, predominantly Arab. Jean-Marie Le Pen, the leader of the extreme right who preaches France for the French, is their enemy; or rather, they are his. He is more extreme in his rabble-rousing than the late Enoch Powell, and less intelligent in his rhetoric. In spite of the stories bequeathed to me by my father, I have never felt the slightest empathy with Le Pen, nor any other xenophobic demagogue, but what I had never reckoned on was the possibility that one of the local Arab workforce would become one of my closest friends and our greatest ally in the dark days that lay ahead for us and Appassionata.

I HAD SETTLED IN FOR the summer, with no plans to travel anywhere. I had my scripts to complete, the hill to maintain, the arrival of guests to prepare for. I could not be more content. Then the telephone rings. It is Michel.

"We have won an award," he announces.

My first book, which we filmed as a miniseries in Australia the previous autumn, has been screened at a film festival in the States and has picked up an award. I am speechless. I had not known the series was being presented.

"The Australians want you to publicize it for them."

"Where?"

"Australia."

"When?"

"Leave on Friday."

The line goes silent while I take this in. Actors are used to this. We live with our passports in our pockets. These calls come at any moment, usually when they are least expected. But this time, I am not prepared. It coincides with another film I shot which is opening across Australia any minute now. I know I should go, but I am in a quandary.

I am thinking about No Name, I am worrying about my schedule which is of no one's making but my own. And the trip, it turns out, is only for one week. I won't even suffer jet-lag because I'll be there and back before it hits me. "Fine," I say eventually.

I begin to set matters in motion. All I need is to close up the house and ask René if he would be kind enough to pop by twice a day to feed No Name. Or as a last resort, I could telephone Amar, who I know will do it for a price. René agrees without a second's hesitation to house my beloved dog, *chez lui*, for a week. No Name will be in loving hands; I have nothing to be concerned about.

It is Thursday. I am leaving at the crack of dawn Friday, flying to Sydney via Paris. Alone in my gecko-infested workspace, I settle down to a day's writing when I hear the whirr of machines start up like an orchestra tuning. They are right beyond the window. Puzzled, I go to take a look, and to my horror, I see three men, their heads and faces masked by plastic helmets, cutting back the strip of land that borders the road to the left of us and lies alongside our olive groves. The jungle of vegetation there has been the only deterrent to entry from that quarter. Recalling the unsavory sensation I felt when I learned that we had been burgled, I throw my pen back onto my desk and go running to stop them.

They have been sent by the *mairie*, one of them informs me. The land has to be cut back. The neighbors along the lane have complained. It is a fire risk, *très sérieux*. I look back along the winding lane to where the man indicates. I cannot even see the house he is pointing at. "What neighbors?" I squawk. Their concern exasperates me. "But we are at more risk than those neighbors should a fire break out," I protest, to no avail.

"Have you been here during a fire?" he asks.

I have to admit that I have not, which seems to be the concluding point.

The workman, who is covered from head to foot with bits of vegetation and sheets of aluminum protective clothing and looks rather like the tin man from *The Wizard of Oz*, shrugs, dons his helmet and is about to walk away.

"Couldn't it wait just one week?" I plead. I am thinking that when I return we could buy some fencing and secure this section of land.

He reiterates that he has been sent by the local council and it has nothing more to do with him. He takes up his machine and begins to cut.

Stones, strips of split bramble, roots, all go flying into the air. I move out of range of traveling herbage and shooting flint. I know there is nothing I can say or do to stop this now. I return to the house and telephone Michel.

"I can't leave," I tell him.

"Don't be foolish. The publicity tour has been arranged. You can't *not* leave." He is right and I know it. "We will have to take our chances. No Name will be there." At this stage I don't bother to explain that I have agreed with René that No Name should stay with him. I drop it. We must continue as planned and hope for the best.

Tormented by the steady drone of the brush cutters baring our home and farm to all and sundry, I give up on my script and set off for the village to buy a week's supply of dog food. As I round the bend, I am forced to halt because the road is blocked by two large trucks parked one in front of the other. There are also several workmen standing in a huddle, pointing and shouting upward to one of their crew who is strapped onto a crane extension and is slicing chunks off the tops of the complaining neighbor's exceedingly spiry pine trees. At first I assume this to be part of their disquiet over possible impending fires until I notice that there are cables swinging freely in the road. Some of the telephone wires seem to have broken loose, or maybe a tree has fallen. Cars are banking up behind me, honking insanely. So few cars ever pass this way that I am bemused by this line and cannot think where it has come from. There must be a road closed somewhere else, other cables down. Musing, I sit patiently, listening to the discordance of chainsaw, whirring brush cutters, French and Arab voices disputing the length of time all this is taking, and asking myself what ever happened to the tranquility of this barely known corner of the coast *arrière*.

Suddenly, I hear two men in front of me begin to shout loudly, "*Non, Monsieur, s'il vous plaît, non!*" I crane my head out of the window and see a car approaching from the opposite direction. It is attempting to pass the parked trucks. This is a perilous insanity, for our narrow little lane drops sheer to a busy road a lethal hundred meters beneath the cliffside.

Everybody takes up the call, Danger! Arms are waving, men are rushing to and fro, yelling, jumping, all engaged in the frenzied business of refusing to allow this driver's impatience to risk lives. I, along with several other motorists, temporarily abandon our cars to wander along the lane and take a closer look, for what else is there to do? Beyond the trucks and the driver hell-bent on getting through no matter the consequences, are several stationary vehicles, their drivers stone-faced, waiting to move on.

Behind this caravan of rising blood pressure and ranting workers, I spy the approach of the postman on his motorbike, weighed down as always with his satchels of letters hanging like floppy leather ears on either side of his post office–yellow scooter. He draws close, weaves his way in and out of the traffic, circling the screaming, hysterical human beings and slips along the lane by the inner side of the trucks. Engaged in their fury, no one notices him, and he pays the show in progress not a blind bit of attention but presses his foot on his accelerator intending to whizz by the trucks on the inner side of the lane. Unfortunately, he has underestimated the portliness of his own figure or misjudged the width of the passage, no wider than the narrowest of mountain defiles, because he finds himself sandwiched, man and bike, between truck and cliff. I alone hear his cries, for his voice is lost among the general furor.

As I hurry to seek out the driver of the offending truck, I throw a final glance at *Monsieur le facteur*, whose arms are now stretched wide and waving high above his head, eyes turned skyward and mouth gaping open in frozen horror. His blue postman's cap has fallen to the ground behind him.

It is only then that I grasp what is about to happen. High above us all, the chainsaw worker in the crane has remained diligently at work. A fairly substantial upper trunk of pine tree is about to give and, any minute now, will come barreling to the ground. Our postman will definitely be its target.

"*Attention!*" I yell. "*Attention!*" My actress's voice booms to full capacity. I am shouting, pointing and running. There is a general cry of "*Mon Dieu*" as half a dozen men scuttle like a twelve-legged beast to save the postman. The obvious move is to shift the truck, but this cannot be done because the driver has disappeared down the lane for a *pipi*, so the crowd is obliged to push and drag postman and scooter. Several others are yelling to the *mec* up on the crane, who eventually gets the message and halts work, leaving a very wobbly-looking pine tree. The driver returns, whistling while closing up his pants, just as the group to the side of his truck is yanking the postman by the shoulders and literally dragging the poor fellow backward off his bike. Everyone, including the postman, is yelling hysterically. He seems barely able to stand, even with the assistance of the rockface behind him, and is rubbing his face with a large spotted handkerchief in an attempt to calm himself.

By now, cars are streaming freely to and fro, while those on foot—the workers—are shaking hands and congratulating themselves and one another. A crisis has been averted.

It is then that I happen upon one of the Arabs who had been lending a hand and who is now making his way toward the house across the lane, our neighbor Jean-Claude's abode. He sees me, nods and returns to his task of trimming the hedges. I watch him for a moment. I have often heeded him there and, more importantly, have frequently remarked on the gardens and well-pruned orange groves. I walk over to him and introduce myself. He smiles shyly, revealing a toothless mouth save for one tobacco-stained front tooth and a golden nugget farther to the back on the upper left side. He also sports a small blue tattoo in the center of his forehead, reminiscent of the red spot worn by Hindu women. His eyes are warm, if yellowed by age. He knows who I am, he says. He has seen us frequently entering and exiting our property. I ask him if he would be interested in doing a spot of work for us. I explain my dilemma, and we both stand and regard the men relentlessly cutting back the triangular strip of land.

He accepts without hesitation and introduces himself. "*Je suis* Harbckuouashua," he says.

Sorry? He repeats his name, and I still cannot grasp it, which tickles him. "Call me Quashia."

He agrees to begin the following morning. I explain what needs to be done. He lists what he requires, and I set off for the builders' merchants in search of meters of meshed wire fencing, cement and iron pickets, as well as the almost forgotten dog food.

The following morning, he arrives late. I fear he is not coming. I will miss my plane and am about to give up on him when I catch sight of his silhouette sauntering along the lane. Trust me, he reassures. And so I do.

When I return from Australia a week later, zapped by an overload of radio, newspaper and television interviews—added to turning my body clock on its head twice in the space of a week—I find the fence in place and completed.

Quashia is there waiting for our return from the airport, keen to display his work. In my absence, Michel and he have become the best of buddies: we have acquired the able-bodied man we spoke of at the start of summer. His skills include masonry, tiling, trimming, tree pruning, as well as any other odd job I can come up with.

Proudly he is claiming Michel and me as "*ma famille française.*" From here on, he addresses Michel as *mon cher frère.* This greeting is followed by four kisses, two on each cheek, much hugging, followed by back-slapping of a force that leaves Michel limp. At first I have to confess to a certain mistrust of such hearty *bonhomie*, but I am soon forced to reconsider my unvoiced reservations.

On the other hand, I am not always regarded as a *chère soeur*, but on occasion, as a potential second wife. When Michel is away or out of sight, even on nothing more than a quick trip to pick up some fresh salad, I have to watch my step. "Sleep with me once, just for the hell of it!" pleads Quashia, and I flee indoors. Glancing back, I catch the tobacco-toothed grin lighting up his sun-cracked face.

HIGH SUMMER IS APPROACHING fast, which means the influx of guests. The first this year will be my parents, who are visiting us for the first time.

After their concerns about the purchase of this farm, I fear they will be testing, rigorous, difficult to please, so their imminent arrival makes me edgy. Added to which, Michel has been called to Paris and will not be back until tomorrow. This leaves me running around alone like a headless chicken. I have never claimed to be a good housekeeper and in fact am pretty hopeless, but here I am now dragging sticks of furniture, such as we have—garden chairs as clotheshorses or dressing tables and the like—from room to room, corner to corner, in a pathetic attempt to create ambience and a home which might realistically be judged as up to snuff.

An hour before I am planning to set off for the airport, believing all is about as together as it is going to get, I flop over the balustraded terrace, breath a deep sigh of relief, peruse the shorn grounds all around me and smile proudly down upon our swimming pool. Michel has spent hours vacuuming and treating it, and now it is crystal-clear. That will impress them, I am thinking, rather too overconfidently. Oh no, they can't call this place a pig in a poke, I am muttering to myself smugly, and then, to my horror, I notice movement. The sanitation cover on the terrace alongside the pool is heaving. An emission of dark brown waste is creeping out from beneath it. Another twenty minutes and the excrement will be slopping like green-jellied aliens into the pool. No, I cry, but the only soul heeding me is No Name, who runs for cover. I scoot inside. My heart is pounding fast. I have to combat this impending disaster before I leave for the airport, or when we return . . . the image does not bear thinking about.

I rip through the pages of our villa address book, searching for the number of Monsieur Di Fazio. Of course, it is eleven in the morning, and he will have left home for work hours ago. Crazed with panic, I ring anyway. I must meet that plane. I have to stop the seepage. There must be an underground leak in the pipes; by this stage, I am yammering to myself. Desperate, my brain is spaghetti. What in heaven's name is the French word for *leak*? I simply cannot recall it.

Madame Di Fazio answers, "*Je vous écoute?*"

I am still trying to get my head around how to explain the excrement oozing across the terrace beneath me. *Truite!* Yes, that's the word I'm searching for! *Truite!*

"'Ello?"

"*TRUITE!*" I yell into the phone.

"'Ello?"

"Hello. *Madame Di Fazio, c'est Madame*—"

"*Bonjour Madame.* Yes, I recognized your accent." She laughs kindly. "Are you all right?"

I have no time for such chitter-chatter this morning. My parents' plane must be sweeping over Lyon by now.

"Madame, I have a serious problem. It's very urgent." I am speaking in French, of course.

"*Oui, Madame?*"

"Please contact your husband and ask him to come over here right away, please. It is *gravement* urgent. There is a huge *truite* which has . . . somehow . . . come up through the plumbing and is now moving along the downstairs terrace. It must have escaped through the . . . er"—I cannot think of how to explain the problem. I have no idea what the translation is, or even the English words for what I am trying to put across are. "*Une truite* . . . in the thing . . . yes, and it's making for the swimming pool, *la piscine.*"

Madame Di Fazio is giggling. "*Une truite, Madame?*"

"Yes, a *truite,* heading for the swimming pool." I am a demented being, shouting and waving my free hand in the air, worse than those lunatics who are convinced that if you speak forcefully enough in English, anyone, no matter what their mother tongue or how nonexistent their grasp of our language, will understand you. "IT'S MOVING TOWARDS THE SWIMMING POOL AND IS ABOUT TO SLIDE INTO THE WATER ANY SECOND NOW AND MY PARENTS WILL BE HERE WITHIN THE HOUR!"

"I'll call my husband." She laughs and puts down the phone.

I cannot drag myself away from the upper balcony. I am standing dead-still, staring at the excrement seeping like poison across the terrace beneath me. No Name approaches it gingerly.

"Get away from there!" I yell from way above her. If she treads in it . . . I scream at her again. "No Name, get away from there!" Her tail disappears beneath her, she glances up at me curiously, regards what from her point of view must be a red and furious face and then slinks away, completely baffled.

Within ten very drawn-out minutes, Mr. Di Fazio's cranky old motor croaks up the drive. He climbs from his van, covered head to toe in soot, as ever, white teeth grinning like piano keys. "Where's this monster fish, then?" he chortles.

"What fish?" I cry, believing this to be yet another of his witty cracks alluding to my television career, or rather the career he continues to insist is mine. Right now I cannot contemplate programs with fish in the title; I am in no mood for it. "Look! Look there!" I lead him to the drainage, and he laughs long and loud. His fat stomach heaving with merriment.

"Why are you laughing, Mr. Di Fazio? This is serious! My parents are on their way. My mother already thinks I have no common sense. Please, do something. HELP!" And help he does. Out of his van, he unwinds meters of thick coiled piping. The underground canal is suctioned and emptied in no time, along with two others situated at various points descending the drive, which according to our plumber could also cause us distress. Then off he goes, explaining happily that he and Michel can discuss a cash price during the weekend. "For the removal of the fish."

I am completely baffled but extraordinarily grateful, and I cannot spend time now trying to get to grips with his sense of humor. I need to leave for the airport instantly. I am late.

I arrive frazzled, zipping like a demented lizard. Naturally, I am not on time. Their plane has landed, they have collected their luggage and are awaiting me outside, smiling and unruffled. "Hello, dear."

Back at the villa, after they are installed in their clean but basic room, which is bettered by plentiful bunches of Marguerite daisies picked from the garden, I take them on a tour. They drink it all in silently. "Well, what do you think?" I ask at last.

"I'm glad you've got big windows," says my mother. "I don't like those small ones the French foreigners always have here." My father's response is "I think you might have bitten off more than you can chew."

WHILE I HAVE BEEN occupied with the tending of my family, word has been spreading fast on the village bush telegraph. I am now known as the actress who can take on the world as Emma Peel but who calls in the plumber to remove a giant trout from her drainage system. In scatterbrained panic, I have muddled my nouns: *fuite*, or leak, and *truite*, trout.

It's time to learn the language, I concede when I hear my linguistic confusion repeated back to me. Sheepishly, I take myself off to Nice, to the university, where I enroll in an intensive summer course.

During my lunch break which, being French, last at least two—if not three—hours, I wander the streets and coastal strip of Nice, keen to learn a little about the city at close quarters. It has flavors to it other than Cannes. For one thing, it is a university city, and even though it is summer and the students have disappeared to the countryside or mountains and the profs are on *congé*, which means the university is only catering to linguistic numbskulls like me, the city still gives off a very different energy. There are myriad bookshops, a healthy majority of young people, a wide choice of movie theaters, an abundance of excellent museums and restaurants and a working population which is not dominated by the idle rich. It teems with bustling life, with inhabitants going about their days trying to make a living, and sports a magnificent harbor where colossal white passenger liners lie in dock preparing departures to Corsica or Italy, even to the Nordic lands or some as far afield as Russia.

Set back from the harbor is the old town, where the street names are written in both French and Niçoise, which is the *patois* language once spoken here. Perhaps the crowning glory of the *vielle ville* is the flower market to be found a few steps from the famous opera house, where *Rigoletto* is to be performed this evening.

The language I am hearing everywhere around me is Italian. Every week, the most avid and passionate of French shoppers cross the border to buy produce and very reasonably priced Italian clothing (and booze) at the frontier market town of Ventimiglia. In turn, the Italians are drawn here on Mondays to spend their lire on antiques and fresh produce every other day of the week.

Along the street Rue St-François-Paule, written in *patois* as Carriera San-Francés-de-Paula, is a *huilerie*, an oil shop, belonging to the Moulin à Huile d'Olive of Nicolas Alziari, a famous name in the business of oil production. His groves are situated in the granite hills up behind this city, and the fruit is a mix of the same small Nice olive, the *cailletier*, as ours and another, the *picholine* olive, which is longer and thinner. *Picholine* olives are named after a Monsieur Picholine, who developed a method of curing green olives using the ash from the green oaks that grow everywhere in this region—we have plenty on our terrain. I would have enjoyed a short browse, but the shop is closed for lunch. Across the street, also gone for lunch, a competitor is situated. The *huilerie* of Caracoles, where it is written—although I have not come across this *maison* before—the products are *regionaux, les articles provençaux.*

Making a short detour along the *rue de la terrasse*, the *carriera de la terrassa*, I am drawn to a hand-painted sign reading *cave, Pierre Bianchi & Cie*, where the painted glass windows are proof of its heritage. It announces proudly three *siècles d'existence*. Three centuries of trading. Quite a feat, considering the history of this city. It means they were here before the French; Nice was ceded to France in 1860.

I step up to the glass to read its hours of business, thinking that I might return after my afternoon course, and am amused to read that it reopens at two and has no particular hour of closing and on Sundays is closed only *si grosse fatigue*. If enormously tired!

The colors and architecture of the tall shuttered buildings crammed alongside one another in streets so narrow a bicycle can barely pass through (certainly not our postman!) are Italian-influenced: vibrant red ocher, yellow ocher and mustard hues, all decorated with faded green or bleached turquoise shutters, or pale dusty lilac, a color so fragrant you can almost inhale it.

Until 1860, this ancient city was governed by the House of Savoy and was adjoined to the kingdom of Sardinia, Piedmont and Liguria. Shortly after this date, these other provinces became part of a new unified Italy. But even today, there is much about Nice that boasts of its Italian heritage, not least its fabulous Mardi Gras carnival, with its masked balls dating back to the thirteenth century and known by the Italian name of *veglioni*. This famous carnival still parties here nonstop during the three weeks leading up to Lent and proudly claims the use of a ton of papier-mâché for every float!

Behind partially shuttered windows, I glimpse local craftsmen beavering away in *ateliers* barely larger than postage stamps. A bald-headed cobbler repairing the soles of a pair of leather sandals puts them to one side and shuts up shop for lunch. Along a crooked dead-end alley leading off one of the many squares, I encounter a mechanic disgorging the engine of an ancient pram-size Fiat Cinquecento. He is seated in the driver's seat with the door hanging open, facing out to the world at large. In his lap is a dish of what looks like pork in a rich, winy sauce. On the ground at his feet are a half-emptied flacon and a glass of rosé wine, fruit, cheese, a half-eaten baguette and two hungry curs salivating at a safe distance, waiting for scraps. Clotheslines of sheets, shirts and undies are festooned like bunting everywhere above me, reaching across the narrow lanes from one side to the other. I hear the hum of a carpenter or cabinetmaker planing great sheets of wood. He must be the only craftsman still at work, for the midday siren has sounded and the world of *les ouvriers* has downed tools.

I am also growing hungry and make for the Cours Saleya, or in *patois,* Lou Cors, to the marketplace. It is sensational. The central square is an amphitheater of ancient colored buildings, the most magnificent of which is now the home of the Préfecture des Alpes-Maritimes and was once the palace of the Dukes of Savoie. The flower market, operating alongside the fish and food stalls, is a glorious blaze of colors and perfumes, crowned with pot after pot of brilliant green, aromatic herbs. It is a feast for all my senses, and I cannot resist a dozen long-stemmed birds of paradise. Now I must hurry and move on to the food. One stall is selling, they tell me— and I take their word for it, since I haven't the time to count—one hundred and fifty different varieties of spice. Each is neatly laid out on dishes dressed in brightly hued Provençal cotton with the name of the spice handwritten in black ink. *Muscade, poivre concassé, poivre Sichuan, exotique,* but they are being whisked away and stored in the rear of a van parked in the cobbled square. Another marketeer offers olives. His array is a *fête!* Among a mind-boggling choice are olives de la Puglia, from Italy. They are the largest I have ever set eyes on and resemble in size, as well as shape, small green lemons. I help myself to one and slip it into my mouth, sucking on it with the glee of a child savoring a piece of hard candy. It is sharp and peppery and delicious.

At various corners and angles in the alleys near the market, there are dozens of busy restaurants where knives and forks clatter, glasses chink, voices chatter, laughter peals and diners await their meals being served *al fresco;* the acoustics of the ritual of lunch are amplified by the tall buildings.

I press my nose against the windows of one or two enticing *traiteurs,* hungry to gorge on everything. I must decide, since everyone is packing up for lunch. I creep inside the second where the flagstone floors are cool and clean, where the pastry smells so warm and soft and yielding you might lie down on it, and where every plate on offer is of psychedelic shades. Mayonnaise has never looked so rich, so yellow and creamy. I want to dive into the large round dish and behave rudely with it.

The dishes of Nice are not necessarily the same as those of Cannes; here again, the Italian and the Provençal influences are in evidence. I buy myself a workingman's portion of *tourte de blea*, which is a local specialty. Still piping from the oven, its pastry is as delicate as *papier poudre*, and I carry my thick slice in a paper bag like a trophy to be consumed with a bottle of mineral water on a bench overlooking the Med, now bobbing with oily, shrieking people.

The beaches along this *Promenade des Anglais* are filling up by the day. To the right, half a kilometer along the coast, the planes sweep low, disgorging yet another batch of holidaymakers. Summer is upon us with its whiffs of suntan lotion, children splashing and screaming with joy, the bells of ice-cream vans ting-a-linging and the ceaseless impatience of drivers leaning on their horns. Two youths, skinheads with radiant pink mohawks, come to a standstill alongside me. The one farther to the left takes an asthmatic drag on a joint, then passes it to his friend, who does the same. They gaze out at the languid sea flopping against the beach in small curls of foam. "S'foockin' grea' 'ere," says one, in a thick, lazy Scottish accent. His pal grunts and they move on.

Within the hazy, heat-drenched distance, I am able to discern the contours of the Alps which are, whatever the season, the magnificent backdrop to this sweeping seafront. Few of these visitors ever see this coastline at its most breathtaking, which, for me, is on a sharp wintry day when the limpid sea is a brilliant turquoise, the coast is depopulated save for a lone inhabitant or two strolling, windblown, close on the heels of racing, excited dogs while behind them the mauve mountains rise up, crisp, clear and snowcapped.

Ambling along a return route previously unknown to me, toward the university, I spot a *poissonnerie* that has reopened and slip in to buy succulent *clovisses* and *praires clams*, perfect for *spaghetti alle vongole*, which I now decide to make this evening and serve on the terrace by candlelight.

As I consider whether my family will enjoy this dish, a memory flashes by of my father's mother, who sat by her fireside in the east end of London, a cigarette smoking between her nicotine-stained fingers, a glass of stout beer on the tiled hearth, picking cockles and winkles with a pin from their shells. Here cockles are known as *fausse praire*. How many worlds make up a life!

In a winding labyrinthine lane somewhere toward the heart of the city, I pass by a butcher specializing in game and poultry and pause to take a closer look. Beyond the glass is a still-life menagerie. It is crowded with heads, curly-tailed haunches and an array of hosed, furry bodies dangling from meat hooks. There are rabbits and hares, unplucked pigeons, quails, chickens and ducks, plump geese alongside tiny birds no bigger than sparrows. And on an oval silver platter in the foreground, like John the Baptist as presented to Salome, the *pièce de résistance,* are the heads of two wild boars. Their fanged teeth jut from semiclosed mouths, smiling with misjudged confidence. Although their days of hunting are over, they remain tusked and bristly but, decapitated, have lost much of their menace. Studying them at close quarters, I have no desire to rekindle an intimacy with any of their cousins living on our land.

BACK AT HOME, DAYS slide by, and the gentle splash of bodies paddling to and fro in the pool is the music of the afternoons. My script moves on apace. No Name grows healthier by the day, springing from one terrace to another like a gazelle in flight. While my mother siestas or reads and my father—with No Name constantly padding or sleeping at his side—snores in the shade or bakes himself a lurid red in the sun and my mother nags him to get in out of the heat before he gets sunstroke, Michel and I wander endlessly and aimlessly, taking stock and sharing our visions. Perching on stones buried in the drying grass, plucking daisy heads, we chalk up lists of projects. Mine are of orchards, fruit trees, farming, vegetable beds to nurture, a compost to dig, terraces furnished with succulents in tall terra-cotta pots; the produce of the earth surrounded by space and tranquility and the freedom to write: self-expression.

Michel's perspective on the future contains a communal *esprit*, and architecture. He has a more structural approach to the place: overview. There it is again, his favorite German word: *überblick*. I am passionately involved at close quarters, while he is pursuing the larger canvas. He reads the lines of the terraces, the symmetry of the olive groves which I haven't even noticed, the shapes and curves of walls. He detects cracks, fissures, the balance or imbalance of windows, aberrations that have been added to the property over the years and have destroyed its overall elegance, its simplicity of form. He draws up plans for future watering systems and reflects upon a practical choice of plants for this mountainous region. Agave cacti, palms, yuccas, citrus fruits, eucalyptus, olives. He never would have handed over cash for a hundred roses to wilt in the hot sun, obliging us to pass half our days hiking hoses or buckets up and down the hill in a never-ending attempt to keep them watered, but we don't talk about my hundred roses, nor about the trader who took my money for them and never returned.

And he talks of artists, filmmakers, writers in wooden huts buried at work in corners of our pine forest . . . here we disagree! But in our shared idyll, all debate is amiable, nothing acrimonious.

Back at the villa, I catch my mother watching us; clearly, she is concerned. My father, who always has a useful aphorism on the tip of his tongue, is baffled: "You've got a career back home, love. A bird in the hand . . ." He has risen from his postlunch slumbers and is playing with the dog, or rather, she yields to him like a puppy, on her back, legs in the air, while he strokes her stomach and examines her. I see him fiddling with her teats, a frown crossing his beetroot-flushed face.

"What's wrong? Is No Name ill?"

I barely hear my mother's concerns: "I've seen you do some daft things, Carol, but . . . if you want a swimming pool, why not work in Hollywood? Think champagne and you'll drink it!"

I giggle. It's true that for the sake of "art," my untamed nature or the whims of *la passion*, I have dived headlong into some "daft things": hung out in Rome doing little better than extra work at Cinecittà and learning Italian, lived a week inside a live volcano, dived the seven seas, had a crack at tracking snowy regions of Lapland with a sleigh and six dogs, got blazing drunk on some deeply suspect concoction with headhunters in a longhouse in Borneo, traveled unaccompanied up the Amazon . . . oh, the list is endless, and I don't regret most of it (the longhouse was a bit precarious; one more glass, and my head might have ended up on a key ring), but the purchase of Appassionata does not equate. It is an exploration of another kind because it requires commitment and faith. It is a canvas, and we are two creating this journey. My parents' final words on the subject are: "Well, I hope you know what you're doing!"

I don't. It would be arrogance to claim that I do. I know where I have come from, what I am attempting to leave behind, the habits and experiences I want to shed like a skin, but not where I am going or even what exactly I am seeking. I am taking it as it comes, making it up as I go along. Pushing the boundaries of identity, hopefully to enrich, deepen, cultivate the spirit. Better to give it a shot than stare at the rain through wrinkled rheumy eyes, sighing *What if* . . .

"This dog is pregnant," my father pronounces. This stops all metaphysical philosophizing. Within seconds, all of us are on our haunches surrounding No Name, who looks from one to the next, uncertain and puzzled. She nuzzles close to Daddy.

"No, it's not possible," I say, staring at her swollen black nipples.

"We should call the vet."

"No, she's fine. There's no way she could be pregnant."

IF QUASHIA IS TO CONTINUE his sterling work of fencing then we must, by law, call in a surveyor, a *géomètre*, to stake out the boundaries of the land. Once this has been done, he will notify our neighbors in writing—including scale maps as drawn up by the department of *cadastration*—

of our decision. If no boundary neighbor (which is only one) contests our rights within a period of twenty-eight days, then the same expert forwards the necessary documents to be signed by the adjoining landowners, which will confirm that they have no claims against the ownership of our land.

All this to fence our property and keep the burglars out! Farmland and buildings—every square meter, every stone fence, every stable—are clearly defined in numbered plots and detailed sketches on the maps and plans filed with both the *notaire* and the local council registers. Still, it has to be done. French bureaucracy is French bureaucracy, and it is tireless!

So the *géomètre* can actually find the boundaries of the property to stake, a traversable pathway needs to be hollowed out of the weeds and jungle. This means hacking land way beyond the acres cut back by Amar, which to our dismay are growing faster than we can earn the cash to keep them at bay. And due to the enormous fire hazards in the area, all landowners are responsible for the safety level of their herbage. I am beginning to get a sense of the never-ending battle that lies ahead if we are to keep the tangle of growth on the farm under control, and the prospect of it exhausts me.

Quashia arrives. He and Michel are going to attack the grounds together. With trimming machines on their shoulders, water bottles in plastic bags and face visors to protect their eyes, the pair hike up the stone track behind the house and disappear into the forest.

As he heads up the hill with Michel at his heels, Quashia points to a mass of small spindly stalks which are growing everywhere. Wild asparagus, he tells me, delicious. I pick a huge bunch and steam them with the idea of adding them to a salad or serving them with prawns or as an accompaniment to another *spaghetti alle vongole*. In fact, I serve them as a first course to my family for lunch. "They're rather bitter, dear," says my mother. I add lemon juice, olive oil and pepper, and we find them . . . bitter.

"I can't eat this! What is it? Some type of grass?" my father says.

I chuck them out and decide to leave the rest in the garden.

WHILE I AM CHEERFULLY chanting verbs in Nice, Michel's parents telephone to say that they have decided to accept his invitation and visit us; they will be arriving in two days. My parents are not due to leave for a while yet, and before their departure, Michel's daughters are flying down. We lack habitable bedrooms. So while my father and Michel work the land with Quashia, my mother offers to help me tear out what Michel and I have christened "the brown room." It remains as we found it, a hideous, smelly space. After scrubbing, buckets of *Eau de Javel* and a slap of whitewash, it has the potential to become a cool, airy retreat with a fine view across the valley and a perfect situation right alongside the swimming pool. Its previous function seems to have been for puppy breeding. The tenant who skipped out on the bills must have run some kind of kennels here—we have come across one or two rather ghastly examples of her workmanship—but in this room she surpassed herself. It has been divided into eight nests that are entirely covered in a foully stained brown carpet. Not only is the entire floor done in this dank rugging but all four walls as well. Lack of air and years of puppy pee seeping into the rotting weave added to an outside temperature of 80°, and you can understand why we have left this room till last.

My mother loves to clean and scrub, to make bonfires and burn great mounds of rubbish. She seems to find fanatical joy in all such activity. I, on the other hand, loathe it, but she soon has me up and at it. Dragged away from my computer, I am armed with mops, sponges, scissors, bread knives, ladders, hammers and hot water. As we rip at the walls, dead plaster and white dust crash down upon with us with the force of an imploding mine. Within minutes, we resemble bakers. My throat is dry as a bone, and I am giddy with trying to hold my breath because the acrid air has me reeling, but worse is yet to come. Living beneath the carpet is an entire microworld of insects and small black worms, disgusting little beings wriggling free from the shock of having been unearthed. Everywhere around us, creatures are on the move.

Perspiration stings my eyes, dust is engrained in my hot, sticky flesh. Spiders and other bodies are marching over my feet, and some are ascending my calves. I shout across to my mother that we should give up. She answers, "Why, dear, we are getting on nicely." I glimpse her across the room. Scraping and scrubbing, ripping and tearing, she is having the time of her life. I can tolerate spiders as long as they are not too large and hairy, but these small black worms look venomous. We begin to lift up the floor covering. Beneath the carpet are twelve-inch gray cement blocks which have been stacked and grouted into a maze of small walls, presumably to discourage the puppies from crossing from one nest to the next. Settled in among them is a mass of black stirring life. I think I am going to throw up and suggest most emphatically that we leave it, but my mother shakes her head. "We're nearly finished, dear," she says. I have to get this over with fast. I cannot bear one more black being mountain-climbing over me. I run to the tool shed, where I dig out a mallet. Back I come. Swinging my arm like a discus thrower, I begin to smash at the cement blocks. I am sweating and heaving, thrusting and crashing. Shards of cement shoot all over the place. Furry and shiny carapaced creatures are whizzing through the air. My mother is yelling at my incompetence. My legs are bleeding. I have no expertise for this, but I am determined until finally even my mother runs for cover. "Stop," she cries, "stop," pleading with me to leave the dislodging and dismantling to Michel or Quashia "before there's an accident."

I am satisfied. With brooms and black bags, we begin to shovel up the mess we have created, stripping the room bare. It is then we notice the floor.

"Look at this!" Yet another original find. The tiles are obviously Italian. Each has a blond stone base with terra-cotta triangular insets and, at the center, sunflowers in brilliant yellow.

They are exquisite and as far as we can tell—given the mountains of general detritus, rotting carpet piled everywhere and insects who won't stay where they have been swept—barely damaged. How could anybody in their right mind have cemented blocks on top of such craftsmanship? I am bemused but thrilled and can picture this bedroom in days to come with crisp white linen and sunflower-yellow walls nestling behind our Matisse-blue slatted shutters. Well-rested guests waking to the music of water trickling into the swimming pool. Open the shutters to a new day, swallows wheeling overhead, and there, on the tiled surround, tall terra-cotta pots ablaze with scarlet-red geraniums to greet them.

It was worth the work and the worms.

We stagger out into the hot afternoon, promising to reconvene for tea. My mother disappears to shower and put the kettle on while my father reminds me we should call the vet, which I agree to do after I have hiked the hill in search of Michel and Quashia. I am too excited to await their return, and I need an oxygen tank full of fresh clean air.

At the summit, it is a veritable rain forest. The broom bushes have been left for so long they are twice any man's height. Even here, there are olive trees hidden in the canopy of rampant growth. Branches whip against my arms, unknown leaves pricking and jabbing as I force my way through. A holly scratches my damp, plastered shoulder. It stings unreasonably. I am calling every few minutes, but the whirring of machines and cicadas drowns out everything. I spy Michel. He is bent over, hacking away with a scythe, liberating strangled trees, disentangling brambles, suckers and vines. Quashia is working at ground level, clearing roots with the strimmer. They crack and thud as they fall.

As I draw near, I pause for breath and take in the staggering beauty of the surrounding hillside. In every direction, there are pines and dusky olive trees, dry stone terraces falling away like snow slopes and, way off in the distance, toward a dense cobalt horizon, the seductive sight of the sun-kissed sea dotted with clear white sails.

Deep hot stillness.

On the terrace beneath me, I spy a twisted, ailing pomegranate engulfed in trumpet vine. Roots and stripped branches lie like dead men on a battlefield. Michel straightens up, lifts his visored head and spies me. Quashia is thankful to switch off the machine, a moment's respite from the sweltering graft. I recount the news of our treasure buried beneath the muck. I watch Michel's delight, the smile spreading and breaking across his sticky, muddied complexion. "We have a surprise, too." He grins, pointing.

Way off to the left of where I am standing is our ruin, uncovered for the first time in at least a decade. We hike over to it and discover the remains of a picturesque little cottage. In what still exists of the living room, there is a fireplace and chimney, terra-cotta tiles—no roof—and crumbling walls; beyond are outhouses where the animals would have bedded down, a fabulous semicircle staircase which leads us up to a higher terrace shaded by a fig tree and a monumental, very ancient Judas tree. I had often wondered why Lawrence Durrell described this magnificent, deep-rose flowering tree as "tragic" until I read legend has it that Judas hanged himself from the branches of one. In the distance, looking back beyond our land, our tiled terraces, the pool where my family is relaxing, swooping down past the olive groves, is a wide blue expanse of Mediterranean. Perfect.

Time for tea.

Quashia and Michel put down their tools, and we trail in single file back down the stony pathway. Quashia pauses to point out a clump of pale green plants which I don't recognize.

"What is it?" I ask him. An aromatic herb. The name he gives is Arabic. "Excellent for the stomach. Drink it as an infusion." The leaves have a pungent scent, sweet yet spicy, but we cannot place it. "Shall I pick some for tea?"

I tell him next time. After the wild asparagus, I prefer to leave well enough alone.

We seat ourselves in the garden and drink Indian tea. I am fascinated to watch my father with No Name forever at his side. Though neither he nor Quashia can understand a word the other says, they are fooling together, and an image returns. I picture myself as a child on his knee, entranced by his exotic tales of those Cairo nights, of that wicked Arab who stole his glasses, and I regard the two men in front of me now, a million worlds apart, clowning like schoolboys. My father is attempting to recall a word or two of Arabic but gives up and instead offers his welcome greeting in Zulu, to which Quashia falls about with toothless, good-natured laughter.

CHAPTER EIGHT

FIRE!

I wake in the sweltering night, perspiration running from my damp body, to the sound of scratching. It seems to be coming from the hill above our rear patio. I lean up on my elbows and peer out at the shadowy shapes of trees, the dark silvery contours of the boskage. What is shuffling or cutting its busy way through the foliage? My first thought is a snake sidling toward our open doors. I tap Michel's shoulder. He mutters in his ocean-deep sleep, wriggles and returns to his dreams, oblivious. Now there is a tiny squeaking to accompany the rustling. I reach for a sarong not out of modesty, for there is no one to see me, but because I fear being attacked or bitten when I am naked. It's illogical. I get up and patter barefoot out onto the terrace. The night is warm. The moon is full and shines across the treetops as though we had forgotten to switch off the lights. The sky is brilliantly clear, not a cloud in sight, galaxies of stars twinkling within a sharp navy heaven. The rustling continues but remains concentrated in the same place, which is at the foot of the largest of our green oaks. I cannot make out any shapes or movement because the trunk is enveloped in deep bushy growth. Fearful of going closer, I sit at the table where we have breakfast, my knees drawn up tight against me, and try to concentrate on other sounds of the night, whiling away time, inhaling the balmy air.

Everywhere smells sweet. Perfume from the twenty-four lavender bushes I have planted—one of the gardeners from our local nursery who knows me well now advised me that lavender planted close to the house keeps the mosquitoes at bay—wafts in heavenly drafts from the lower terraces. High on the hill, there is a bird trilling even at this hour. I catch an owl's hoot, and then again the squeaking. It must be mice. I wander back to bed and lay listlessly on top of the sheet. I turn and watch Michel, his peaceful handsome face. It never ceases to amaze me how anyone can sleep so deeply. Nothing troubles him.

The squeaking is growing more insistent, the intervals more regular as though it is multiplying, and the rustling continues. If it is mice, there are plenty of them, and they do not trip lightly on their feet. I rise from the bed a second time and search for sandals and a wrap. Slowly, I make my way the few meters up the hill to the tree, crouch low on my haunches and discover No Name surrounded by a writhing mass of life. At close quarters, the sweetly cloying smell of blood thickens the humid night. She glances my way but makes no effort to greet or even acknowledge me. I move in close, and she growls. It is not a real threat, more an atavistic maternal response. In any case, she seems exhausted. Birthed out.

Gingerly, I touch her head and find her coat wet and sticky. Viscid fluff heaves against my arm. Overhead branches dapple the moonlight. Dawn has not yet broken, so I cannot make out how many whelped puppies there are. Five, maybe even six. I sit on the ground and keep watch with her. Pride surges within me for my elegant procreating Belgian shepherd. I quell a longing to rush around the rooms, beat on the doors and rouse every sleeping person. I doubt that Michel or our parents would welcome my rude awakening, it is not yet five o'clock. Still, I am too overwhelmed to go back to bed. So I decide to stay here, keep guard over the newborns and await their first sunrise.

Around seven A.M. Michel finds me conked out, curled up amid the stones and dusty dry earth at the foot of the tree. Twigs tangle my hair, indentations and dirt have creased and daubed my cheeks. I am brushed with blood and bits of gummy afterbirth, scantily clad in a bedraggled sarong.

"*Chérie?*" He is gently shaking me. "What are you doing up here? I have been looking for you everywhere." No Name's halfhearted growl draws his attention to the nest of life alongside me while I wake slowly, aching and sore, stones piercing my back, trying to work out where in heaven's name I am. And then I remember. "The puppies, have you seen them?" I cry.

Aside from a zillion worms and ants and spiders and caterpillars and ladybirds and bats and lizards and geckos, and carp and those horrid feral cats, which took off the day after we found them, and probably snakes, but I prefer not to consider them, and thousands of rabbits and hopefully dozens of those almond-munching bushy-tailed red squirrels, these blind little mewling beings are the first, the very *first* life born to us on our farm. No Name's puppies.

"How many are there?" I ask sleepily.

Michel puts his hand into the nest, which has been extraordinarily well fitted out. She must have been secretly foraging for days, when we were not around to notice. "Seven, I think." He is moving furry balls aside to see if there is yet another furry ball beneath. "It's hard to say, but you know, I don't think she's finished."

"How can you tell?"

He shakes his head. "Look."

I cannot see anything besides a mass of shining wet pelt which resembles a damp moth-eaten fox wrap unearthed from a long-forgotten attic.

A second look reveals ejected placenta and a substance similar to a plastic bag filled with murky water. And No Name is not moving.

"We should wake my father."

"HOW MANY NOW?"

"Ten."

"*Ten!*"

"I think so. There won't be any more." My father pronounces this with such certainty that no one questions him, and he has a way about him with dogs. After all, until our splendid vet confirmed my father's suspicions, none of us believed the dog was pregnant.

So ten is the final count. "See how she cleans them with her tongue."

Now the puppies are as round and pristine and furry as mink tennis balls. Michel is taking photos while my father and Michel's mother, Anni, keep watch, communicating with each other through sign language and intricate mimes. My mother is making tea, and Michel's father is sitting at the table awaiting his breakfast, scribbling a list of ingredients for the cake he plans to bake later today. As for me, I am taking on board the reality of eleven dogs gunning all over the farm.

By evening, there are nine puppies. The general opinion seems to be that it was not a miscount. Either No Name ate one or it perished and she has buried it somewhere, although, as far as we know, she hasn't left her site all day long. Any day now, Clarisse and Vanessa will arrive. They will be entranced, although I am not altogether sure how Pamela will respond. We will be eight people, two dogs and nine puppies in addition to the prehistoric carp surviving in our murky pond. Our menagerie grows. It's becoming exactly the home I craved as a child. Carefree and casual, with animals and people falling over one another, books everywhere, guests dropping by to while away a happy hour or two, jam a few tunes with whoever can play whatever instrument, nobody being quite sure where anyone else has disappeared to because there's loads of space and everyone is quietly getting on with their own thing. Heaven—just so long as I can creep off to my cool stone room and write in peace!

The farmyard spirit is taking hold of Michel, too. He is eulogizing about the possibility of planting a vineyard, acquiring a donkey, goats and bees. "Think of it—our own honey! And the goats can roam the terraces and eat the vegetation. It will save us the cost of cutting back the land."

Yes, and of ironing the laundry!

Alas, his suggestions are impractical. The olive does not need baby-sitting, the animals do. And we are both still on the move, living our itinerant professional lives. Somewhere beyond summer, beyond days drenched with heat and familes and scrubbing walls (and fumigating the brown room before the girls get here) and endless puppy care, we have another life, all too easily forgotten as the days drift listlessly by and we swelter and burn under the relentlessly seducing sun. Retirement, even as producers of olive oil rather than television, is not yet in the cards. I think of the scarecrow farmer and his weekly visit to the village *crémerie*. I can't quite picture myself in that role, yet after a sleepless night in the garden, I do resemble him!

What does amuse me is a shift I notice taking place. I have never been a practical creature, whereas Michel is far more down-to-earth, but there is a pendulum swing happening here. We are changing places, changing roles. He begins to fancy while I place feet on the ground.

LATER, TOWARD THE END of a sun-blessed afternoon, while still enamored by our new family of fluffballs, we receive a call from the girls. They want to confirm the hour of their arrival two days ahead of when we had agreed. In other words, tomorrow, and can they, please, please, Papa, bring two of their cousins with them, Julia and Hajo.

"But where we will sleep everyone?" I ask.

The plumbing is creaking, the water has turned a rusty autumnal shade—we cannot work out why—and half the house is crumbling. The cottage has not been touched yet, the brown room has barely moved on since my mother and I attacked it and we are, as ever, almost out of money. Even if we could afford rooms at our favorite hilltop hotel, they are no longer available, for he has sold his *petite affaire* to a restaurant owner from New York who has closed the place down for extensive renovation, intending to reopen it in readiness for next year's film festival as an exclusive hideaway, set back in the hills overlooking the glamorous bay of Cannes.

"They are bringing tents and will sleep in the garden, and before you say another word, they want to. It will be an adventure."

Tents arrive and, with them, a quartet of teenagers. How is it possible that only last year two prepubescent girls spent a summer with us and this year two stunning young creatures appear? The French have the perfect word to describe that awakening flush: *pulpeuse.* I love it. Pulpy, ripe. Their bodies and senses have woken up to the world. Of course, with such awareness come hazards. Julia, with her nubile figure, bewitching blue eyes and swaths of long, flowing blonde hair, is two years their senior and a sleek and enticing temptress she is. Hajo, her younger brother, is a few months their junior and, as so frequently happens with boys, seems to be five years younger. He is a Boy Scout of a boy. He helps Michel and Anni in the garden, collects wood, treats his grandparents with extraordinary love and respect and, when evening falls, happily accompanies the trio of girls to town but remains completely, innocently oblivious to their real interests: *Les mecs. Boys!*

DAYS SPIN OUT. Contented guests laze, doing nothing in particular or find themselves chores to help us out while I write like a driven fury. My scripts are ready to first-draft. Michel is reading them, and I have set to work on my novel. And then, a delicious diversion—*Klaxon! Klaxon!*—as a truck coughs up the drive, stripping sprawling fig branches and denuding ripening fruit as it ascends. We have all been awaiting this delivery, I more feverishly than the rest. Finally, I am to have my ancient wooden table the size of a railway sleeper. At last. At last. We bought it in sorry condition months back from a fabulously eccentric secondhand furniture store on the Left Bank in Paris, near St. Sulpice, where the shop owner arranged to have it restored for us by an artisan carpenter in Mougins. But when he delivers it, he takes one look at the exterior stairs, the terraces, the length of the arched walkway and pronounces his work done. He and his two associates, with the aid of a pulley system within the van, unload our precious teak table, deposit it in the driveway and depart.

It requires six men to carry it and deliver it to its place. Quashia's Arab colleagues rally to the call, shouting to one another in a language that none of us understand, with their dark faces and their assortment of hats. Polite men with decaying teeth, shabby clothes and shy expressions on tobacco-ravaged faces, always willing to lend a helping hand if there are francs in it for smokes. A makeshift team, troops up the hill, shaking hands with one another, shaking hands with us, then they go to work, moving as one, like our train of caterpillars, at the yell of an order—nasal high-pitched cries— until the table has been hoisted up the steps and positioned beneath the towering, majestic magnolia grandiflora, with its shiny bottle-green leaves and perfume from heaven, and there it will stay, we hope, for a hundred years. Sweating, resolutely keeping their gaze away from the three tender beauties sunbathing in itsy bits of string by the pool, the men refuse refreshment.

Each lines up solemnly for his fifty-franc *billet* dished out by Michel, nods his thanks, then wanders off contentedly down the drive, slapping his fellow countrymen on the back and Quashia, too, who has found them this rare moment of employment.

Pamela is the first to settle beneath the table. She waddles over and takes up residence like a rotund queen bee, then drops like a log and begins instantly to snore.

By and by, the puppies begin to appear. They creep forward inquisitively, one by one or in twos or threes, unkempt fluffy curiosity converging from everywhere. One cocks its little leg against a great wooden beam of table leg. I run, screaming, to chase it away, and they all scatter like a swarm of frightened rabbits, tumbling over one another in a mix of confusion and uncertainty only to sneak back again as soon as they sniff my absence.

They are still so gauche, so unsteady on their limbs, making nuisances of themselves at every turn, chewing feet, climbing bronzed legs, uprooting flowers and covering everything in earth. One little culprit steals one of Anni's new sandals, which makes her laugh, but when she settles back into her book he drags it to the murky fishpond, where it is lost until a carp surfaces with a sandal strap trailing from its torso—do fish have torsos? At feeding time the pups are easy to locate, nine hungry mouths packed greedily beneath No Name with splayed legs, sucking at her tired chewed teats. Still, she is a model, patient mother.

But how my father indulges them! Whenever I mention the inevitable, finding homes for them, he offers to take all nine of them back to England until my mother shrieks and quite sensibly reminds him that there is a quarantine into the United Kingdom. Vanessa has volunteered to take one, a golden-russet chap she has christened Whisky. The other eight, heavenly as they are, will have to be given away.

MEALS ARE A HULLABALLOO of pleasure. Our long-awaited table is the focus of life, the epicenter of the day. Like a clock striking, a yellow or cobalt blue ceramic and terra-cotta plate clatters lightly onto its surface. The salad contained within it is a masterpiece of Michel's cuisinary art: variegated leaves, striated, mottled, speckled reds and greens seasoned with herbs, olive oil, lemon or lime and garlic. A cork is drawn, liquid shot through with sunlight tumbles into glasses, a rainbow of fruit appears and each one of us, no matter what we are about, recognizes the signal. A meal is waiting to be devoured. Hajo returns from the village, laden with warm bread that divides at the touch. The epitome of the perfect house guest, Hajo also roams the inclines searching out kindling to bolster Michel's collection of sacks of pine and magnolia cones stored and dried during the winter for the specific purpose of fueling our summer kitchen: the barbecue, which is working overtime.

We eat and drink and talk and go silent at the pleasure of the delicacies being passed from one length of our table to the other. As the days progress, we eat and drink in greater quantity, and the meals grow longer and more cheerfully abandoned. We have three languages here: French, English and German. At night, candles flicker and the warm light glows and dances across our faces, animated by conversation and flushed with wine. The bats swoop low and spin off, flying "after summer merrily." Jazz reaches across the terrace from a makeshift system Michel has rigged up in the cool storeroom.

When Michel's parents first arrived, my mother came looking for me to ask what language they were speaking.

"German," I replied absentmindedly, busy with my work.

"For God's sake, don't tell your father!"

I glanced up, not really paying attention.

"Why?"

"We fought them in the war."

Here at this table, we pass bottles and lift empty glasses to accept yet another refill, and such frontiers don't exist. Michel is the conductor, for he is the only one of us who speaks all three languages fluently. With a turn of his head, he switches tongues. A glance to the left and he is with us in English; to the right and words unknown to me flow from his lips. His French daughters and their German cousins, Julia and Hajo, are able to converse workmanlike in whichever language is currently being spoken, but we Anglo-Saxons and Irish are a sorry lot. A lack of language is a poverty, and I resolve to add German classes to my list of chores and brush up on my Italian and Spanish, both as rusty as the plumbing. The odd German word is growing familiar. *Essen* is a meal or to eat; *schnecken* is being repeated frequently and debated on a great deal this evening, but I have not heard it before. "What is Anni saying?" I ask Michel.

"She is talking about the snails."

"Ah, *schnecken* means snails, does it?" I sigh. Yes, the plants are infested with snails. I have passed several hours on different dewy mornings picking them off the stalks of various shrubs only to find that, by evening, they are back in greater numbers. Crustaceans crowded on top of one another, like bracelets of hippie jewelery.

"She is telling us that she has a solution for them and that I must take her shopping in the morning."

I look at Anni, and she nods wisely.

"What is it?"

"You'll see." She laughs, and her merriment rings loudly across the valley, absorbed within the mauve hills.

THE NEXT DAY IS A brittle, dry day. Baking. Eerily still, deep heat which often precedes a *mistral*. My father and I are returning from the vet, where we have delivered a cardboard box full of restless puppies to be inspected. All are in good order, and as far as Dr. Marschang can say at this stage, these little ones are also purebreds. No Name must have been days, even minutes, pregnant when I discovered her. He has agreed to put up a notice in his surgery requesting homes for them. No Name is hovering, concerned by the disappearance of her brood, when Michel comes rattling up the drive with Anni. They have been shopping. As well as the usual provisions and the daily mountains of fresh food being consumed by our party, they have bought black pepper. Not one container, but twenty! This is Anni's answer to the *schnecken*.

"They can't abide pepper," she explains to me.

I shake my head in wonder. How can she possibly know such a thing? Is it black pepper they are allergic to, or all peppers? Are they fine with salt?

I take myself upstairs to my den.

Toward noon, as I stare idly from the window and nurse in thought my work in progress, I notice our various guests at their holiday activities. My father-in-law, Robert, I know, is absent. I can hear the clatter of tins and pans in the upstairs makeshift kitchen, where he is baking yet another round of cakes and creating utter chaos, showering flour and sugar every-where, transforming our inadequate cooking space into a ski resort. My father is by the pool sleeping, dogs crawling over him like flies on a cow's rump; the girls are perched in an elegant trio alongside the pool, polished toes dangling in the water to keep cool, sunglasses hiding the mischief in their eyes, whispering hot secrets to one another and laughing skittishly. I discern wind in the trees. It looks as though a weather change is coming in, brought by the wind that blows in from Africa. Hajo and my mother are both alone in private worlds. He is whittling a branch or a piece of tree trunk he has retrieved from somewhere on the land, while she, under the pretext of reading, is frowning at her feet, worrying about something.

Observing folk busy about their leisure is endlessly fascinating to me. But where are Michel and Anni? Leaning closer to the glass, I catch sight of Anni bent low, vigorously shaking pepper over twisting flowers. She moves on to the tender young orange trees, which are shooting up at a remarkable pace and soughing in the wind. Michel trails behind her, shirt flapping, with a tray of pots. Half are empty. He accepts an empty con-tainer and hands her another full one, and so they continue. I will be fas-cinated to learn the outcome. My guess is that the wind will pick up and the pepper will be blown away while the snails will continue to cling fast.

I return to the world of the novel I am writing. In my imagination, I am on a sugar plantation in Fiji and a young arsonist has set fire to the crops. "Fire!"

LATER, I HAVE NO IDEA how much later, minutes or hours, Michel is at my door. "Carol! *Chérie!*" I look up but barely register his presence, lost as I am again in my invented scenario.

"Mmm?"

"There's a fire. We should prepare ourselves."

It sounds too incredible to be true.

"A fire?" I repeat stupidly. Michel has no idea what I am writing, and his news has confused me. "What fire?"

"*Chérie,* there's a fire on the other side of the main road. Can't you hear the planes?"

I have heard nothing. I rise from my trestle table, padding after Michel, then scoot back to save and switch off my work.

"The others are getting dressed."

It is Saturday, midafternoon. I exit the house after Michel and am hit by a blanket of windy heat and by the roar of engines coming directly toward me. I lift my head and look skyward, and there, probably no more than twenty meters above our heads, a red plane swoops low and shaves the flat roof of our house, sending the gravel stones laid by Di Fazio into rising whorls before they clatter like running feet onto the terraces. Dust is everywhere, leaves are whipped from the trees and swirl about. This feels like an attack.

"I think we should drive to the end of the lane and find out what's going on."

Our little lane has been cut off by the fire brigade. No one can enter, and we cannot pass. A barrier erected within the last hour is being watched over by half a dozen hulking young members of the local fire brigade. Clots of people are huddled in groups. There is great activity, much argument. Most look like Parisians, lean and mean, smoking furiously, dressed in chic shorts, bathing suits with silk shirts thrown on hastily, jogging clothes, gold watches, designer purses clutched tight to their well-honed, neat-bosomed bodies. They are probably occupants of summer villas, living behind us or along the multitude of narrow tracks which wind inland toward the heart of Mougins. I ask one of the fireman what the chances are that the fire will leap the bridge over the road. He shrugs. "So long as the wind does not change direction, you are safe."

"And if it does?"

"If it does, get into the swimming pool and wait for an airlift out."

We are not to worry, he assures us, they know where and how many-we are. "How many are you?" he asks then as an afterthought.

"Ten, and two dogs and nine puppies." One very fat dog, I am thinking, who will not be able to run for her life. If worst comes to worst, one of us will be obliged to carry Pamela. And what of all those puppies? I will have to pack them back into the cardboard box and try to keep them calm.

We hurry back down the lane to the house, where the cinders are falling like huge dove-colored snowflakes and are settling on the surface of the pool. All around us, the sky is changing colors. Our loved ones are grouped together clutching bags and various bits of belongings. They are staring skyward, where the reflection of the fire has twisted nature out of recognition. It is impossible to concentrate on anything except the fire. The distant cries of people carry on the wind, the force of which sends a towel left by the pool flying into the water, where it sinks like dead meat.

Michel moves to and fro, making mental notes about the wind's direction. He is unwinding every hose we own, calling to anyone listening for assistance, and is attaching them at strategic points in the garden. Hajo is dismantling the three tents and taking them into the house for safety. I cannot stop myself from studying the scene, deciding what I might extract from the occasion for my story. The fear, the uncertainty and the threatening sky. Almost every word is shouted or drowned out by the skirring of the brilliant red Canadair planes (the color of the double-decker London buses), purchased from the Canadians and used to fight fires to great effect. Their presence is everywhere. If they are not overhead or passing to the rear of the hill, they are before us, diving into the sea, swooping like dragonflies. Their presence gives an urgency to the fire, which is still out of sight. The roar of their engines, no more than a few feet above our heads, brings real terror to the mood of things.

"I think it wouldn't be a bad idea to begin to soak the vegetation,"

Michel suggests, which is what he and I, along with Hajo, are about to do when Quashia appears, damp from exertion, wearing a battered old Panama hat. "I think you need help."

"How did you get through?" calls Michel.

"I saw the flames from the village and followed the towpath by the stream in the valley. The bridge has been cut off. There are fire engines everywhere."

I am relieved that our parents cannot understand this, for I fear it would distress them. "The wind's picking up, too."

We all look out to sea, where the waves are foamy and white, a sure sign that a gale-force wind is blowing in.

"How much water do we have in the *bassin*?" Michel shouts to Quashia.

"I switched on the pump on my way up here."

Michel nods, relieved, and hands out hoses. "We can manage this, *chérie*, you ought to stay with the family."

I retreat as the men begin to run the hoses up and down the hill, watering wherever the nozzles will reach. The sussuration of water spraying and falling on a day as relentless as this has a cooling, tranquilizing effect which I am grateful for; whatever posture of artistic detachment I might be laying on the occasion, the truth is I am scared and trembling.

There is nothing more we can do but wait. We sit silently listening to the crackling, even though for the moment the fire is still on the opposite side of the bridge, or we make inane jokes to keep the fear at bay. Eleven of us, plus the terrified animals, staring at an aubergine sky. Those who smoke are smoking too much. The rest of us are trying to remain calm. Quashia, perhaps because he is too restless to sit or does not feel comfortable being a part of the family, has gone to climb the hill. Michel tries to stop him, but he insists that he can better warn us from there.

It is a question of the wind which is building. Trees are bowing and swaying as though attempting to tear themselves from the earth and fly unencumbered with the wind. And then it changes direction, an instant turn about as immediate as switching still-life into animation. Within seconds the flames leap the bridge which crosses the road and are now right behind us, burning fast toward the pinnacle of our hill. We are all on our feet.

"FIRE! FIRE!" It is Quashia.

We run to the rear of the house, and at the very summit, beyond the unfenced limit of our own terrain where the vegetation has not been so rigorously cut back, is a scorching wall of fire which reaches the tips of the tallest pines ascending toward a confused, overwrought heaven. It is the most terrifying sight I have ever witnessed. The flames leaping toward the bruised and moody sky seem to be performing a war dance. I stand gazing up the hill, horrified and petrified.

Beneath us, the first of the fire engines hurtles up the drive. It is shortly followed by a second and then a third.

Michel tells us to collect our passports and keep them at the ready. Clarisse admits to being scared and wraps an arm tight around my waist. I love her for the confidence. Pamela whines like a frightened baby. Robert, munching on one of his cakes, is still covered in flour. Anni, stalwart and unafraid, empties the last remaining pot of pepper onto a rose bush and lights yet another cigarette.

"The hills are on fire and you are cut off," announces the hirsute chief of the four *pompiers* who have descended from the fire engine. "Someone set light to the trees in the pine forest over on the other side of the hill. We almost had it under control, but *le mistral* is picking up fast, changing direction and we can't contain it."

My eyes are weeping now from the smoke as well as these words. The heat is beating like a drum and tightening my skin. It is raining ashes. They are drifting through the air and falling on the terraces and floating in the swimming pool. It is like a blanket of gray snow. I have no idea what will happen to us. "Should we dive into the pool?" I ask weakly.

"No, go on with whatever you were doing. We'll keep you informed."

Continue with what we were doing! Even those rare moments of literary inspiration pale in comparison with this real-life drama.

An army of men pours out of the red vehicles and begins pounding up the hill. Each man carries what looks like a knapsack on his back. In all, approximately one hundred and twenty men are beating their way toward the summit of our hill. I have never seen so many fine-looking, fit fellows. Whatever fear had taken hold of Julia and our two girls has been forgotten. They are giggling and posing as dozens of handsome, lithe, young firefighters in their navy-blue uniforms go charging by. I confess to also being thrilled by them, their maleness and phenomenal physical prowess.

Now the pool is being sucked dry, and the chlorinated water transmitted up the hill by meter after meter of ample piping to be sprayed onto the fire. The dogs won't stop barking. Puppies are peeing and scooting all over the place. We are overwhelmed by noise and activity and chaotic fear.

What will happen when the pool is emptied? I ask myself. Certainly there is not enough to quench this conflagration. Will the fire then beat its way down the hill, killing the men and burning all in its wake? How can they hold such a fury at bay? Never mind, put a stop to it.

Suddenly, three or four of the small planes are arriving, droning and circling like great angry insects. They fly low, barely ten meters above the treetops, dropping tons of red powder on the wall of flames. Then they circle back, heading for the bay. I watch them dive, plunging their noses into the sea, nozzling up gallons of salty water. They return, one after another, a ceaseless aggressive procession hell-bent on beating back this twist of nature. Gallons of the Mediterranean Sea mixed with the red powder are dropped like bombs onto the flames. And so it goes on. Four planes, each making ten or fifteen trips an hour. It is a mesmerizing spectacle.

"Rather puts to shame those air shows you took me to when I was a kid," I whisper to my father, who is as always deeply impressed by such displays of organization.

"You've got to hand it to the French," he mutters, but he's not really talking to me. He's somewhere else, lost in his war, perhaps. I cannot say. I lean in and give his hot, peeling flesh a stroke.

I want to walk up the hill to get a closer look, but Michel and Quashia call me back. The weight of the red avalanche, they warn me, is sufficient to kill anyone foolish enough to be standing beneath a plane's load. I listen to one shrill crack after another as whining trunks snap and collapse to the needled earth, and I consider the fate of those firefighters, all of whom are at risk should the plane misdirect its lethal cargo. I have always harboured a child's romantic regard for firefighters and lifeboat men. They have always been my heroes, and nothing today dents that illusion.

BY EVENING, THE FLAMES have been beaten back. Slowly, the engines begin to reverse and depart. We are left with an empty pool, exhaustion and a strange sensation of deflation mingled with immense relief. Something tremendous and sinister has roared through our day, and now a disconcerting, cautious tranquility has taken its place.

"We'll be back tomorrow," the chief tells us, "to refill your pool. We'll be keeping a couple of men on the hill tonight in case the wind picks up. It needs only one burning ember . . ." It is usual here for the *mistral* to drop at night. No matter what gale force it has blown during the day, by evening it quietens. I have always found it one of those curious feats of nature—how the wind knows when the sun is setting—but it is so. We are left with a view that is as clear and pure as freshly drawn water.

Michel and I hike the steep, stony track to survey the extent of the damage. Four young men are standing together. Their eyes shine blue and bright beneath faces smeared with soot and sweat. Everyone shakes hands. They are welcome to join us for dinner. They thank us but do not accept. It is not possible for them to leave the site. In any case, as always, they are well prepared. Stores of water and food have been lodged beneath a living tree. Its verdant life is almost jarring amid so much blackness. Charred tree trunks are lying like history everywhere the eye can see, but not on our land. Not one tree, barely a blade of grass has been touched. Now I understand why the local councils are so strict about keeping the land cut back. There was nothing for the fire to take hold of, nothing to burn.

Still, the sickening aroma of fire is everywhere. My cheeks are burning just from standing so close. Heat rises like a sauna from the charcoaled earth. Everywhere, tortured black skeletons of trees are etched against the fast-fading day. Our water *bassin* has been drenched in red powder.

"You should cover that," a young fireman remarks.

It is true. Quashia has been nagging us about it all summer. I step up onto a three-rung ladder attached to the side of the *bassin* and peer in. The water within is tinted pink, and there are several birds floating lifelessly at surface level. Did the fire carbonize them, were they caught in a slipstream of wind and heat or have they fallen victim to a normal day's drowning? Pine needles are inches thick on the bed of the basin. The water looks stagnant as well as pink. Its murkiness could well be the reason for our rusty water.

"We'll clean it out for you tomorrow," one of our night-watch team reassures us.

A curl of smoke can still be seen here and there among the embers in what remains of the dwindling light and curling roots, snapped and torn from the dry earth. Pines that were dead but not burned have been uprooted, ripped from the earth by the sheer weight of the water falling on them. The newly dead surround us in an arboreal cemetery. Life laid waste against a ruined sky.

We should leave them to it.

"*Bonsoir.* If there's anything we can do . . ." calls Michel.

They shrug shyly and then an earnest-faced, dark-haired fellow in his early twenties steps forward. "Monsieur?"

Michel turns.

"*Nous avons vu les chiots . . . ils sont à vendre?*"

The puppies, are they for sale? they are asking.

We have eight to give away, I tell them.

Two young men now step keenly toward us, assuring us they would give them good homes. *Sans doute.* It is agreed, they will take one each. Tomorrow morning, before they go off duty, they will choose their puppies.

THE FOLLOWING MORNING, Sunday, is almost as eventful as the previous day. Cars arrive, a huge tanker bearing almost a reservoir of water negotiates the winding drive, splintering what's left of the fig branches in its wake, to refill the pool. This is followed by an official from the council administration, who arrives in a sleek silver-gray Renault. He is a short, stocky individual who wears a dark gray mustache and struts like royalty with his hands clasped behind his back. Most unusual, I think, because a true Provençal's hands are half his conversation. When I run downstairs to greet him, he asks to speak to the man of the house, which infuriates me. It is typical of a certain machismo which is prevalent on this Riviera coast.

"He is busy," I insist. "How can I help?"

He shrugs, wearied by the knowledge that he must deal with a woman. "I need to inspect," he informs me curtly.

"The fire damage?"

He nods impatiently. But of course! Squinting, he looks about him with a calibrating eye, ascertaining what we have or rather what we have not, because that certain turn of the mouth and pout of the lips tell me that he considers the place a ruin. "*Beaucoup de travail*" is his informed opinion. It makes me laugh because it recalls the estate agent, Charpy, who fled at the prospect of the work needed here. I am way past bothering to explain that as far as we are concerned, renovation is part of the joy of the place. Instead, I offer to escort him up the hill. We make our way to the back of the house, where he halts and tilts his head skyward. It is clear that he was not expecting such exercise. Glancing at his watch with a monumental sigh, he begins the climb, leading, not following.

The young men who have kept guard all night look very weary and desperately in need of showers and clean clothes but are as cheerful as the evening before. We all go through the handshaking routine, and they lead the council official on a guided tour of charcoaled tree trunks and grizzled brush. I stay where I am, taking in the view. The dense scent of charred wood pervades the early-morning air with the same persistence as last night. He takes his time, this official, crunching across acres of ravaged land before he finally returns to me.

"You are to be congratulated," he announces.

I am quite taken aback.

"*Vous, votre mari, vous êtes des bons citoyens,* and you are most welcome here in our commune." He shakes my hand warmly. "I want to meet your husband."

We traipse back down the hill, and I feel as though I am in the company of a different human being. He is whistling, looking about, pointing at this and that, nodding at the ruin and our olive terraces. The young men follow, carrying their rucksacks and moving wearily. Michel offers everyone coffee, but the firemen prefer to get off home. They leave, promising to return later to choose their puppies. Over a glass of *vin rouge*—it is not yet ten o'clock, and our parents regard this man with shock—the council official asks Michel what we do for a living (*ah, les artistes, maintenant je comprends!*) and if we would object to a photographer from the local gazette, the *Nice Matin,* dropping by. Not to photograph us, he reassures, but to take shots of the damage. Our privacy is sacred. Michel gives our consent.

The rest of Sunday is a series of comings and goings. The fire brigade returns to make a reconnoiter and decides that two more men are to be posted. "There is a light wind, and you can never be too sure."

The photographer arrives, an unshaven scruffy chap, who appears far more interested in the girls in their bikinis, who lap up every glance of attention as though it gives credibility to and feeds the rising temperature of their sexual awakening. And then the crowning moment of the day, the four firemen return late in the afternoon, spruced, shaved, showered and dressed in civvies. Handsome as mythological gods. Four of them in one battered outdated car. The girls rush to and fro, combing their hair, changing their clothes, searching out lipstick, snitching mine, and then return to posed composure in deck chairs in the garden, making quite sure that every puppy has been dragged to their sides.

Much bending and caressing and displaying of helplessly adorable creatures takes place and, I suspect, arrangements to meet later in Cannes for cups of coffee. Finally, four yawning puppies are chosen. They cannot be taken tonight, as they must spend a little while longer with their mother, which means that each of the young men promises to return at regular intervals to keep an eye on "his chosen companion." One young fellow must have lost out, I mutter amused to Michel, who is blithely unaware of what I am talking about.

After supper at our table, the girls, with dear Hajo as their escort, scuttle off to the bright lights of Cannes while we, the veterans, settle sedately on the upper terrace to watch the new moon and the stars appear. After a *mistral,* the view is always crystalline, as though the whole of nature has been polished. We can see every detail on every hill. Fortunately for the girls, we cannot see what they are up to in Cannes!

Tomorrow our parents are leaving. It is a sad yet complete moment. We have experienced the gamut of life's offerings together here: birth and death and time shared. As always, farewells create a deep and melancholy emptiness within me, and I feel the loss swelling as Michel opens the final bottle to be shared between us all for this summer. We sit in silence, quaffing, listening, appreciating the soft sounds of evening. And then, suddenly, there is a noise that none of us recognize. Short, sharp, tiny and repeated.

"What's that?" asks Anni.

We all of us listen concentratedly. Frowns and bemused expressions take shape in the candlelight.

I watch the families puzzling over the distant hiccuping and I simply cannot resist. "It's the *schnecken*, Anni, the snails."

"What about them?"

"They're sneezing!"

CHAPTER NINE

TRACKING THE OLIVE

Summer is slipping away, like the silent falling of petals. Everyone has left. We are on our own. The swallows gather, autumn sets in, rustic and rather rainy. The land grows green again, revivified. Grass, dry and brittle as old bones during all those hot months, shoots up overnight, and daisies sprout everywhere. They are crisply white, innocent and child-like, an unpretentious flower. I stroll along the terraces, studying the ripening olives, which are a light violet now, or piebald green and mauve, picking slender-stalked handfuls of wildflowers. I carry these back to the house to place in jars on the tables. They swoop and lift toward the first tendrils of sunlight creeping round the corner of the house, and I am delighted by their ordinariness.

It is Saturday morning. Herby scents in an immaculately well-washed day. Michel is somewhere at the foot of the hill, planting a wheelbarrow

full of purple and white irises which we have dug up from numerous terraces where they are multiplying in wild profusion. He is using them to
create a border to our new fence and the *arbuste* of laurel.

René arrives, bearing two plastic shopping bags full of small black
grapes. "*Framboises,*" he announces. I am confused.

He laughs at my expression. "These grapes are known as raspberries."

"Why?"

"Taste them."

Surprisingly, they taste exactly like raspberries.

He is about to escort us—we were expecting him the day before yesterday, but no matter—on a visit to one of the farms he tends in the
arrière-pays, the hinterland. He and I make ourselves comfortable on the
upstairs terrace and settle down to *un verre* while we wait for Michel to
complete his gardening chores. I glance at my watch as René pours our
chilled beers, and I smile silently. It is not yet ten-thirty. Years of restraint,
of broken diets followed by insufferable guilt, sleepless nights and a sense
of inadequacy, all to stuff myself into costumes a size too small but befit-
ting the television or silver screen: someone else's notion of sex appeal. And
here I am, bright and early on a Saturday morning, dressed like a Mediterranean construction worker in boots and shorts, facing with delight the
frothy liquid on the table in front of me, learning to live at peace with
the hedonist in my soul.

"Thirsty work," proclaims René, lifting his glass. For a second I think
he must be referring to my inner reflections, and then I notice his attention is directed toward poor Michel, whose silhouette moves in and out of
view as he bends and rises in the process of digging and planting.

René begins to recount tales of his life as a truck driver before he
retired. He has an extraordinary assortment to tell of the years of German
occupation here on the coast, when he and his truck were used by the
Resistance to ferry food from place to place after curfew, so no French
families went without. He paints a tantalizing picture of "man and his

trusty steed"—in this case his truck—of rations redirected, *une petite escro-querie* here and *une petite escroquerie* there. He must have been hard at work on the trail of Robin Hood.

Escroquerie. I love this word. Although it is not specifically a Provençal noun, it does seem to sum up so much of the way of life here. *Une escro-querie* is a swindle . . .

My attention returns to our sanguine-complexioned olive man. He is now describing to me in detail, using his hands for dramatic effect, how to skin and eat a hedgehog. The cooking is not complicated, he assures me. Is he thinking I might rush to the butchers and give this a go?

Boil it first in a bouillon, then slit it open down the middle of its soft side—its belly side—"as though cutting open a cushion," and peel the skin off the same way you would a diving suit!

"What about its quills?"

"Bah, they fall away as easily as picking out cotton stitching once the animal has been boiled."

I cannot picture adding this recipe to the cookbook, but I refrain from saying so. Another staple food here during the Second World War, again during the occupation, was the guinea pig. According to René, guinea pigs, *cochons d'inde*, are an excellent source of fat. This was an important factor, because fat was always in short supply, and it made the meat edible, too. Any animal that has plenty of fat on it makes good eating, he explains. I am beginning to think I prefer the rigors of the actress's diet!

He reaches for another bottle of the blond beer, tops up his glass and embarks on his descriptions of the occupation of the grand hotels and *maisons particulières* along the coast, of shells exploding, of the *Maquis* preparing for the liberation. Here he interrupts himself: "Do you know why the Resistance or underground forces were called *Maquis?*" he asks, but does not wait for my response. "Because that is the name of the brush or scrubland that grows all along these Mediterranean and Corsican coast-lines—to take to the bush, to go underground. And so they were named *le Maquis.* They were very active here in Provence, and without them it is unlikely that the Allied invasion of '44 would have proved such a success." I had known this, but I feign surprise and René shrugs that Provençal shrug. He genuinely delights in telling tales, and I seem to be his perfect audience. He goes on, swiftly describing nights spent in the shelters—not all misery, according to him, which leads him quite naturally to the wartime romancing of a nightclub singer in Marseille.

"*Diable,* she had great legs!" He grins and begins a saucy observation about his height and the length of her legs, seems to think better of it, glances at me in an impish way, blushes and deflects. Now he is describing the courting of a local girl, and paints pictures of their lovemaking on the beaches while guns were firing all around them. She was three years his senior and, in those days, was deemed a daring and romantic choice. Later, she became his wife and is housebound now.

Michel is ascending the drive with the wheelbarrow. He waves.

René turns his attention to more pressing matters: plants and *l'entretien* of the *oliviers.* The pruning and maintenance of all plants and the olive trees in particular clearly ignites his passion as readily as his reminiscenes of the good old days. While I listen and watch, I perceive in his piercingly blue eyes the joy of a life richly lived.

"Quite a lady's man, eh, René?" I tease.

"Ah, yes, I'm very lucky," he mutters, gazing out across the view, sipping his beer. "You don't know the half of it."

WHEN MICHEL IS READY, we set off on the first trip of what is to be our pre-harvest *petit pèlerinage,* our olive pilgrimage. This morning we are driving inland, winding up and around the leafy corkscrew lanes, gazing back onto spectacular coastal scenery: sweeping bays, a lone helicopter traversing an electric-blue sky, forests of sailboats like miniature flags waving back at us from the glassy expanses of the Med. We are climbing to a cooler altitude, a remoter province, a rural world where little traffic passes save for a few trucks and grunting soil-beaten tractors. Everywhere, with the exception of the olive and the cypress, the trees are turning striking tones of amber and ruby red. There is a remarkable stillness in the air. Twenty minutes inland, and we might have turned back the clock a half a century.

This particular olive farm is approached along a well-hidden track, a bumpy, rutted trail better suited to tractors than René's diesel-powered Renault. The gate is well worn, askew and held fast with with a rusted padlock and chain. Inside the grounds there is a long straight drive climbing a steep stony path, flanked by terraced groves on either side. This leads directly to the farmhouse, set, rather like ours, halfway up the hillside.

The salmon-pink house, with its fading grass-green shutters, is an ancient *bastide* all but forgotten in this deep countryside. Situated south of a rocky mass of land known as the Pre-Alpes of Castellane, it looks out in sunlit seclusion across the valley toward a hilltop village named Gourdon.

Its edifice is cracked and aging. The Parisian proprietor, now well into his eighties, visits the farm for only one month during the year, in the height of summer. For the other eleven months, the place is locked up and unused. No one except René comes near it, which saddens me, recalling how neglected Appassionata had been when we first found her. To the left of the farmhouse are the stables. These have been converted into a bathroom—there is another in the main house—so that the old gentleman can shave in peace and not be pestered by his grandchildren first thing in the morning. A vine laden with pendulous green grapes gives shade to a cracked concrete patio. The look of the place reminds me of one of those early Dubonnet commercials I used to see on television when I was tiny. I had never visited France in those days, but the pictures struck me as so gloriously foreign, so happy-go-lucky, so much the French idyll. Perhaps that's why I'm here!

This farm boasts one hundred and thirty trees, thirty of which are the originals and have grown on these terraces for somewhere in the region of two hundred and fifty to three hundred years. Their trunks are wrinkled and gnarled like old elephant skin. The younger trees, planted by our absent proprietor, are barely twenty-five years old but for the most part are fruiting well. They are of a different variety known as *tanche*. The ancients, with their thick tormented trunks, are of the variety known as *cailletier*, the variety we have inherited.

René picks off a drupe and hands it to me to examine. "The *cailletier* is renowned for the rich golden oil it produces as well as its superior quality. It is a tree *rustiqe* perfectly capable of sustaining long periods of drought, and in times gone by, its oil was sought after by the perfume houses, particularly those in Grasse, because that golden hue was judged a marvelous addition to any scent." Locally, it is known as the Nice olive and exists predominantly along this coastal strip. It grows taller than any other variety of olive tree yet produces the smallest fruit. Take a trip deeper into the hills of Provence, and you will discover shorter, stubbier varieties. This is a natural protection against the harsh *mistral* winds which blow fierce and unrelenting farther inland, at higher altitudes.

We trail from terrace to terrace, watching while René checks on the progress of his purpling fruit. Suddenly he stops, pulls a mottled leaf from one of the young zinc-gray trees and turns it over with a frown.

"*Paon,*" he says sombrely.

"*Paon?*" I repeat, surprised, looking about for exotic birds. The word means peacock.

He nods, then explains. The peacock was a domestic animal on many farms in this part of France. When the male struts and screeches and fans open its tail, the compelling blue and green plumage reveals a series of circular black spots. There is an olive tree malady, *Cyclocodium Oleaginum,* known in layman's terms as *oeil de paon,* eye of peacock, because its fungus scars the silvery green foliage with round black spots before jaundicing the leaves, which eventually drop from the branches. He hands us the leaf, and we both examine it. "Watch out for it on your trees."

Even to us amateurs, it is obvious that the leaf has turned a dusty yellow and is dappled with dark brown blotches. I am concerned for the welfare of the fruit, but he assures us that this particular ailment will not harm the olives at all. However, if ignored, the leaves will fall, denuding every branch. Within a year, he warns us soberly, the entire tree will be bald. And it spreads fast. It is highly contagious.

"After the harvest—it is too late for this season, I would risk poisoning the fruit—I will be obliged to treat every tree on every terrace here on this farm."

Naive on my part, of course, but I had not even considered the dangers of olive tree maladies, and I am rather horrified to learn from René that there are nine insect or fungus diseases for which we will need to keep a wary eye out. Some of these can be carried by the tools used to prune the trees. In such cases, the tools need to be disinfected after the pruning of each and every tree. He laughs when he sees my expression and assures me that such cases are rare here, more common in Algeria.

During the drive home, I remark on the number of hilltop villages in this part of southern France and learn from Michel that most are built on sites originally chosen by marauding Saracens as strategic lookout points best suited for the building of fortresses. Once these bloodthirsty invaders had been defeated and the region reclaimed, villages were constructed on the ruins of the defeated territories to protect the people against the return of their enemies or the arrival of future aggressors.

The Saracens—a collective name for Arabs, Moors, Berbers and Turks—have been painted by history as a thoroughly disreputable lot, invaders who did nothing for the region besides rape and pillage, but in fact made certain contributions to local learning and tradition. They taught the Provençal people much about natural medicines and how to utilize the bark of the cork oaks to make cork—where would the wine industry have been without it?—and to extract resin from the numerous regional pines. Their other significant addition to local culture was to

teach the native people how to play the tambourine—not that I can own
to having noticed a single sun-wrinkled Provençal roaming about the village streets or his *places des boules*, watched over by the silent shadows of
towering plane trees, happily tapping his tambourine.

Dropping back toward the sea, descending into a gentler clime, we
drive by squads of people mustering in the numerous country lanes and
hidden grasslands. They are sporting baskets and sticks and do not look as
though they are embarking on jolly weekend rambles; they seem intent on
some far more serious activity. And indeed they are.

"It's the *funghi* season," Michel reminds me. Ah yes, I remember the
group I confronted on our own hill the previous autumn and suggest to
Michel that it might be fun to try our hands at mushroom picking.

There is a village in Italy in the Apennines named Piteglio where, in
the late nineteenth century, the inhabitants used to gather during the
funghi season and collect three thousand pounds of mushrooms every day.
We are neither so actively committed nor in possession of a hill quite so
fecund. Nevertheless, on Sunday morning, a gentle, sunny late-October
day, we go mushroom picking. Clad in Wellingtons as protection against
the brambles and damp undergrowth, we pick our way up to the brow of
our hill, where blocks of sunlight cut sharp right angles through the lofty
trees. This is a delightful way of working up a thirst and an appetite for
lunch, I soon discover. I hear and then catch sight of a woodpecker and a
pair of whoopees. The earth is spongy underfoot and crackly from the
sinking layers of pine needles. The scent of humid pine hangs in the air as
we bend and forage. Fat cones, like sleeping Humpty Dumptys, turn and
roll in our wake. The mushrooms are everywhere, barely hidden, soft and
slippery, pushing up through the damp earth and pine needles. I have to
watch my step or I squash them, or the big brown snails I find hidden on
twigs and runkled leaves. Rich dark soil slides beneath my fingernails
as I scratch and scoop at its surface. I want to feel the silky mushroom
textures, but I am unsure about touching them. I am no expert and have

little idea which of the *funghi*, the *champignons*, are edible and which are poisonous, and Michel is barely better informed. But, we tramp the woods merrily, searching and gathering with vigor, storing our hoard in woven wooden baskets. Once back at the house, working at our long table in the garden, we sort them carefully into floppy heaps according to their shape, size and possible variety. We have done rather well, and I fear we may end up wasting them.

"No, if they are all edible," Michel says, "we'll cook some in vinegar to preserve as antipasto."

We place one example of each onto a tray, careful not to damage them, then hasten to the village. Our regular *pharmacie* is closed on Sunday mornings, so we visit another, where a thin, stooped pharmacist with greased flat hair peers at our pickings with disdain.

"I wouldn't touch any of them" is his pronouncement.

We are silenced by disappointment.

"Are you sure, none at all?"

With the tips of two tweezerlike fingers, his pinky curled in the air like an old maid sipping tea, he begins lifting one after another by their tufted or fleshy stems still thick with dried earth. He twizzles each one in turn, glares at it and then tutts.

"*Faux, faux,*" he accuses, damning each poor vegetable before dropping it as though it were excrement back onto the tray. "Eat them if you like, but I wouldn't."

Michel picks up a vaguely mottled ocher example and offers it for consideration. "I thought perhaps this might be *un lactaire, non?*"

"Perhaps it is, perhaps it isn't."

Michel turns the mushroom over to convince the pharmacist. Beneath its fleshy cap, its corrugated belly, the gills are undeniably reddish. He breaks the stalk in two. The flesh inside is also red.

"*Oui, peut-être ça c'est de la variété lactaire,*" this dry-spirited chemist concedes without enthusisam. "You might try that one but none of the others. They are *champignons vénéneux*. Even that one might be riddled with maggots." And with that he disappears, determined not to be moved to any height of joy.

"*Merci, Monsieur,*" we call after him with a twinkle.

We return home carrying our tray heavy with assorted poisons, to our table in the autumnal garden piled high with our seven stacks.

"I think he may have been a little damning of our efforts, but we better not risk it." Dear Michel, he patiently gathers up our morning's efforts and dumps the entire harvest into the dustbin. One dustbin full of decomposing, deadly mushrooms, and eight edible *lactaire*. Hardly competition for the Italian peasants in the village of Piteglio, but more than sufficient for our own consumption. Not even vaguely downhearted, we lunch sumptuously on our eight home-grown mushrooms, sliced into slivers and simmered lightly in olive oil seasoned with garlic, salt and pepper and chopped herbs from the garden, served with grated Parmesan and washed down with a bottle of red from Châteauneuf-du-Pape, all on the terrace in the autumn sunshine.

We learn later from our own pharmacist that the mushrooms we have eaten are known as *lactaire délicieux* or, in English, saffron milk-caps. "They grow beneath pine trees and are excellent."

We vouch for their delicious nutty flavor and confirm that we gathered them from the summit of our hill in the pine forest.

"The Russians preserve them in salt, you know." He shows us the chart he keeps on display for ignoramuses such as us, and we see at least one from those we threw in the dustbin. It is the large white variety known here as *faux mousseron* or, in English, fairy-ring mushroom. I am very taken with the notion that we have fairy rings of any sort on the land. On our way home, still in a mushroom mood, we stop off at the vegetable market and buy half a kilo of ceps to add to a risotto.

It is a perfect evening at the end of a tranquil, uneventful and too-short day, even though the clocks have gone back an hour. Already the sun is setting, and it is growing chilly. Lights on the hills are illuminated. Everywhere the comforting whiff of wood smoke trails the dusk. Michel is stoking the fire while, a terrace beneath him, I creep naked into the pool. A fig leaf turned saffron with the season falls from the tree and floats into the water to accompany me. The cold shocks my system, and my toes and fingers start to tingle. I splash and throw my body in unflinchingly, swimming fast and determinedly, growing accustomed to the icy temperature. I pound up and down, not daring to slow in case my flesh numbs. Then I leave the pool, heart pounding, flesh zinging, and run around the garden whooping and calling like an Indian on the warpath. The dogs are barking at me, and Michel runs out onto the terrace to see what is up. I am laughing lightheartedly.

"I think there must have been hallucinogens in the mushrooms," he calls and returns inside to more constructive chores.

A DELUGE OF RAIN descends. Tropical in its intensity, it shocks. Day after day, it sheets across the hills making it impossible to discern the line of horizon between sea and sky. The sky glowers blackly. The days are somber. Drops the size of dinner plates splash into the pool, which looks as though it may burst its banks and roll like Niagara onto the terraces.

We are confined to the house, to our books and projects. To wine and food, to each other. I am at work on my scripts again, reshaping them to include Michel's observations, but there are times when the labor goes slowly and I lose confidence and spend restless hours pressed against the long, steamy windows staring out at the clouds which have hidden the valley from sight. We are very short of money. I need to press on if we are to secure a contract to shoot next summer. The rain drips and sloshes, gushing and gurgling urgently from every pipe. Lightning strikes; the electricity goes dead. We run through the rain to the garage and switch the trip back on. It flicks on and then off again. We live by candlelight. Thunder rolls and roars. The dogs howl and whine, terrified. We drag them in by the fire to soothe and dry them. The rooms are pervaded with the smell of wet dog.

The baked land welcomes the weather. The plants suck it up greedily, but we are less grateful, for we are discovering cracks and fissures we didn't know existed. Under the French doors, the water sneaks in and settles in puddles on the tiles. I hasten to the bathroom to fetch towels. I hear dripping and running and splashing everywhere, a cacophony of water music. Back and forth I go, armed with bowls and plastic pails to plug the invasive percussion. Fortunately, Di Fazio's roof is holding. At every minute, I expect the whole thing to come crashing down on top of us, but this is an ancient house built of sterner stuff. It may shift and leak and groan like an old man sleeping, but it will never fall down.

Eventually, the rain stops. The sky clears instantly and returns to its crisp laundered blue. It smiles seductively as though the torrents never happened. The sun bursts brightly forth, the days grow warm again and my mood lifts.

The wise men of the olive world say that, as with the grape, the sun of September determines the quality of the fruit, but here is the difference: rain in October and early November is essential to give the drupe that final, essential burst of growth. Unlike most northern-hemisphere produce, the olive is not harvested in the autumn. It still has another six weeks' to two months' growth, and a nicely plumped olive, with its pulp rich in minerals and vitamins, produces a greater quantity of quality oil.

But this year, nature's waterwork has overreached itself.

We stalk the terraces, taking note of the damage and the phenomenal growth that has taken place in the space of a week. Fascinated by the light and the luxuriance of the vegetation, I seek out the scents and sounds of a rain-washed world like a dog trained for truffle hunting. The orange trees, dead as mummies when we bought the house and which we have watched creeping back to life throughout the summer months, are now sharp, five feet tall, brilliant green spears of life. And, what is more miraculous to me, they are laden with round green balls. Minuscule oranges.

Such renascence hardly seems possible. I close my eyes. Like a squirrel preparing for harsh days, I store the fact that rebirth is a resource of life. Some creeping shadow warns me that I will need to keep it in mind.

A few feet to the left of the oranges, among the tufted grass at the root of the prehistoric olive trunks, I detect puddles of purple and green, tiny hard pellets. I pick one up to examine it and identify it as unripened olive fruit which the force of the rain has driven from the branches. I call to Michel, who is bent on his haunches to photograph a harvest of bulbs which have metamorphosed into dwarf-size narcissi overnight.

"We ought to net the trees before we lose the crop," he suggests.

I try to reach René, but he is not home. His wife promises to "*faire le commission*," which means that she will tell him we called. He does not ring back, not today or the next. We make a tour of the sodden springy earth around the roots of the trees again and agree that the ratio of fruit on the ground to fruit on the branches is shifting in balance. Whether the rain started the downward flow, the olives have been attacked by a fly or another of the nine maladies René mentioned that we know nothing about, or they have simply ripened too early, our inexperience cannot guide us, but we decide that the grounds must be netted.

I am confident we can manage this part of the operation on our own and suggest to Michel that the *Coopérative Agricole* might be the very place to guide us with our needs. He agrees and waves me off in the Renault, which is becoming a greater health hazard every day, to purchase netting while he reads through my latest pages of work. Naturally, the purchase is not as straightforward as I had hoped.

The chief gardener at the cooperative, a ruddy-cheeked, bespectacled young man, is sent out to deal with me, the foreigner attempting to go native. His patience for such an animal clearly ran out seasons ago.

"*Oui?*"

"I would like to buy netting, please, for our olive trees."

"Which color?"

Color!

Price, quality, even dimensions, I was vaguely prepared for, but not color. The French bourgeois obsession for matching and designing every item of house and gardenware cannot, surely, have stretched to the color of olive grove nets, can it?

"Does it matter?" I ask sheepishly, certain that my response is only going to confirm his already formed opinion that I am a city-bred ninny wasting his precious time. He sighs theatrically and stomps off. I hesitantly stay where I am until he spins around and orders me to follow him, which, obediently, I do. We arrive in front of a massive roll of bright red netting spooled onto an iron bar operated by a rusting handle which looks as though it has been plucked from a nineteenth-century laundry wringer.

"*Rouge,*" he says.

I could not disagree.

"Is this the one you want?"

"*Oui, peut-être.*" I am doing my best.

"*Deux francs vingt,*" he tells me, as though, for someone as ignorant as myself, cost would be the deciding factor. I am taken aback by the price, which strikes me as extremely reasonable at approximately twenty-two pence.

"A meter?" I feel I should confirm the good news.

"*Par six, le longeur.*"

By six in length. We are getting somewhere. Sounds good, I tell him. He looks disappointed and vaguely impatient with me and proceeds to tug at the red netting with his fingers until a small strip of it begins to split.

"*Eh, voilà!*"

I assume he has made this little test to prove to me that the net is not too difficult to cut, but no.

"You see, if you had decided upon the green . . ."

"Ah, the green?"

"Two francs ninety."

Tucked away at the back of an enormous hangar area, protected by corrugated roofing, is the green. Similarly rolled, marginally longer, but otherwise identical to my eye. He strides toward it, unfurls a few feet and begins tugging. Nothing happens.

"*Costaud*," I confirm with the nod of a sage who knows what she is talking about. It is tougher, more resilient. It won't rip when, by mistake, someone—me—treads all over it. I understand, and he is pleased with me. At least I think he is, because he grunts and begins to unroll a length of many meters in readiness for the cut.

"How many meters would you like?"

I smile, attempting charm. "Well, I'm not exactly sure."

The netting is dropped to the ground. A fellow gardener from somewhere far off calls, "Frédéric!"

"*J'arrive!*"

I feel my time is running out. I begin to talk fast. "We have sixty-four trees, so that would be . . ."

"What are the size, the reach of the branches? What age are the trees? Are they facing south? Have you measured the circumference of the root areas? What variety?"

To each question, I shake my head.

Poor Frédéric is growing exasperated, and I am mortified, knowing that I have played my part of the amateur olive farmer only too convincingly.

"I tell you what," he suggests with a warmth I had not counted on at this stage. "Buy a roll! *Pourquoi pas?* It is considerably cheaper, and that way you can measure the lengths at home and cut the nets accordingly."

It sounds like an excellent idea and lets us both off the hook. I agree wholeheartedly. He points me to the *caisse* situated inside in the shop and asks which car is mine. I signal the wreck parked near the gate and hurry off to pay. While in the shop, I pick up the odd extra purchases—oil for the chainsaw, blocks of olive oil soap as hefty as building bricks, thirty kilos of dog biscuits—and pull out my check book. The girl rings up the items and announces a figure which is a little short of five thousand francs.

"Five thou . . . ?"

It is then that I learn that I have just purchased a thousand meters of green netting. I dare not change my mind, so I smile wanly and write out the check, which will just about empty my account.

Outside, I find Frédéric and his colleague closing up the car, which looks as though it has sprouted wings. Not surprisingly, the roll could not be squeezed into the trunk; nor would it fit in the car's interior, so it has been wedged between the front passenger seat and the rear seat directly behind my driving place. In each case, it is protuding from the open windows a full eighteen inches or more.

"Isn't this a little dangerous?" I mutter. Frédéric is not interested; he is now serving someone else. I start up the engine, blue smoke billows forth and off I roar, trying not to take the garden center gates with me.

By the time I haul up the drive, I am exhausted and my nervous system has been shot to pieces. Half of Provence has hooted or yelled at me, and while I was being rudely overtaken on a roundabout by a very impatient gentleman, my precious netting actually dislodged his passenger-side driving mirror and he was about ready to run me into the gutter. Still, I am home more or less in one piece, and more importantly, we have our filets. Michel is laughing loudly, No Name and her three remaining puppies are scrambling around my ankles, barking and mewling enthusiastically—they can smell biscuits—but nothing we do, no matter how we shove or pull or tug, will shift the thousand-meter roll of netting.

Exhausted, we finally manage to contact René. When he arrives and sees the netting, he stops and stares at it in puzzled amazement. "But why didn't you buy the white?" he demands.

HOW DIFFICULT CAN it be to lay a length of netting around the foot of a tree? Is it feasible that this work could take three men and myself as many days? There is a skill to it that I would not have fathomed. First, the brush-cutting machines need to clear a circle of approximately six meters in every direction around the foot of each tree. This is to make sure the net doesn't get tangled in growing herbage and to facilitate the collection of the fallen olives later. After Michel and Quashia have completed this part of the process, the first day is almost over, and the evening air has an oniony scent to it. I love it; freshly mown grass never had quite that same piquancy. I assume it is the mixture of those extra ingredients: felled wild garlic, dandelion for mesclun, wild and unidentified Provençal herbs.

When the auspicious moment arrives for the laying of the first net, René explains that the ground needs to be covered to the farthest reach of every branch, wasting no meterage, cutting the netting as infrequently as possible and marking out the lengths immediately, by numbering both tree and net, so that next year the whole process is not a complete muddle while we *casse* our *têtes* trying to work out which length goes where. And while all this is going on, how best to keep the overexcited puppies from sitting on the netting or your feet every time you want to unroll a length or readjust the positioning of it? How much netting can three puppies chew and destroy while your back is turned for five minutes? The men allocate me the task of puppy patrol.

René's white netting is harder and less flexible but not necessarily more durable. And it doesn't blend into the colors of nature so naturally. I prefer the green, but I keep that opinion very close to my chest—that is, until the sun shines through the branches, which hang low like full skirts, and the nets and the silvery underside of the leaves begin to glint, and the entire effect resembles a cascading platinum sea. Green or white, nature creates magnificence.

Toward dusk on the third day, when the nets are in place, carefully symmetrical so that not one poor migrant olive can escape, we lay boulders and sticks at strategic points to hinder movement and to create a basin effect, a cradle, so that with any wind or heavy rain, the fruit will not roll away. I place a large stone at the border of a net and rise, worn out in a positive, healthy way. The men are at work one terrace beneath me, unrolling the last of the meters, shouting to one another, debating. René, Quashia and Michel and the netting, bathed in the golden light of evening: that late-autumn sunlight, honeyed and still, which is particular to this climate. The sight of the men on the land and meters of netting calls to mind preparations for a rural wedding feast, with veils and dresses and local produce. A feast, yes, for at the end of all this, the ritual of the harvesting and pressing, there will be a grand *fête*, a street party held in the villages, a Mediterranean thanksgiving to *l'arbre roi de Provence* or *l'arbre immortel.*

The work we are doing here is keeping faith with the past. It has been acted out for thousands of years, the labors of the land. The olive is *un arbre noble*, a noble tree. According to biblical legend, it survived the great deluge of Noah and his ark; the dove brought its branch as a sign of peace and that the rains had finally subsided. There is no other artisan who works with tools which are several hundred years old. Indeed, in the eyes of the *oléiculteur*, the older the better.

There is dignity and humility in this work, in the yielding to it, the power and force and, on occasion, the cruelty of nature as well as its phenomenal generosity. Its fruits should not be wasted. I read somewhere this morning, in one of the many French books on *horticulture pratique* that litter the wooden table in my still-undecorated *atelier*, yet another version of those bygone beginnings of olive farming: the cultivation of olive groves and the pressing of the fruit began in Iran long before it was thought of in

Greece. Old Testament territory. The Iranians took the olive to Greece. But it was the inhabitants of Phoenicia, an ancient territory which consisted of a narrow strip of coastal land bordering Syria, to the northwest of Palestine, who brought the trees to France some eight hundred years before Christ, approximately three hundred years before the Greeks arrived here. Or was it the Greeks those three centuries later, as most contend? The fact is that the history of the olive is so buried in the distant past that no one seems certain of its precise beginnings. What is certain is that we are here today, Arab and European, embarking on a method of farming—revered in both the Koran and the Bible—a gathering and pressing, almost as old as life itself.

CHAPTER TEN

PRESSING THE OLIVE

Finally, at long last, the moment has arrived. We are about to begin our very first harvest: *la cueillette des olives*. It is a critical period because the fruit has to be gathered at precisely the right moment and in the correct manner. The olives do not produce top-quality oil if picked too green. On the other hand, if the fruit is left on the trees too long and it overripens or grows wrinkled, then the drupes begin to oxidize, which gives a bitter, unpleasant taste to the oil.

This year, our first as olive farmers, we have a bumper crop. We will lose some of the fruit if it is not gathered and delivered to the *moulin* within forty-eight hours. René says we will need help, particularly in light of our lack of experience. We accept his counsel, and the following morning—the first occasion since we met him that he turns up on the day he said he would—he brings with him a motley collection of harvesters. Each of the five gatherers, one woman and four men, is presented to us, and each steps forward to give us his or her name and profession. They treat us deferentially, with what we suppose is the respect normally shown to proprietors, *oléiculteurs*, of a *grand domaine*. This puzzling behavior makes us both a little awkward. We have not come across this class barrier here before. We would prefer a rather less formal relationship, and I offer them bottles of water, for the day is warm and I want to lighten the mood.

"*Nous avons, nous avons tous,*" they assure us politely and retreat. They set about unloading their cars, parked on a flat grassy bank which skirts the base of the hill and the lowest of the terraces. It is a beautiful morning. The birds are chirping. There is heat in this late-November day. We leave them to their work and head off to begin our share of the picking at the top end of the land, promising to return later to see how their share of the *récolte* is progressing. I suspect René has divided us into two groups so that should we, with our city fingers and clumsy unskilled ways, damage the fruit—all too easily done—our basket loads need not be mixed in with those collected by the professionals and won't destroy the acid balance at the pressing.

What excites me is the thought of that first taste. There are over fifty different varieties of olives, and I have bought and tasted and cooked with an assortment of oils. Some were virgin, others were extra-virgin, while a few bottles were of a lesser quality or mixed varieties of olives. We will soon be trying a single-variety oil cold-pressed exclusively from our *cailletier* olives. Perhaps at some point in my life I have used oil pressed from this southern French variety, these rocky coastal hills, without being aware of it. Even if that were the case, they were not from here, not from this very hill. A modest geographical nuance, but it makes a world of difference to us. Part of the thrill lies in the expectation. Does this farm, our humble terraces, produce fruit that can be classed as first-class oil? We can only wait and see. Until then, there is hard work to be done.

The gathering is backbreaking. And time-consuming. And there is no way around it. René does not hold with wooden rakes. No, every olive is gathered from the trees by hand, stretching from ladders or climbing up in the branches and reaching out to pick each olive individually, for they do not grow in bunches.

"But I read that the wooden rakes are good. They're used on many of the well-known estates," I protest.

He shakes his head adamantly. "No. Whatever anyone says, the rakes can cause damage. Two or three olives growing close to one another, almost a cluster, the rake is bound to bruise at least one. No, we will climb the trees. You, Carol, can take a ladder."

So here I am, battling with branches flicking me in the face, wobbling and gripping for dear life. On top of which, when I have managed to clutch hold of an olive or two, I must take care not to squeeze it too hard or hold it too long in my sticky palms and overheat it. And the nets, both white and green, that encircle the base of the trees have to be considered for fear they may split. Worse, if the foot of the ladder gets caught up in the netting, I and the ladder will topple over, spilling two hours' work on to the ground. It is about now that I am beginning to wish we had bought a vineyard. At least cultivation and harvest are at ground level.

OUR FIRST VISIT TO the *moulin*. Heading off into the hills with René once more, we are planning to visit two mills, about twenty minutes apart. René wants us to choose where our fruit is to be pressed, particularly given my preference for all matters organic. Our first stop is at the mill he recommended. He brings the harvests from his other farms here, and like so many of these traditional land matters, it is family-run. Altogether, on his four farms, including ours, he is husbanding seven hundred and twenty trees, so, not surprisingly, he is a familiar and well-loved face at the mill. When we arrive, he takes us first to the shop that the family runs above the mill. Set on a cobbled hill, this is the tourist arm of their trade.

Once inside, everybody kisses and embraces and we are introduced as the *patrons* of the villa-farm in the hills overlooking the coast. During a brief tour of the merchandise—Provençal napkins, various jams and soaps and objects such as pepper and salt shakers carved out of olive wood—we observe the steady flow of men with children, or lone adolescents, bringing their farms' early season pickings. Their olives are delivered in large woven *panniers,* about the size of a modest laundry basket, resembling those which in bygone days were strapped to the sides of donkeys or packhorses. Other loads are delivered in plastic crates, and a few arrive in bulging sacks that look like outmoded coal bags—though these are discouraged now because they do not meet the latest European Union standards of hygiene. The fruit is placed on a whacking, great metal scale, where it is weighed and then stacked on the floor in a line alongside a chute which will shunt the gathered drupes down to the level of the mill.

While all this weighing and stacking is taking place, a cashier is filling in lilac tickets and handing them out. The tickets provide each farmer or gatherer of the fruit with a receipt which states the precise quantity of olives delivered. Later, after the *pression*, it will also confirm the quantity of oil pressed from those olives.

How the oil is measured is fascinating but somewhat difficult to grasp—convoluted, I'd say—and dates back to the days when farmers arrived with their olives in measures known as *une motte*. Literally translated, a *motte* is a mound. One measure, *une mesure*, is equal to twelve and a half kilos of olives, the cashier—one of only two staff at the mill who is not a member of the family—explains to us.

"Why twelve and a half kilos?" I ask ingenuously. It seems a curious figure for calculation. René then jumps in to explain that the containers used in the olden days carried precisely twelve and a half kilos. (I refrain from asking why.) Across the lip was a measuring stick. When the loaded olives were even with the measuring stick, it contained twelve and a half kilos. Twenty of these containers equal *une motte*.

"I see." Up to this point, I wasn't confused. Now it grows a bit foggy, at least for a pea brain such as mine, which is quietly trying to multiply twenty by twelve and a half!

Until today, I have always blithely assumed that so many kilos of pressed olives liquified into so many liters of oil. When I mention this, Michel nods his agreement but René and the staff of the *moulin* shake their heads gravely. "*Mais, non,*" they tell us. "The production of oil is valued and measured by weight."

What!

One liter of oil, we learn, weighs nine hundred grams, or nine tenths of a kilo.

Lord!

If the fruit is ripe and healthy and plump, therefore rich in oil, it is hoped that a measure (twelve and a half kilos) will achieve 2.7 kilos of oil which, divided by nine hundred, translates at approximately three liters of oil. In other words, after a phenomenally complicated calculation, the ideal is to produce fruit which will yield three liters of oil for every twelve and a half kilos of olives, or sixty liters for every "mound."

Phew! We are exhausted, my head is spinning and it is not yet half past eight in the morning. I am about to ask why the system is calculated in such a mind-bogglingly difficult way when Michel grabs me by the shirtsleeve and says, "While we're here, *chérie,* why don't we buy some of their *tapénade?*" Anything to stop me from further scrambling our brains.

To reach the level where the mill is operating, René ushers us back out of the shop onto the cobbled street, through another door to the left of the one we have just exited and down a rickety flight of narrow wooden stairs. I feel as if I am going backward in time. Added to which, the temperature is falling. At the mill level, it is almost arctic. Every exhalation is visible.

We *have* gone backward in time.

As we enter the mill, our senses are socked by the thumping and turning of a whole array of machines, and the air is so thick and heavy with the dense aroma of freshly pulped olive paste you feel you want to shove it off you, just like a blanket. At eight-thirty in the morning, it makes my head reel, as does the rough red wine handed to us to accompany thick wedges of locally baked bread topped with ham cured from a pig reared and slaughtered in the village. It is a peasant's breakfast offered to us by a wan girl of no more than fourteen, who is accompanied by her brother of about nine.

Once we have been fed, the children retreat politely to stand guard at the table groaning with the family produce. Silently, arms at their sides like small soldiers, they await the next batch of ravenous *oléiculteurs*. René is battling against the din to explain the mechanics of the machinery, but I am more fascinated by the children. They look like waifs, serious-faced with dark penetrating eyes that, though kindly, might have witnessed a thousand hard seasons. It seems incredible to me that our farm is situated somewhere equidistant between this world and the gaudy glitz and *escroquerie* of Cannes.

The noise down here is impossible. I cannot hear or understand a word that is being spoken. René talks on, lips moving. I have no idea what he is explaining. I turn to the miller, who says nothing. He has returned to his work. Both he and his assistant are wrapped in scarves knotted at the neck and substantial jackets, although they are moving continuously, shunting trays of mashed olive paste and enormous bottles filled with the freshly pressed green oil. All around me, machines are milling, thrumming, spewing out liquid or excreting dried paste. A fire is roaring behind a small glass window, no bigger than a portable television screen. It is fueled by dried olive waste. Each ancient machine feeds the next, it seems. They are interconnected as though it were some enormous Rube Goldberg invention which today, according to the miller—who beckons us over into a corner away from the racket—is taking four and a half kilos of olives to press one liter of virgin oil. Most of these early-season fruits are not quite ripe enough, he explains. The fruit arriving after Christmas, when it has had longer on the trees to plumpen and grow black, should be better and produce the optimum.

We are led through to a cave where labeled bottles glow with oil growing gold instead of green as the sediment settles. They await the return of their owners, who will cart them away and store them safely in cool, darkened depositories. This mill, I see, is rigorous about making certain that no grower's olives are mixed with another's if they are a single-estate press such as ours will be.

I am fascinated by how the remains are put to good purpose. Olive oil soap is made from the residue of the third or even fourth pressings, and the desiccated paste is burned in the fire which heats the water and operates as the central heating system, such as it is here. Ecologically speaking, the olive is an all-rounder. Nothing goes to waste. Every last drop of oil is wrung out of the fruit, and only in the making of *tapénade* is the pit extracted and thrown away.

Before we set off for the second mill, the longer-established of the two, everybody shakes hands enthusiastically. "Next time, Christophe will be here," we are assured. He is the *patron* and has "*parti pour faire la chasse.*" Gone hunting. There is much kissing and backslapping and promises to meet again soon. They enjoy the idea that foreigners take an interest in this most venerable of trades.

"*Beaucoup d'Americains visitent içi,*" we are told. Thumbs and fingers are rubbed together, heads nod gravely, all to express the sums of money handed over by the Americans in return for trinkets, souvenirs and glossy books detailing the history of the olive and Provençal life.

"And the English?" I ask hopefully.

As one, the family shakes their heads. I appear to have touched upon a sensitive and sorry subject. "*Mais, non,*" returns Madame in a conspiratorial tone. "*Les Anglais* have no interest in anything!"

THE SECOND *MOULIN* IS an altogether different affair. Situated in a field at the end of a deserted lane in the middle of nowhere, it was founded in 1706. It looks as though it originally must have been a peasant farm with an outbarn, which at some early stage was transformed into a mill and never decorated since. The crumbling outer walls of the edifice are of a washed pink which is popular in certain parts here but which I feel belongs more comfortably in Suffolk. First impression: there is little about this place aside from the surrounding countryside and mountainous backdrop, that is welcoming.

One step in the door and we are directly in the mill, a cavernous space, with a room temperature barely above above 40°F. It is sunless and gloomy. There is no shop here, no tourist attractions of any sort, which rather pleases me. As before, we are instantly knocked backward by that dense, palpable odor of crushed olives. Here, though, there is no offer of comforting slabs of bread and ham and red wine to douse our senses. There are no trimmings whatsoever. The place has one function: the cold-pressing of extra-virgin oil.

The pressing wheel and floor have been honed out of massive slabs of craggy stone rendered smooth by centuries of use. Somehow, the heavy stone adds to the keen wintry atmosphere. I exhale and watch my breath rise like smoke. Ahead of us are two farmers engaged in business with the lady miller, or the miller's wife, who appears to be discussing their accounts. René, because he has visited here only once before, is not quite sure who she is. We are all strangers, which suits me because it allows a sense of discovery.

René guides our attention toward the stone wheel that crushes the fruit. It is so imposing, almost monolithic, that I shiver at the thought of getting any body parts trapped beneath it. It is stained with what look like clumps of dark peat, but on closer inspection we see that, of course, it is coated with trapped olive paste. Passing along to another completely indescribable contraption, we find oil at its base, trickling at a snail's pace into a dustpan-like box made of olive wood. The arrival of the oil appears to be a discreet, low-key affair; none of the slosh and flow of the last establishment or the horrendous ear-splitting noise, but then, to be fair, the machines here have completed their last pressing for the day, even though it is only a little after half past ten.

Looking closely, with René drawing our attention here and there, we learn that this system requires more fruit for less yield. It takes approximately six kilos of fruit to produce a liter of oil here, even with the ripest and richest of drupes. René closes his eyes and goes through a swift mental calculation. If we use the other *moulin,* Appassionata can expect, on average—depending on the weather and the harvest—to press approximately two hundred and fifty liters of oil a year. Here we would net fewer than two hundred.

"Yes, but here it is cold-pressed, extra-virgin."

"The other, too," he assures us.

"In any case, two hundred liters is more than sufficient for our needs," I counter.

Michel quietly reminds me that our share would be, in the first instance, eighty-three or -four liters, while here, somewhere around sixty-five. The remainder is René's. I glance at René, who merely shrugs.

The miller woman, who wears her gray hair slicked back in a tight, uncompromising bun, boots, a full woollen skirt and velveteen shirt, is paying us no attention, engaged as she is with her clients. They are weighing *panniers* of violet olives and calculating figures: the cost of the pressing, no doubt. Perhaps for the first time, I am made acutely aware of this as a business, not a dream. Olive farming and oil pressing is a livelihood, and these people are close to the land, bearing its vagaries and hardships.

They cannot afford the romance that swims about in my head. I wander off to investigate further, and to be alone.

Beyond the mill, though still under the same roof, I discover a cave with storage spaces dug out of rock and cut with stone-shelved corners. It is windowless and dark. Two or three dozen glass jars cased in wicker are stored there. Each must be capable of holding fifteen or twenty liters of liquid.

"They are called *bonbonnes à goulot large*. In the olden days, the Romans stored their oil in tall clay jars which were originally turned or baked in Spain and then shipped to Italy. They were not dissimilar to the oval terra-cotta pots you keep in your garden and fill with flowers. These are a more modern version, if you can describe anything in here as modern." It is René. He and Michel are once again at my side.

Some of these thick-necked demijohns, the *bonbonnes,* are still empty, while others have already been filled with the deep green, freshly pressed oil, which from this distance and in this crepuscular light, resembles seawater or steeped seaweed juice. Judging by its color and the juice slipping heavily into the dustpan apparatus, the quality of the oil here is richer, more luscious and aromatic.

"I like this place better," I whisper to Michel, who laughs and replies, "*Mais, oui, chérie.* The question is which mill would better suit our needs. Not which would serve us as a film set!"

"I still prefer this one," I confirm calmly.

Outside, the morning is warming to a bright clear day, so clear that we can see the shrubby details on the surrounding hills and valleys and the snow caps on the high, distant alps. I close my eyes and inhale the fresh air, rich with the smell of pine resin. The heat of the sun against my eyelids is a comforting relief.

STROLLING BACK TO OUR car, we learn from René that there is an olive tree growing in Roquebrune which we might like to take a look at. There are several villages down here with that name, but the one he refers to is the rather glamorous Roquebrune-Cap-Martin situated, on the mountainous road between Monte Carlo and Italy. Michel knows the place. In fact, he has visited it on several occasions. Its marvelous restaurant, le Roquebrune, which has been owned and managed by the family of Mama Marinovich since its inception, has been a favorite of his for years. The village is also known for its medieval houses cut into the rocks. There, a few kilometers from Menton, the gateway to Italy, grows an olive tree believed to be a thousand years old. Who planted it? I ask. Does anyone know? Who would have looked upon it?

It is fifteen hundred years too young to be a souvenir left by the Greeks and almost a millennium too young to have been planted by the Romans during their marches north from the heart of their empire while constructing the Via Aurelia, the great highway stretching from Ventimiglia to Aix. The Romans, with Agrippa as their consul, were building roads and tracing out this land of Provincia, creating cadastral surveys and scientific mappings before the tree was ever in existence. Even Charlemagne, crowned emperor of the West in 800 A.D., preceded it, as did the Saracens, who were looting and sacking the littoral even while Charlemagne and his children were dividing up the country for their heirs.

Might it have been a peace offering to the counts of Provence from Rome?

A thousand years after the birth of Christ, somewhere around the date the tree was planted, Provence was being returned to Rome and inaugurated as part of the Holy Roman Empire. The Saracens, having created havoc and terror for a hundred years, had been conquered and driven out, and Provence, though back under the ruling thumb of Rome, was enjoying a certain independence, a bit of peace and quiet after so many centuries of strife. Alas, it was not to last. Within a century or two, the counts of Provence ceded the province to the counts of Toulouse and they to the counts of Barcelona and so the chain goes on, right up to the liberation of

Provence by the Allies from the Germans in August 1944, which our friend, René, standing beside us now, bore witness to.

Still, this noble tree is believed to be one of the oldest in the world.

By what stroke of fortune has that one single specimen survived? Michel suggests we make a detour, a slightly elongated one, approximately one hundred and ten kilometers round-trip, and pay homage to this most holy of trees. This I agree to wholeheartedly. René, who does not want to come with us, bids us *bon appétit* and leaves us to it.

Less than an hour later, our car is swooping and turning like a bird in flight along the mountain road. It is a giddy, spectacular altitude. The endless hairpin bends on this infamous descent, then ascent, from La Turbie, with its magnificent Roman ruins, make you catch your breath when you look down to sea level and pray to God your brakes won't fail. There's precious little chance to enjoy the view if you are driving. Michel is at the wheel. He drives fast, but with great skill, and I am leaning out the window, unafraid, hair flying in the wind and whipping my face, eyes watering, thrilled by the panorama all around me, following the sweep of hundreds of meters of rocky face which lead dramatically to the Med.

Somewhere near here, Princess Grace of Monaco lost her life when her sports car went over the cliffside. She was killed instantly. From where I am now, you see why. The memory of that accident sobers me for an instant, and I crawl back into my seat and gaze at the rock faces towering to the left of us.

It's then that I spot the village high above us, rising out of the stone toward a linen-blue sky. It resembles a picture from a book of fairy tales illustrated by Arthur Rackham; even more so when I realize that, perched atop its pinnacle, is a castle with a tower.

We park the car at the foot of the village in what was the ancient castle's barbican and hike the winding lane to the *vieux village*. Much to our dismay, because we are starving, every single restaurant is closed. This is not about being closed for lunch. It is that time of year, *la fermerture annuelle*, November 15 to December 15, when so many buinesses shut up shop in preparation for the upcoming festivities; Christmas and the New Year are a busy season on the Côte d'Azur. But we are not too disappointed, even if our stomachs are rumbling. Our noontime is flooded with warm winter sunshine.

We stride and puff and arrive at a perfectly empty place, and what strikes me instantly is that there is not a soul about, though there is no sense of this as a ghost town. In the center of this pleasingly airy square is an olive tree, fenced and surrounded by benches. It is unquestionably an aged specimen and well preserved, but I had expected something more spectacular. The girth of its trunk is probably three meters which is barely more than our own trees. I stroll to the cliff's edge and look out across the rippling water, lambent in the sunlight, toward Cap Martin and, in the other direction, to the kingdom of Monaco with its curiously out-of-place skyscrapers. Michel comes up behind me and wraps his arms around me.

"I've had a good look. I don't think that's the tree we're after," he says. "Let's investigate."

We make our way through the *vieux village* up a hill, down a winding stairwell—everywhere tiled and cobbled and polished with the gleaming shine of a proud housewife's stoop—passing through Place Ernest Vincent with its obsolete prison until we spot a sign for the *olivier millénaire*.

"Look," I cry.

Triumphantly, with the air of adventurers whose navigations are confirmed on track, we begin to descend. A profusion of hillside trees fluffy with green leaves similar to the willow—a variety of tamarisk, if I am not mistaken—overhang the pathway. We are plunging down a steep path. In former days a donkey trail, no doubt, used to transport victuals from the fields at sea level up to the homes carved out of the rocks. We are walking in the footsteps traced by a billion and more travelers, by soldiers, other lovers, by farmers and farmhands, to pay homage to a tree. And lo and behold, two hundred or so meters farther along, there it is, growing out of a wall on the terraced cliffside. This elephantine miracle is not fenced in. It is not on display. It is simply there. Being. Its roots, like a banyan tree's, sprawl everywhere. Branches, roots, reaching out like an octopus, stretching, bursting its banks with the sheer determination to live, to survive. Its force is taking earth and stone with it.

Michel and I stand side by side, silenced, gazing in awe at this monumental symbol of creation. Then we spin around, seaward, to take in the view unfolding before us; flocks of starlings swoop and tack against a vigorous blue sky. Even at this precipitous height, we can hear the gentle lap of the water washing the coastal rocks and beaches so far beneath us. We incline our heads and gaze down upon the coastline, eyes eastward to the cap of St. Martin, where Yeats once spent a holiday, Queen Victoria was a regular visitor and the architect Le Corbusier drowned.

Everywhere is warm and still and calm; *calme* in the French sense, meaning untroubled and at peace. Without a word, we reach for each other, and I feel the warmth of the sun on Michel's skin.

"Je t'aime."

Rarely have I felt so in harmony with life, so humbled by its magnificence. I pace out the distance between the farthest visible reaches of the trunk extensions and measure fifteen meters. Here we are, some nine hundred feet above sea level, in the presence of a growing organism that has stood sentry over this landscape for ten centuries. I can comprehend the millennia of reverence given to the olive tree, to its wisdom and unmatched nobility.

For a heartbeat, all seems clear. The world is pure, and the miracle of life washes through me.

We return to the village, deciding to continue our ascent to the castle, moving closer to the sun, passing open windows which overlook one of the most breathtaking coastal views I have ever laid eyes on. I pause and catch snippets of language, barely audible radios transmitting in both French and Italian. We are on the border of both cultures, yet so much about this village was born of times when France and Italy were not divided as they are today.

The climb is winding, the lanes cobbled and tiled and pristine. From the keep, the views are yet again stupendous. Several hang gliders are drifting on slipstreams and silence out over the water. What a spot for hang gliding; to take off from here like a bird!

We walk on. I read aloud from a booklet given to us by the friendly lady at the ticket booth that we are about to discover the oldest castle in France, the sole example of the Carolingian style. It was built by a count from Ventimiglia, Conrad I, to keep those dratted Saracens at bay. Later, it was remodeled by the Grimaldi family, who, of course, still reigns over Monte Carlo.

What a coup for one small village to be in possession of the oldest castle in France and a tree claimed to be the oldest living olive in the world!

The leaflet also informs us that the inhabitants of Roquebrune believe that the creation of the world is a "thought from God," and that while he was creating this village, his mind was particularly well disposed to man. For that reason, they value their good fortune and make it their business to honor their environment. Too right! With such a philosophy, they deserve their daily sightings of this seascape and their miraculous olive tree.

RENÉ TELEPHONES TO inform us that the *moulin* of my choice is to be closed down. Founded close to three hundred years ago, the very winter we choose to take our custom there, it is closing!

"But how can that be?" I cry.

"Because it does not meet the European Union health standards."

His advice is that we take our olives to the mill he frequents, which is what we do. Frankly, aside from driving around the countryside in search of another mill, we have little choice. Half a dozen crates of olives are sitting in the dark at the back of our garage, waiting to be pressed. If we delay, they will oxidize. Though stung by an initial bout of mistrust and suspicion, I have no reason to be disappointed. The proprietor—the chap we did not meet the first time around—is a splendid fellow with cheeks as red as his checkered shirts and a paunch which flops over his sinking jeans. He welcomes us extravagantly, takes care of us admirably. And I warm to him all over again when that long-awaited first trickle of oil from our own pressed olives drizzles from the onyx tap.

"*Venez vite, mes amis!*" he bellows. "*Venez vite!*"

By now, it is spluttering and gushing green-gold gallons in fits and starts.

Nervously, excitedly, we pick our way across the mill floor—skidding and skating because the surface is an ice rink from the dregs of a season's oil and paste—to taste, please God, our ambrosial liquid. It is a tense moment.

Michel, *Monsieur le Propriétaire*, known to us now as Christophe, and I lean in close over one single dessert spoon and inhale its aroma.

Will we like it? Will we be satisfied? We sip in turns. I go first. Six eyes meet apprehensively, but there is not a shadow of doubt. The texture is velvet-smooth with a flavor of lightly peppered lemons.

"Oh God, it's delicious!" I croon.

Oh, we are mightily proud. Christophe, after filling a wooden spoon with another precious few drops, dunks a chunk of the local rough bread into the cloudy liquid and chews pensively. Save for the thundersome turning and clunking of machines, there is a gripping silence. His *fils*, the young miller we met the first time around, watches on while a motley clutter of farmers who are awaiting the results of their own *pression* flock around us eagerly. How they love these *petit* dramas. And then, in a thick Provençal accent, Christophe declares our produce "*Beurre du soleil.*" Butter of the sun, he cries loudly, followed by the all-important quality distinction, "*Extra!*"

Everybody cheers. There is much shaking of hands, slapping of backs, kissing and hugging and, of course, pouring of wine while Michel and I, grinning from ear to ear with the pride and happiness of a birth, are also doing our damnedest not to fall about laughing.

OUTSIDE, AT OUR TABLE in the garden, lashings of our very own burnished oil are being decanted by Vanessa and Michel from the five-liter plastic containers supplied by Christophe into numerous elegant or uniquely shaped wine bottles. All year we have been merrily quaffing their contents, cleaning them, collecting them and storing them away, for this most auspicious day. Christmas is upon us once more, and this one is to be celebrated. Clarisse is designing the delicate, exquisite labels, and while the others pour, we are spending our hours in front of a roaring fire ticketing the full bottles and dating them before Vanessa's friend Jerôme carts them off and stows them away in the cool of the summer kitchen downstairs. Over the coming weeks, the olive fruit sediment will settle and the clear oil will become a glorious primrose gold.

Mellifluous music, carols broadcast live from Notre-Dame Cathedral in Paris, is playing on the radio. A blue fir tree perfumes our home with a spicy happiness. Michel purchased it from a bankrupt antique dealer in the square opposite the old port in Cannes where, aside from this festive season, retired gentlemen with dubious histories pass their afternoons playing boules. To honor this, our very first harvest, he has decorated it entirely in swathes of golden trimmings and glass.

The girls are spending their holidays with us this year, and along with them has arrived Jerôme, who is eighteen and disturbingly gorgeous. Twice I have invited him to come and help me in the kitchen, and on both occasions Vanessa has lovingly whispered in my ear, "Please, *chère* Carol, resist flirting with my friend." In a day or two, Anni and Robert, Michel's parents, will arrive, followed by my mother for St. Sylvestre, New Year's Eve. My father and sister, both being in the entertainment business, are employed and staying in England. Still, Appassionata is stocked for a full house, and the holidays are set to be a joyous affair. Our turkey, for now we are in possession of an oven which stands alone in our empty, still-to-be-constructed kitchen, is being lubricated with oil from our own reserve. It is a moving and significant moment which we honor appropriately with flutes of champagne. To accompany our *apéritif,* as a prelunch appetizer, I prepare bruschetta, toasting thick slices of six-grain bread which I top with sliced tomatoes straight from my thriving vines and season with dried herbs and salt and then grill. While the toasts are still warm, I decorate them with strips of fresh basil leaves picked from our herb garden and generously oil them as a topping—Appassionata oil, naturally—adding only black pepper.

We gather at the table in the garden and eat in the end-of-year sunshine, chattering noisily in French—French language, French manners; we are knitting together as a French family—knowing that when the winter sun has begun to sink behind the cypress tops, slipping out of sight beyond the mountains, we can curl up indoors with books and music and doze in front of the fire. While the others clear the table and stack the washing, I disappear to my den for a few hours, to print out my scripts for Michel to take back to Paris after Christmas. He has clients waiting to read them. After, I intend to close the door on my work and forget about it for a few days. I need to rest, relax and partake of the holiday season with our loved ones.

As evening falls, the wintry sunset patterns the sky a pale, streaky rose. My work is done. I run my fingers across the stacks of freshly printed pages standing on my table in thirteen neat piles and turn to gaze out of the window. The Mediterranean coast is growing dark and still. I cannot see the fortress and dungeons where the Man in the Iron Mask was imprisoned, cannot even detect the silhouettes of the islands, but the images live on in my memory and have fed my story; thirteen episodes, partially set on that isle of Ste. Marguerite.

Beyond this private space, I hear the ripple of laughter. I smell that woody smokiness of crackling logs burning briskly. The others await me. Michel and his teenage girls, so staggeringly grown up, so suddenly filled with a confidence I am sure I have never known, and Jerôme, the first of what no doubt will be a long procession of handsome young visitors over the summers and winters to come. Summers to come. . . .

I don't go to join them, not directly. I linger by the window, aware of my reflection, of me looking back at myself. I am in pensive mood, assessing what has been achieved. That's often the way after a long work stint.

After so many years of wandering, I have found my base. We have our shabby home. We have produce, too—oil—and found good men to help us. We have a story to sell; with luck, it will be our way forward. With luck, it will settle our affairs with Madame B. Maintaining the house, its upkeep, is a struggle, but we are just about managing. It has been a productive year, and I am grateful for it. Still, something is nagging at me, tugging at my floating balloon. Can life really turn out this well? Can I really be this happy? What if it should all fall apart? I have opened myself up now. Yielded to love. Trusted someone. The loss would be twice as devastating.

Steeped in these dark evening musings, I am not immediately aware of the diesel van hiking the drive. I stare at it almost without seeing it and then move through to the *salon*, where the others are gathered.

Michel jumps to his feet. "*Jerôme, s'il te plaît.*"

"Who's that?" I ask no one in particular. "Are we expecting somebody?"

The men hurry from the house while the girls, basking on cushions, pay me no attention. I stare at their concentration. Clarisse is sketching; Vanessa, ears plugged to her Walkman, is learning Russian from a tape; Whisky, the last of the puppies and no longer a puppy, is snuggled in her lap, and I hear several male voices shouting.

"Do we know what's happening?" I ask again. Neither girl responds. Curious and bewildered by their lack of interest, I stride back to my *atelier,* to the window which overlooks the driveway, to find out what is happening. Quashia has arrived. He is accompanied by a faithful quartet of Arab colleagues who are all hovering by the rear doors of the van. I frown, puzzled. Michel is climbing into the van while he and Quashia converse. Two of the Arabs are then instructed to cross the driveway and collect a wooden pallet, which they place at the foot of the rear doors on the bitumened ground. Something is being delivered, that is clear, but what?

"Do either of you girls know what this is all about?" I shout.

They do not seem to have heard me. I am about to get cross when from out of the van comes a curious-looking plant, sitting in a saucer-shaped terra-cotta pot the size of an early television satellite dish. The plant must be exceptionally heavy, because it is lowered painstakingly onto the work pallet. Then slowly, awkwardly, Jerôme and the Arabs hump it along the walkway beside the pool and mount the outside staircase to our open front door, which is where I am now eagerly awaiting them.

"What in heaven's name . . . ?"

"Where shall we put it?" begs Michel.

I turn, swamped in indecision. Half the room is already taken up by the Christmas tree. There are cushions everywhere. Presents, shoes, sweaters, general holiday detritus have all spread across the room. Michel does not wait for me to respond. The men are sweating and staggering.

"There," he commands, and the plant is delivered into the house, lifted ever so carefully from the pallet and placed on the tiled floor. Quashia and the men bid us *bonsoir,* shake hands and retreat. Michel sees them out and returns to survey his gift. Or rather mine, for clearly I am the recipient: the only one who has not been cognizant of the arrival of this wonder.

"Happy Christmas, *chérie,*" he whispers and kisses me. "It's not as ancient as the *olivier millénaire,* but as close as I could find."

I am speechless, gazing at this extraordinary gift which stands six feet tall, has a trunk like a sculpted rhino's leg and, according to its label, is South American and a hundred and fifty years old. What most puzzles me is that this spectacular exotic is growing in a saucer-deep pot. Doesn't it have roots?

All eyes are upon me, waiting, girls grinning, as I turn to my husband and kiss him. "*Merci*," I whisper, for I can barely speak, so overwhelmed am I by the sheer craziness of this man's love. All niggling fears evaporate. What am I worrying about? It has been a wonderful year.

CHAPTER ELEVEN

DARK DAYS

After the holidays, sometime around late January (the month Matisse described as possessing a "rich and silvered light essential to the spirit of the artist"), when every last straggly olive has been culled from the trees, pruning will begin. Alas, Michel and I cannot stay for it. Quashia, who took the train to Marseille a few days ago, bound for the boat which, by now, will have transported him home to the town of Constantin in northern Algeria—where he is spending the remainder of the season of Ramadan with his wife, seven sons, one daughter and sixteen grand-children—will return to look after No Name and caretake for us. Vanessa and Jerôme have agreed to stay on a day or two to await his return. She is taking Whisky with her when she leaves. Michel and I have work to do. For this year, our very first as olive farmers, our contribution is sadly at an end. Alas, we will even be absent from the celebrations of the *fête des oliviers* held on the last Saturday in January, in the streets of many of the inland Provençal villages. Strangers and natives alike are all invited to tastings from the various mills and single-estate oils or simply to celebrate. The one near to us is to be held in the streets of the village of Vallauris, and we understand from René that our own mill is represented. As is their tradition, Christophe and his three sons will deck themselves out in local Provençal costumes and offer *dégustations* of the various oils they have produced. They even display a small working model of the mill, which actually presses olives! We are sorry to miss what promises to be a socially fascinating event, but work calls, and Quashia and René are more than equipped to attack the rigorous buiness of pruning the trees.

As for Michel and me, we are returning to our separate lives of London and Paris, back to our bachelor-style existences, meeting when and where we can, grabbing a day or a weekend here or there, burying ourselves and our desire for each other in professional energies. Returning to our real lives—but can that other, the cut and thrust of the metropolis, still be thought of as real life? It is confusing. I have often heard friends who hailed from various far-flung corners of the globe and ended up in London complain that they don't know where they belong. I am beginning to understand that displacement, although I have been a traveler all my adult life. But now I have put down roots. My heart is in France. Here I wake in the mornings, thinking: I am where I want to be. Here I swim, garden, spend hours at the outdoor markets shopping for vegetables and fresh fish, natter with the local stallholders about the quality of this or that home-grown produce, marvel over the range and choice on display and then bury myself away in my studio, writing stories.

My work and history remain in England. Back there I stare out of rehearsal-room windows, dreaming of what? Shrubs and herbs, the possibility of rearing goats and vines, the man I love so passionately. At the end of the day, I race to the local store, grab some prewashed salads, negotiating a cart around row upon row of shelves and neon lighting, then gratefully close the door of my little flat, which these days feels as impermanent as a hotel, shutting out the fractious bustle of city life. I prepare a solitary meal, unless I have managed to catch up with a frantically busy friend or two not seen for months, and when I set off again for work, some kind lady plasters my face in makeup while I fret about my figure and ever-increasing wrinkles and the problems of an actress who is fast saying *au revoir* to forty.

I am more than fortunate to have both the gregarious life of an actress and the solitary days of a writer, but from time to time, it is confusing and sometimes unsettling. And there is no doubt that, because I am in England less and less, the circles and worlds I have inhabited are slowly plugging up the spaces which I had staked out as mine. Friends call less regularly, unless they happen to be passing through the south of France and decide to drop by for a few days. My agent calls less frequently—actresses who are on the spot are offered the roles I might have played had I been there. Sometimes I feel people think I have emigrated to the moon!

When I mention my dilemma to Michel, he says, "I don't know why you feel you have to choose. Why can't you encompass the whole? A woman who has a multilayered existence." And perhaps it really is that simple. It's I who complicates it!

IT IS VALENTINE'S DAY. Michel is attending a television festival in Monte Carlo, which means that he can spend a week at the farm. I am on location in Wales and cannot get away. I send a dozen red roses and receive a dozen from him. And then the telephone rings in my hotel room. I catch the background bustle of festival activity, the chink of *apéritif* glasses issuing from the hotel bar, and I hear excitement in Michel's voice. I miss him so badly it hurts.

"The English are in!" he says. For a moment I am confused. And then it dawns on me. My thirteen-part series will need several partners, but, given that it is the story of a thirteen-year-old English girl, it would be almost impossible to film without an English network on board. Monte

Carlo was to be Michel's first attempt to finance the production. I am staggered.

"Any chance that you could fly down here for a couple of days and meet up with him?"

Well, I am not filming on the weekend. I could drive to London and take the plane . . . yes!

Saturday lunch at Appassionata is the date. The English television executive, always delighted to have an excuse to linger in the south of France an extra day or two, to wriggle out of the mind-grinding business of buying and flogging programs, is more than happy to lunch with us at our home.

February is traditionally a wet month on the Côte d'Azur. Just in case, I prepare lunch at the table inside. From the dining room, through tall French windows which command a view over the front terraces across to the sea and distant horizon, I gaze down upon the splendidly pruned olive trees. They are a magnificent spectacle. With their height lopped and their remaining branches hanging low and wide, tumbling almost to ground level, they remind me of whirling dervishes.

One of the great joys of Appassionata is its ability to surprise; the ever-evolving, complex shift and balance of the surrounding nature. Determined by time of day, season and the weather, the hills, mountains, forests and the sweep of the watery bay transform themselves. We live in a world of kaleidoscopic colors, softening or deepening shades and an array of perfumes, tantalizingly sweet, fragrant, musky or dusky. In this month, when the sun is busy elsewhere and the dove-gray skies lower and clouds bank up thickly above us, the deciduous trees are naked skeletons tightly withholding any promise of spring—save for the almond which, though leafless, has already begun to burst with the palest of pastel pink blossoms. Beyond our farm, the distant mountains appear as dense, stubby shadows while the sea, an ominous battleship gray, is lifted to poetry by slender rays of nacreous silver.

This is an altogether unencountered tapestry. These nuances of shadow and light are steelier than in the brighter, warmer seasons. But February justly claims its own stark beauty, and it is always wonderful to be home again.

My sole concern is No Name, who is angry with me and will not draw close. She glowers at me from various corners of the room or peers in through windows from the terraces, refusing to approach. Whether her anger is born of grieving for her puppies or my absence, I cannot tell, but nothing I do consoles or appeases her. And what is worse, while her reproach of me is unrelenting, with Michel she is playful and tender.

I hear the smoky cough of Michel's old powder-blue Mercedes. He is returning from the train station in Cannes, where he has collected Harold. I have met Harold before. In fact, I have worked with him, as an actress. He is a well-meaning Brit who has spent his entire career in the poorly paid service of children's and adolescent drama. (Why it is that networks feel obliged to cut the cloth so tightly when it comes to creating programs for the young, I have never quite understood.) I hurry out onto the terrace to greet them. Harold calls out, "Yooey!" I smile at the sight of him: even in this season, he has arrived dressed in a crumpled off-white linen suit and Panama, with his *Times* clutched tightly in the crook of his arm. I find his appearance touching, so wonderfully British. He looks as though he has ambled out of the pages of a Somerset Maugham short story.

He has read my scripts and likes them very much. We talk of the filming as though we might be commencing the following day. I am thrilled by his enthusiasm, and he is delighted with lunch and the wines on offer. As far as he is concerned, we can begin picking the key members of the production team and start the joyful process of location hunting. The development budget he offers is generous. It is sufficient to take us into preproduction. This leaves Michel with ample time to slot the remaining financial partners into place. Business matters are concluded satisfactorily. As a natural accompaniment to the cheese, glazed apple tart and dessert wine, Harold's conversation grows more frivolous, turns to gossip within the British television industry. He revels in his topic, attacking it and the *brie de Meaux* with a lusty appetite.

As afternoon pitches toward deepening dusk, Harold is transported back down the drive. Disappearing out of view, head poking out of the car window, he gazes back up at me on the upper terrace, waving his Panama in the air like a man setting sail for the ends of the earth.

Later, alone by the fireside, Michel and I discuss two essential matters: the first is my distress about No Name. Was it thoughtless to have given all the puppies away? Should we have kept one for her? Whisky was her companion for many months, and now she is lonely and bereaved and I feel wretched about it. The second is that as soon as my work in Wales has been completed, Michel will employ a production manager—he has the ideal man in mind—and with luck, by summer, we will be in production on my first entire series as screenwriter.

MIRACULOUSLY—ANYONE operating in the world of film finance will know that these affairs are usually tortuous—the money falls into place with ease. By April, everyone has committed the sums Michel has requested of them. We have a major French network, our Englishman abroad, Polish national television and a prestigious German company. I am both excited and over-whelmed. My summer is to be spent traveling with the producer and designer to the various countries, meeting with the networks, listening to their requirements and making any requested script adjustments. Then later, toward autumn, once principal photography is underway, I will be employed to play the role of the mother in the series. I have structured the scripts so that most of her scenes take place on the Île Ste. Marguerite. I will be able to work from home. The future looks rosy.

Michel bases the production office in Paris. Early in May, we find a very pretty girl to play the main role. During those same weeks, many of the other major players are also contracted. Three weeks from now, carpenters will start building sets in London; from there the crew moves on to Paris. I am finding this early process of filmmaking very exciting. There is much to be said for being on the other side of the camera.

I, with the producer and designer, am bound for Warsaw, Kraców and Gdansk and then on to Bialystok, close to the Russian border. We are in need of a Polish propertymaster and master carpenter. There are props to be built, most importantly a huge wooden windmill to be constructed in a remote field in the countryside outside Bialystok, which, during the course of the film, will be set alight and burned. In Paris and London, a team of design assistants, propertymakers, set dressers and costumers have already been brought onto the payroll and are out shopping, sewing, constructing, measuring and painting.

My plane is flying out from Paris the following morning. I am in my element and happy as a lark, but during our last supper together for a few weeks to come, Michel mentions to me that "there is one small concern clouding the horizon. The English money hasn't arrived. Well, yes, the early development funds have, but nothing since." According to the contracts, which as far as I can comprehend are built like a pack of cards, the English money was scheduled to be the first to arrive, followed by the French who are due to come in at a slightly later stage, followed by the Poles and so on and so forth right through to postproduction.

In my naïveté and perhaps blind excitement, I don't pick up on the gravity of the situation. Harold and Michel have shot numerous television film series together, one or two of which have picked up awards, and the station he represents in England is solid and wealthy. Whatever the delay, it can be nothing more than a minor bank hiccup, surely? Then I learn that the contract has not been returned. This has never been a concern before. On at least two of the programs they have shot together, the contracts arrived only after the films were delivered. Well, then? But in each of those cases, though the contracts were delayed, the money was not.

I place my fork back onto my plate. I fear I am beginning to get the gist of this. "Are you worried?" I ask, attempting desperately to keep the jitters out of my voice.

"Well . . . no, not really."

I recognize that bluff, that smoothing-over, mellifluous tone that Michel has fine-tuned over the years. One emotion a producer can simply *never* convey is panic. Rather like the captain of a torpedoed ship, he cannot fall to pieces and bellow with fear. I am staring across the table in shocked silence.

"Give me the worst scenario," I say, barely audibly.

This rattles him, which is certainly not what I had intended to do. "Why do you have to look for the worst in everything?" he snaps.

"No, don't!" My hand has leaped the distance and is attempting to meet his, but he withdraws, rises from the table and goes in search of a corkscrew. I rest where I am, listening to the opening and closing of drawers beyond the room, silently calculating how many members of the team in how many countries across Europe have already been contracted. And what of those already on salary? If the English funds are not covering all their fees . . . who is?

"That early development budget must have run out . . ." My palate is dry. My words stick in my throat. I cannot complete the sentence because Michel has returned to the table and, while opening our dinner wine, is looking at me in a way I have never seen before.

"The French network advanced several hundred thousand francs," he replies, pouring the glasses.

"So there's no real problem, then?" I hear the plea in my question, the need to know that everything is right with the world. It is quite pathetic.

"No, probably not. I shouldn't have mentioned it," he mutters, and the subject is closed.

I lie awake while Michel sleeps. I am the perennial insomniac, and our evening together has given me plenty to toss and turn over.

The following day, we say our good-byes. I promise to call from Warsaw. He promises to keep me abreast of what is happening. It is a muddled, unsatisfactory parting and I hate to go like this.

"Everything will be fine," he assures. I nod and set off for Charles de Gaulle Airport, leaving him on the telephone.

WARSAW IS EXTRAORDINARY. Poland is a heady mix of reformation, modernization and long-lost chivalry. Every color shrieks like a drunken song in streets which have known only the grayness and deprivation of communism for so many years. I am fascinated and attracted and, occasionally, repelled by the weight of recent history here. Blocks of ugly buildings lean in over me as though they will squeeze my presence right off the streets, and I want to run for my life. And then I stroll to the old town, entirely rebuilt after its wartime bombings, and sit in a quaint café and listen to the accordion players and the bell-like chatter of waitresses, plump and girlish and innocent whatever their ages, pleasing and polite, and I am seduced. I love the fact that we are here to film and create and fuse with these people who see the world through eyes that are so different than mine. Artists who have known mental and creative imprisonment. I know I can add this vision to my story.

Poland is a country emerging. My tale is of a girl emerging from the pain caused by the breakup of her parents' marriage.

The work process is going well; both teams are enjoying each other's contribution. The only drawback is that everything takes twice as long as I would have expected because we are being translated. Our interpeter, not always accurate, I fear, sits between us or trots alongside as we hurry from meeting to meeting, location to location, and repeats in Polish all that we have said and vice versa. Dear Gruzna, whose shiny plump face seems buried beneath layers of bright blue eyeshadow and thick black mascara, has been assigned to us by the local production company. She is a rather lazy girl who has no truck with our Western ways and longs to return to the security of the old regime, where she knew that at half past four she could go home, her work for the day done. All day long, she jabbers empty-headedly of romance and tells us how she and her husband are starving and surviving on love alone, but her heavily painted eyes light up like a magpie's when she sees currency or jewelry, and she sidles close, hoping for a gift. She, like everything here, is a curious paradox.

One evening, after traveling eleven hours in a van without suspension on country roads that seem never to have been completed, so rutted are they with deep potholes, I stagger exhaustedly to the hotel reception desk to collect my key. The porter hands me a message, left early that morning, asking me to call Michel. Frustratingly, but not unusually, it takes me a while to get an international line out of Poland. I know instantly by the tone of his voice that all is not well, so the words—the English have withdrawn—only partially stuns me. I have no idea what to say. "Why?" is all I can think of.

"Restructuring within the network. It looks as though Harold might be given early retirement."

"Poor Harold," I bleat, unable to contemplate where it leaves us.

Michel is used to the roller coaster of film production crises. Unless an actor has invested his own money in a film, he is rarely, if ever, burdened with such problems. Actors are cushioned, cosseted, so this is a completely new and rather scary scenario for me, but I remind myself silently that I am sitting on the other side of the fence now. I have to take the blows with the rest of the team. "What now?" I ask eventually.

My question is returned by a silence broken only by the crackling on a very inadequate and antiquated telephone line. Eventually he says, "I've spoken to the French and German networks today. Both are willing to up their investment and make first payments earlier than originally scheduled. It doesn't cover the shortfall, but it will pay the production salaries and keep us going for the time being. I'm flying into Warsaw tomorrow and I'll meet with Agnes midafternoon."

Agnes is the head of Drama here. One of the other discoveries that has surprised and pleased me about Poland is the power given to women here. I am thrilled to know that Michel is coming, but I am very troubled by the reason for his trip. We say good night and he sounds as tired as a thousand-year-old man. I cannot sleep.

OVER A DRINK IN THE darkly lit bar, I hear from Michel and our producer that the meeting with the Polish network has gone smoothly. They are still very keen and are offering to double their commitment to the project. I, in my naïveté, am thrilled, believing this to mean that we have jumped this tricky hurdle and are out of trouble. Michel gently explains that because the Poles are not rich and are operating in a currency which has no buying power on the international market, they are offering "their extra commitment to us in below-the-line costs."

I stare blankly.

"It means to say the Poles will make extra services available to us here in Poland. Hotels, crew, facilities . . ."

The three men sitting with me around the table read the confused look on my face. I have never been confronted by this problem before, but I am not so blind that I cannot discern from the lack of overabounding joy at the table that the matter is not fully resolved. I attempt a lighter approach. "Such matters never concern actresses. We learn our lines, climb into our frocks and are driven to the set . . ." I look from one to the other. "Help me," I add.

"We will shoot a greater chunk of the story here, more than we had originally envisaged. This means that we, or rather you," says the producer, "will have to relocate certain episodes."

"Relocate?" I repeat stupidly.

"The story will not begin in London. It will begin in Paris, and then, instead of two episodes in Poland, we will have four set here."

I silently take this in. "But it's not possible . . ."

"It has to be, or—"

"Fine," I mumble, having absolutely no idea how I will achieve this unexpected order.

Later, alone with Michel in my hotel room, I learn that there is still a shortfall of over half a million pounds. He is returning to Paris at first light to begin the process of finding another source of finance to cover it.

"Wouldn't it be better to cancel the series?" I ask. No. We are already committed to such an extent and to so many contracts still to be paid that, ironically, it is cheaper and less risky to keep going.

"I see," I mutter, but I don't.

Michel leaves, and I am driven to the studios to meet with Agnes and a script editor before being put to work. Apparently, there is a considerable amount of Polish history that I must learn and include in the storyline. I dare not ask what Polish history has to do with our rites-of-passage tale. I am at the point where I think the best course of action is to just do as I am told.

We are ten days away from principal photography, and I am five scripts short of my thirteen. The thirteen which it took me the best part of a year to write and polish. If I cannot produce four acceptable Polish scripts, we will have no film, and then what? I do not allow myself to dwell on it.

I am put to work. Everything I need is installed in my hotel room. Food is brought in at intervals, as well as limitless supplies of dark, stewed coffee. Squires of paper arrive to feed a monstrous printer which barely succeeds the original printing press. In Paris, it would sell in a fashionable Marais boutique, a techno-antique converted into some natty home device, but here it is dumped on the floor because there is no shelf or tabletop in the room spacious enough to contain it. Cables festoon the room. Every time I stand up from my work, I trip over them or the printer.

For forty-eight hours, I work without sleep, feeling guilty if I pause to brush my teeth, and emerge at dawn on the third day having produced two newly rewritten scripts. I am gibbering with exhaustion, and to remind myself of what is wonderful in life, I pick up the phone and call Quashia. Extraordinarily, I get through without a problem. The chuckle in his voice, his lighthearted good humor, warm and relax me.

"How are you?" he hollers. Quashia still seems to believe that talking long-distance on the phone involves a great deal of shouting. But it's part of who he is, and I am deeply glad to be in touch. It all seems a lifetime away.

"Terrific," I lie. "How is No Name?"

All is well back at the farm, and I am buoyed by the news. No Name is in good form and has adopted Ella, the small golden retriever puppy we bought for her, who is now four months old. I close my eyes and picture them prancing across the terraces in the bright sunlight. I try to draw energy from the tranquility there. Whoopee birds flitting to and fro in the garden, the two white doves who have appeared since Christmas and fly in and out daily, cooing and nuzzling on the phone line by our bedroom terrace, buzzards wheeling high in the deep blue sky. All is right with the world back there, and I am so profoundly grateful for it.

During my retreat it has been decided by the drama department that what the story lacks is a plane sequence and a chase set in one of the famous Polish opal mines.

"What?" I mutter, barely able to comprehend what is being suggested to me. "But this is the story of a thirteen-year-old girl in search of her father." No matter, I am assured, the newly proposed sequence will dovetail into the story nicely. I am given a sheath of material which tells me (in halting English) all I need to know about the local mining industry and sent away to write the scenes. Back I go to my room, encased once again within four walls and my imagination.

I am cheered by news from Michel. He has found an independent company in Paris that has guaranteed the missing financing. Everything is back on track. I return to the opal sequence with optimism in my heart. Perhaps my heroine can find a stone or two! Why not?

By Friday, I am certain that if I do not get out of the hotel I will not be held responsible for my state of mind. I have had four hours' sleep in as many days. I stagger down to reception, where the sight of so many people milling to and fro in a brightly lit, bustling area almost sends me into trauma. I leave a note for the producer, telling him that I have four scripts. They are ready to be read, and I don't care what he says, I want to go out to dinner this evening, and will he and the designer please accompany me because I am starved of human contact and laughter!

Later that evening, along with the English director, who has flown in from London the day before, we stroll to the old town and order vodka and fresh fish and settle to our evening. They are priming me on all that has happened during my missing days, but I am so tired, so punch-drunk and, after one straight vodka, so slewed that I can barely take in the sequence of events. The mayor of Bialystok has telephoned to discuss the newly constructed windmill which he has spotted in one of the surrounding village fields. He is refusing to allow us to burn it. The designer is laughing as he recounts the conversation. Why? Is there a local fire risk? No, not all. He is so taken with it, with its unusual design—essential for the story—that he wants to buy it and keep it there as a tourist attraction! We laugh wildly and order more vodka, a blissful palliative to me this evening. The restaurant grows packed, candles are lit, accordionists in national costume are serenading us at our benched table, searingly sweet romantic tunes. We are talking and giggling hysterically because we are all tired and stressed. And so I chill out and heal. The money is back in place. The English director, a gentle, intelligent soul, is an excellent addition to our small team, and in one week, so long as my new scripts are accepted, I will return to the haven of Appassionata and write the remaining changes from there. My work, for the time being in Poland, will have been accomplished. The film will have reached the starting gate. Life is not so bad after all.

My thoughts drift to the garden, to the olive trees and dogs and how well I shall feel writing in my own precious space, my sanctum, surrounded by shelf after shelf of books and warm shafts of moted sunbeams. Of course, if the scripts are not accepted, the start of principal photography will be delayed, the budget will be at risk, jobs on the line . . . I choose not to dwell on such negatives tonight, or the incredible weight of responsibility I feel. Tomorrow—no, today; it is now Saturday—there is to be a mammoth script conference at the studios in the afternoon where my work will be discussed and, probably, dissected. What a baptism by fire for any young scriptwriter this is proving to be.

It is two A.M. when we enter the lobby of the hotel, and I find an urgent message waiting for me to call Michel.

Back in my room, dubious about calling at such a late hour, I pick up the phone. His voice is grave, and I know before he utters a word that what I am about to hear will not be good. "It's your father," he says.

"My . . . ?" The effect of the vodka, which left me sleepy, slurry and mellow, is whipped from me just as surely as though someone has slapped me with a cold metal object.

"You better ring England." I crash the receiver down clumsily almost before he has finished speaking and telephone my mother. It takes a frustrating age before I can get another line out and then an age before she answers.

"We've just returned from the hospital." I hear her breathlessness, caused by rushing to the phone, no doubt.

"The hospital?" I seem incapable of uttering anything other than parrotlike responses.

"There's nothing you can do."

My father has had a stroke. He is unconscious and paralyzed. He could live a day, he could go on for an indeterminate period. "If you came, he wouldn't know you were here, and we know you have difficulties there. There's no sense in risking everything you have been working for."

"No."

We say good night and I promise to call again in the morning. I walk to the window, tripping over the cursed printer on my way, dragging a carver chair with me, which I place facing the leafy deserted square beyond the hotel. There I sit for the entire night. Exhausted, spent as I am, I cannot go to bed, would not sleep. I think of my father and try to comprehend the reality of what has happened to him way across the waters in a land of Englishness so alien to this place, with its remnants of gray communism, its fast-growing mafia, its distant grim echoes of concentration camps and its desperate hungry hand reaching out to a new world where pop music is not banned, kids smoke dope and, supposedly, salvation lies. My story is of a thirteen-year-old in search of her musician father, and in the Polish episodes, she finds him and loses him again. The streets beyond the window are deadly quiet. My own father, dying in a hospital bed in a place my mind refuses to conjure, is a musician and has been the inspiration for the central theme of my story. It was to have been a spiritual present to him; a gift of my work. I had been looking forward to talking to him about it, to taking him to the islands, to the fortress where the resolution of the story is to take place. I close my aching eyes and picture him at Appassionata, sleeping in the sun with No Name at his side, loyal companions, his sunburned, sleeping body covered in puppies.

At first light, I make my way to the dining room. There is not a soul in sight. When the waiter comes by, I order coffee and stare at the phenomenal buffet on offer, which includes mountains of caviar and every marinated herring you could dream of, all so at odds with the miserable poverty and deprivation I have witnessed everywhere in this land. I stare at it blindly and then, in my mind's ear, I hear a voice. Indisputably. It is my father's. *Carol, Carol, darling, it's Daddy.* And I know that whatever the weight of responsibility here, no matter how many actors' and technicians' jobs are at risk, no matter if the Poles hate every word I have written and call this huge production machine to a halt, I must go. If only for a day. Today is Saturday. I could take the weekend and be back to face the music on Monday morning.

At reception, I learn that access in and out of Poland is not the simple affair I had thoughtlessly anticipated. There is one flight to London later this afternoon and another back tomorrow evening. They are fully booked. In fact, there is not a flight with a single seat available in any class for the next five days. What if I went through Paris? Or Amsterdam? Or Frankfurt? In my vulnerable, barely coherent exhaustion, I blurt out my dilemma, unbosoming myself to the desk clerk. He is kindly and sympathetic and promises to look into the matter and get back to me. I return to the dining room and drink several more black coffees before calling the producer's room.

"Of course, you must go," he tells me when I disturb him at eight-thirty. "I will drive you to the airport."

By whatever miracles make these matters possible, flights are found, and I am booked to London via Berlin. There is no time to waste. The producer has read the scripts overnight and seems relatively happy with them. He envisages few, if any, problems. We grab a hurried bite, or rather he does while talking through various scenes. He intends to attend the pre-arranged weekend script meetings on my behalf and take notes; upon my return, he and I will collaborate on whatever has been requested by the television network, and I will deliver the corrected scripts to the network by Monday morning. I merely nod my agreement to this insane schedule. I cannot think beyond what awaits me in England. I have moved into a different pace, another zone.

STANDING IN THE CENTER of my hotel room on Sunday evening, I survey my temporary habitat. Nothing has changed except the bed, which has been made during my thirty-six-hour absence, and my papers, which were strewn everywhere and have been tidied into bundles. I stare at nothing in particular except its orderliness. I have a meeting in the bar in fifteen minutes with director, designer and producer who have passed practically the entire weekend at the studio. I have begged the time to wash and to phone my mother. I slept, or rather didn't at the hospital at my father's side. Now I have just replaced the receiver, having learned from her that my father died two hours earlier. I would have been flying somewhere between Berlin to Warsaw. I gather up my scripts and head for the elevator. In the bar, my three colleagues await me with a tall glass of champagne which costs the earth here.

"Ready to go back to work?"

I nod and decide to hold off my news until we have worked through the scripts. It is four in the morning when our powwow breaks up and we head toward the elevators. I am clutching my papers tight against my chest. Bleak emotions are churning up my guts. Questions unable to be answered hang in my mind like smoke trails. One phone call and life has taken on an entirely different perspective. The men are talking among themselves. Small talk, the banter that is born of exhaustion. As we exit the elevator, the producer and I say good night to the others, whose rooms are elsewhere. He accompanies me, knowing.

"It's curious. When you rang my room on Saturday morning, I was lying awake thinking about my own father. He's not well. I was wondering what I'd do if I got that call. You were luckier. Mine's in Australia."

I drop my eyes and stare at the carpet. Luckier?

"Have you told Michel?"

I shake my head. "Not yet," I murmur. "The funeral's next Monday. I'm going," I snap, too sharply.

"Of course. In any case, you should be out of here by then. You've done well. Against all bloody odds. Thanks for it." He leans in and gives me an awkward hug.

THE DAYS BANK UP, each one like the last. We attend meeting after meeting. While the others talk and debate, the producer fighting in my corner with a ferocious loyalty to the story we had set out to tell and which now seems to be disappearing behind action sequences that bare no relationship to anything as far as I can see, I close down. I stare at the blank, faded white walls or the conference table around which we sit. None of this seems relevant, and yet I know that it is. So many livelihoods at stake. And a story dedicated to the father I have just lost. As we approach the end of the week, I learn that there are no flights. Not at any price. I will walk if I have to, I tell no one in particular and set about trying to rent a car. I shall drive to London or drive across the frontier and pick up a plane in Germany. I am going, I repeat angrily. These dark days have crept up without warning. No pointers to alert me that they were approaching; I was not prepared for this. I am hurting with life and ready to lash out.

Miraculously, yet again, flights are found. But this time the route is more circuitous. Warsaw to Frankfurt, Frankfurt to Nice and then Nice to London. This extraordinary tour includes an overnight in Nice which means, incredibly, that I can go home. I am grateful, profoundly grateful, for the opportunity to touch base.

I phone Quashia to alert him of my imminent arrival and learn that No Name has gone missing. In between script sessions, budget and design meetings, I begin to ring all the refuge centers in the south of France. No one has found her. I am beside myself with concern. I call the police and the fire brigade. They also respond with negatives. I telephone the vet. What shall I do? He has a record there of the numbered reference he tattooed in her ear when I first found her. He will call the central office and alert them. He reminds me that when I gave him the signed photo he had requested, I also gave him a photograph Michel had taken of No Name running in the garden. He offers to have photocopies made and distribute them in our local shops and put one up in his surgery. My heart is troubled as well as numb, but I am thankful for his support. "I'll see you when I arrive," I mumble and replace the phone.

A BLANKET OF HEAT greets my weary arrival. Here at home, it is a blazing, glorious summer. It had been warm in Warsaw as well, but because I had been incarcerated in meetings and cold with grieving, I had not noticed. The tropicality of the Côte d'Azur takes me by surprise. For the first time ever, I feel a stranger to the plumes of palm fronds while the gloss and bustle of Riviera life rather turns my stomach after the poverty of Poland, but as I climb up into the winding twilit hills, breathe in the fragrance of scarlet and pink oleandar and the sky-blue plumbago, my heart begins to settle. By the time I have reached the land of olive groves, our own in particular, a great weight seems to lift from me and a peace descends, albeit a lamenting peace.

Upon arrival, I find a fax from the producer saying all four scripts have been accepted. The network is delighted with them. Once I have shared with my family our farewell to my father, I can return to Appassionata and begin to write the new first script, now to be set in Paris, from the serenity of my own stone-walled space. Any last-minute changes requested by the Poles can be achieved by fax. Principal photography has been given the green light. The task has been accomplished.

CHAPTER TWELVE

LOSS

Soon the weather will begin to break. Already, the crush of holiday-makers with children have packed up and left, and with them has gone that distinctly pungent tang of suntan lotion which has dominated the Riviera coastline for the past two months. Michel and I are lunching on the beach. Early autumnal winds, driving off that heavy summer lethargy and previewing the shift of season, have blown in, bringing with them fragrant whiffs of late-summer flowers. Light gusts lift and settle the paper napkins on the table in front of us. Dragging a stray wisp of hair from off my face, I glance about me. On the shore, at water's edge, two wiry setters are barking incessantly at a retired couple in matching swimming caps splashing lazily on their backs in the warm sea. Cries of distant voices drift toward us on the welcome breeze. Closer by, well-fed bronzed bodies—Nords, Dutch, Germans, Brits—chatter and prattle, ordering drinks, lighting cigarettes, oiling one another, while tame waves spume and curl just a few yards from our feet. We have barely seen each other for weeks. Our eyes shaded by Raybans; we gaze across the table but do not smile. Michel looks shot to hell, in need of a haircut and a break, while I am shell-shocked by the news he has just imparted. Behind me, the steady thwack-thwack of ball hitting bat acts like a salty metronome. Time to make a decision.

"What are we going to do?" I ask eventually.

An entire film crew is on its way. Shooting will finish in Hamburg in a week, which means that the full caravan of actors, makeup and costume, camera, lights, electrics is about to converge on this resort by road and air. In the meantime, the advance team of designers, carpenters, buyers, et cetera, has already been installed in a small hotel three streets back from the main coastal drag. The film material in the can—the rushes—has been well received by all the various international networks involved, and the young girl playing the leading role has been described as "magic" onscreen. We should be delighted. And so we were, I thought in a worn-out sort of way, until this morning.

In short, the French company who stepped in to cover the deficit incurred by the loss of the British network has gone bankrupt. They are not alone. During these past few months in Paris, somewhere in the region of twenty independent production companies have gone to the wall, and we are likely to join them if we cannot find a solution to this crisis. Michel learned this news three days ago. He said nothing to me but went immediately to his bankers in Paris, who have, after much wrangling, telephoned this morning to say that they agree to advance the monies and keep the production running—which right now means to get a host of salaries paid before the middle of next week—on one condition.

"And that is?" I ask as a plate of freshly grilled sizzling sardines seasoned with curls of fresh parsley is set in front of me and the waitress, a pretty, darkly tanned, middle-aged blonde in shorts, refills my glass of rosé.

"That we give them the farm as a guarantee."

"Give them Appassionata? No!"

Sleek heads at nearby tables turn at the sound of my raised voice. I sigh. We are both exhausted.

Since collecting Michel from the airport, while driving along the busy stretch of coast road, negotiating corkscrew curves in the old fortressed port of Antibes, swinging by the palm-fringed, art deco villas along the cap, I have chattered without pause about various horticultural difficulties I have been experiencing, as well as my preparations for the arrival of the girls, who are flying in later today. This was to have been our first home-based family weekend in months. I was excited. Having completed the rewrites on my scripts weeks ago, I have spent my late-August days immersed in affairs of the garden and wanted to share my news.

"*Cicadelles.* They are small white flies, smaller than moths. They're everywhere and lethal. According to René, there's a local epidemic. They've laid their eggs on our orange trees. The underside of the foliage has been invaded, robbing the leaves of their color; all viridescence sucked out. I treated them twice. Quashia has, too, but it's made no difference. They just fly off and settle somewhere else. Watching them move is like seeing a soft pale gray blanket fluttering across the terraces. Now they are on the roses and the bougainvillea. When you touch the plants, they are all sticky. I was scared they'd attack the olive trees, but they haven't gone near them. And just when I was beginning to feel safe about that, I discovered *paon*— you remember René showed us when we went to visit that farm near Castellane? Remember he told us to watch out for it—leaves turning yellow, round brown spots? Well, I have found the fungus on nine of our olive trees. You're very quiet, Michel. I'm talking too much. I'm so pleased to see you. Are you all right?" And that was when he broached the subject. By then we had parked my little car and were crossing the street, heading beachward for this café.

"We can't give them Appassionata," I repeat. My voice is quieter now, almost strangled but emphatic. Behind my dark glasses, tears prick my eyes. Michel picks up his wine and takes a sip. He smiles at the waitress as she places Parma ham and a mesclun salad in front of him. *"Merci."*

We begin to eat, but the delicious fish tastes like cardboard in my mouth.

"If you don't mind going back to the airport later and picking up the girls, I'll begin to make some calls to see what else I can come up with."

"Such as?"

"I have plenty of contacts in Germany. I'll try to pick up a cable sale. I'll talk to the Swiss. A children's channel in Italy. I don't know yet, I'll think of something."

THE GIRLS ARE CLEARING the table after dinner when the row begins. I do not know from where it explodes. I'm feeling fraught and deeply upset because we have decided to go ahead and sign Appassionata to the bank as a guarantee. Frankly, we have no choice. Salaries have to paid, hotel bills met. Whatever solutions Michel can cobble together, they will not solve our immediate dilemma. We agreed at the beginning of the evening and then promised ourselves to leave it until Sunday, when we will put aside part of our afternoon to arrange the paperwork.

Now, suddenly, here we are, standing around the table shouting at one another. I am quick-tempered by nature, volatile, but Michel is more steady in his emotions. Vanessa lunges forward and screams unkind words at me which send me reeling. "No," I stammer. "No, you don't understand."

Have I been unkind to Michel, did I speak too sharply to him? Do I act as though I blame him for what has happened even though I know that the difficulties are not of his making? The girls must think me culpable. They side with their father. Naturally. And yet, in so many ways, I had thought us a family. I wanted to believe it. I am more sensitive to cutting words, accusations, because I am not their mother. Were we family, flesh and blood, I could dismiss the unkindnesses more easily. As it is, dishcloth in hand, greasy plates clutched before me, I turn and flee to the kitchen.

Glancing back, hazy with tears, I see a sight which curdles my heart. Michel standing at the head of the table staring at the floor, lips puckered, frozen in speech, one daughter on either side of him clutching him fast, their heads pressed against his chest. I settle the dishes in the sink and, without washing them, creep off to bury myself beneath a cave of sheets and pillows.

EVERYONE IS SLEEPING. The dew on the early-morning grass glints in the sun like crystal stones. The soles of my feet are damp from walking in it. A cock crows in the far distance. The blue of the sky is as smooth as velvet. It caresses my fractured senses.

"They will hold all deeds of the farm until the film has been completed and sufficient profits have been made to pay them back, plus their interest, of course." Michel's words of yesterday echo in my mind.

This must be hurting him as much as it is me.

Seated on one of our many drystone walls, I scan the misty morning hillsides, drinking in our ravishing land and seascape, and my heart swims sickly. Even without a cent to renovate, even crumbling alongside its romantic ruin, this place is magnificent, magical. To lose it all—myriad moments of crazy happiness—does not bear contemplation. Our lives had seemed golden until this summer.

Ella, our little puppy, is nudging her cold nose against my naked arms, begging for attention. I stroke her soft russet-auburn head absentmindedly. We never found No Name. We advertised everywhere. She just walked away, disappeared out of our lives. We cannot fathom even how she got loose. She must have made a hole in a fence somewhere. I looked for it, spent hours scouting the terraces in search of a point of exit, a clue, but without luck. I still blame myself, even though, in place of her, the most extraordinary incident occurred. I might almost claim it a *petit* miracle.

It was my father's birthday, two weeks ago now. I was aching from the loss of him. A hot sultry lunchtime; I sauntered down the drive, taking heart from the birdsong, to collect the mail from our mailbox. I unlocked the great iron gates, which Michel has painted that Matisse blue of our house shutters, and there, curled up like a snake in a shaded corner among the irises and beneath the bird's-egg-blue plumbago which festoon the cedar trees, was another shepherd. For one glad second I thought it was No Name returned, blackened with mud or tar, and then I saw that the shivering, skeletal creature was darker and smaller, a German rather than a Belgian shepherd; her fur is not as long. I put my hand out, but she growled ferociously. I was reminded of that first encounter with No Name, a damaged fawny mess who feared to trust. What is this dog doing here, settled right outside our gate, miles from anywhere? I could not contain the thought that she had been brought to us by the spirit of my father, on his birthday, to keep our little Ella company.

I bent low and she bared her teeth, so I decided to leave her be and turned to retrieve our mail. As I locked the gates, she staggered to her feet. She was unsteady and limping, in pain, but she trod the length of the hilly driveway, a shadow stalking me, keeping her distance. What a scrawny sight. I hurried to the stables and dug out No Name's bowl, which I loaded with chunks of meat, biscuits and water. I offered her this, but she backed off mistrustfully. I placed the food on the ground and returned to my writing room, where I could survey her discreetly through the window. She did not touch the meal but slumped on the ground about three yards away from it and glowered at it, as though waiting for the aluminum dish to approach or challenge her. It made me smile. I noticed then for the first time that her left side and haunch were completely bald. I wondered if she belonged to anyone and telephoned the vet. She wasn't wearing a collar.

She bore no tattoo. Lucky is her name. Or so I have christened her. She is still with the vet. She was suffering from internal bleeding, a perforation, stomach problems from where she had been kicked repeatedly. Two broken ribs, worms and a highly strung, nervy disposition which Dr. Marschang suggests is the result of repeated maltreatment. It is why she is still with him. He wants to be sure before we take her in and foster her alongside a small puppy that she will not turn nasty.

I was intending to collect her later. I had been looking forward to introducing her to the girls.

Wordsworth said "the past, present and future are strung together, as it were, on the thread of the wish that runs through them." Running through my mind this morning is everything we have achieved, the contentment I feel here and the happiness Michel has brought me, but the future now looms large with hurdles and fears. And this morning, reasonable or not, I blame myself.

Ella at my side begins to wag her tail as arms reach around me and hug me tight, drawing me back to the present, to this "spot in time," from my memories and misery and from an uncertain future. It is Vanessa. She says nothing; neither do I. We only hold each other tight, and the sun, flooding through the treetops beyond the flat roof of the house, begins to heat our backs, invigorating us, healing us with the promise of a whole new day.

THE WEATHER IS BREAKING. Pale rain falls across the hills and turns the sea bluish and opalescent. Michel has gone traveling, to sell our now-completed series. He is working all the hours God sends, traveling as though he is trying to squeeze in a second day elsewhere, catching the sunrise on both sides of the world. He never rests, never takes a day off. He behaves as though he could keep it up forever, as though he were invincible. I want to tell him that he'll wear himself down, make himself ill, but I know that such negatives will only incapacitate him. I want to believe that he is as powerful and capable as he is forcing himself to be. I want to believe in his strength because I dare not consider the alternatives. But most of all, I think we should relinquish the farm, sell it, hand it over to the bank. Throw it at them, release us, but Michel won't hear of it. We'll get there, he keeps saying to me as though it were a secret mantra which, the more he repeats, the truer he begs it to become. It is a heavy burden to carry. I am anxious and depressed for him, and I see our dreams turning to dust.

Quashia leaves for Algeria. He is preparing for his retirement early next year. His departure all but finishes me. I have no idea how I will manage without him, but I lie to him, tell him I've found someone, because he has his own life and family in Africa and it is not for me to hold him back.

"If you need me," he says when he comes to say good-bye, "call the village café, *comme d'habitude*. I'll come back." I nod and wish him well, knowing that I will not call.

"Remember, we are family, you and I. I will never let you down." I nod again and kiss him on both cheeks, twice, fighting back great blubbing tears.

This is beginning to feel like the Year of Loss.

Loss. The fear that has haunted me. It is why every farewell, every parting, no matter how trivial or short-lived, seems to tear at me. It's why I never found the courage to love until I met Michel.

"Say hello to your wife and children," I manage. I have never met them, but he talks of them so frequently that I feel as though we are old friends.

"You tell Michel from me to stop working so hard. He's needed here."

I smile bravely and nod again, wondering if he has any idea of the deep trouble we are in. I suspect so. He has a wise man's instinct. I watch while he descends the drive, fur hat on his balding head, waving as he goes and smiling that warm, toothless grin of his.

I stay alone at the farm, thinking out devices for the salvation of Appassionata, living from hand to mouth. The bank is growing impatient with us. They are threatening us. They muscle us regularly with registered letters, promising to snatch the farm and put it up for auction. Worry haunts me. I pace the tiled, sun-slanted rooms and windy terraces like a lost spirit who has a code to decipher but cannot find the root clue. The fears and responsibilities churn in my mind like souring milk. Some nights, before the first cock crows, sleepless with concern, I press my face against the glass, staring out at the moon while, down in the farthest valley, the Arabs are at their prayer, their *muezzin*. Their cry to God.

"Count me in," I whisper.

I write from dawn till dead of night, alone in the ancient creaking house, candles burning, logs crackling, staring into Bible-black darkness. Stories, children's books, script synopses, beavering away, wearing myself out in an attempt to change the tide of our fortunes.

And I seek out small day-to-day joys to elate me. I jump in the pool to save the life of a drowning bee, twitching his legs every which way, backside down on the surface of the water. I talk at length to a surprisingly large cicada who has pitched up out of season in the bathroom, lonely in a corner like a displaced twig. I chance upon a pair of hornets copulating against one of the flowerbed walls; one behind the other. Embracing her, he is moving rhythmically while she strokes her small black insect face with her front feet until, suddenly, she begins to emit high-pitched noises. A love song delivered with passion on a warm Sunday afternoon. Lucky is a miracle, too. Nervy and snappy, but less so. She requires much tending with creams and potions, but her fur is beginning to grow back, and she is proving herself a loyal and loving guard dog. I tell her how thankful I am for her company, her gratitude and needing of me, and I stroke fluffy little Ella and reassure her that I feel the same way about her, too.

RENÉ DROPS BY TO take a look at the *paon*, which he won't treat now because the spray he is suggesting—which I absolutely oppose because we have been running our farm by organic methods—might damage the fruit. He hands me a set of papers given to him by Christophe, the mill owner.

"What are these?" I ask, puzzled and barely interested.

"Forms to fill out and send to Brussels. Christophe mentioned your names specifically."

I stare at them in a lonely, unmotivated way. They appear as complicated and long-winded as all French bureacracy, so I stuff them in my jeans pocket.

"Don't ignore tham, Carol. In an attempt to support the olive industry here in France, Brussels is offering every *oléiculteur* financial assistance."

"How?"

"For each liter of oil pressed, we will all receive a designated sum."

My eyes light up, my attention drawn back. I am considering our crisis. Could this, miraculously, be the answer to our problems? "How much?" I ask.

"Well, it is not retroactive, but if this farm produces the same volume of oil this coming season as last, then it would be approximately six hundred francs." Six hundred francs! That's about sixty pounds. He must read the disappointment in my face.

"It's not a great deal, but . . ." He shrugs his wonderful Provençal shrug, and that canny look of his tells me that anything is better than nothing, which is true, of course.

"I'll fill it in." I smile. "I won't forget."

Before climbing into his Renault, which is laden with the largest, frizziest lettuces I have ever set eyes on—the size of lavender bushes—he reminds me that before too long we will need to begin netting again; the harvesting season will be upon us once more. A swift tour of the terraces shows us that the trees are laden with bullet-hard green olives. We are in for another bumper crop.

"With that load, you might even make seven hundred francs from Brussels," he jokes as we return to his car. "Do you want a salad?" He is pointing at the produce cluttering up his trunk. I shake my head, explaining that I bought mesclun and lettuce earlier at the market. Still, I cannot help but remark on the size of them. His eyes glint with pride and that knowledge of a *bonne affaire* as he explains that he grows his salad on someone else's *terrain* where the water is free because the owner has a private *source*.

"And don't forget," he calls as he leaves, "we can't do this alone."

It is a fact. Without Quashia, and with Michel away for weeks at a time, René and I will need extra help. We were so blessed in the early days, the way both he and Quashia seemed to turn up out of thin air, that I have no idea how to go about finding anybody. Finally, I decide to scribble a card, a four-line *annonce,* to pin up at the local *épicerie.* I drive it over. I have always been rather fond of this particular store because it reminds me of countless village shops my grandparents took me to when I was a country child back home in Ireland. They would sell their great clanking churns of milk, and it seemed to me that every item in the world was on sale for us to choose from, particularly sweets; jar after tall glass jar of rainbow-colored sweets.

The burly wife of the owner of this particular grocery, pregnant again, greets me loudly and, having glanced at my advertisement, tells me that there's no need to post it. I can take their chappie.

"But what about you?"

"Winter's coming. There's nothing for him to do here 'cept rake leaves and burn. Manuel is his name."

"And you recommend him?"

"*Mais, bien sûr,* he has worked for us for six years." She quotes the hourly rate they pay him, which seems affordable—the olive crop will pay it—and I can think of no objection to offering him the job.

"*Bon,* we'll tell him to be ready for you tomorrow morning. You can drive him back with you."

Relieved, I agree and proceed to do a bit of shopping. This includes a dozen small bottles of lager. Madame shakes her head. *Désolé,* she tells me. "We have run out."

I am puzzled, for I had requested the same only a few days earlier, at which time she had informed me that she was expecting a delivery the following afternoon. We have long passed the full throes of summer. Tourists with tongues hanging out are no longer raiding the fridges of every corner shop and leaving them bare.

"Your delivery never came, then?" I remark innocently. She glances at me sheepishly and heads off to collect the coffee I need.

"Don't forget Manuel," she calls after me as I close the door.

When I return for Manuel the following day, as arranged, I find no one and head into the store to inquire after him. Monsieur, usually a fairly convivial fellow, who is proprietor, *boulanger* and *pâtissier* and is right now covered in flour, glowers at his full-bellied wife in an accusatory fashion and disappears in to his backroom bakery without a word.

"Try the woodshed," Madame mutters, pointing toward a section of the grounds I have never visited before.

I am a little taken aback to discover not a Spaniard or a Portuguese as I had been expecting but a scruffy weatherbeaten Arab, no bigger than a sparrow, fast asleep on a pile of logs. At his feet is a small frayed satchel.

I hover a short distance in front of him. "Manuel?"

Startled, he cusses incomprehensible words and drags himself up onto unsteady feet. Staring at me, he has the air of a guilty child. He grabs the satchel and raises one arm in the air as though leading a posse to the charge.

It is only when he is seated beside me in the car, lighting a cigarette without checking that I have no objection, that I notice his bloodshot eyes and inhale the fumes of alcohol on his breath which are so overwhelming I fear the flame from his lighter might blow us and my little car sky-high.

I need this man. I need this to work. We have been shopping in that little corner store ever since we moved here. Madame wouldn't palm us off with a drunk, would she?

It appears that she would.

When we arrive back at the villa, once Lucky has been chained because Manuel refuses to get out of the car while the dog is at liberty, he asks immediately to be shown to his room.

"Room?" I retort, for it had never been my intention to take him in.

He lifts his beaten satchel in the air and swings it as though he intends to set up residence wherever it lands, or smash a window or two.

"I need a shower and then I'll go to work," he says, groaning.

I am uncertain what to do for the best. Should I just shove him in the car again and deliver him back to the corner shop? Should I release Lucky and hope that he runs off in terror, thus relieving me of the problem altogether? Or am I being hasty? I decide to humor him until I can speak to Madame on the phone. "Why not work now and shower later?" I suggest. He humphs, throws the satchel on the ground, kicks it, lights a cigarette and shrugs. "What do you want doing, then?"

I look around in desperation. Nothing that could break or get damaged, certainly not the preparation of the olive nets. "A bit of weeding" is my reply, and I point to the greater of the various flowerbeds. I unchain the dog when Manuel is not looking and leave them to it, making for my workroom where I can discuss the matter in privacy.

Searching for the number, I realize that although we have shopped there since our arrival here, participated in their Christmas raffles, bought numerous tickets for gallon-size chocolate Easter bunnies and generally been neighborly with this couple, I have never noted the name of the shop. It is the only one on a manicured private estate set in the hills to the rear of our home, but that does not help me. I have no way of finding it out. Short of going back there and leaving Manuel here alone, I can think of no other way of settling the situation. I have been careless in this arrangement, and I am grumpy with myself. And I have so much work of my own to be getting on with, I wail silently. Finally, I hurry downstairs intending to explain to him that I will be back in a few minutes, but he is not in the garden and I cannot find him anywhere.

"Manuel!" I call.

Lucky comes loping toward me, barking.

"Manuel!" There is no response. Eventually, I find him hovering like a specter in the darkness of our windowless garage which, with two cars as ancient as ours, never houses vehicles but is packed to the gills with gardening equipment and a beaten-up but useful fridge.

"What are you doing?" I ask rather crossly.

"Looking for a hoe," he explains. I point out the switch for the electric light and hurtle off down the drive in the car, hastening along lanes to be there before the shop shuts at midday. This *épicerie* is one of those small family businesses that closes at noon and does not reopen until four in the afternoon. When I arrive it is closed. I bang on the door and call out. No one answers. I wander around back to the area with the woodshed and rap my fist against a glass door. Still no reply. It is only a few minutes after twelve, but the place is as silent as a deserted ship. Infuriated, I pile into the car and hurry back to the farm. Manuel is nowhere to be found. His satchel, which had been ditched on one of the terraces, has also gone. The only sign that tells me he was even here is the hoe, which I find in the flowerbed, slung carelessly across a cluster of now-wilting tiger lilies. No weeding to speak of has been achieved. I call his name several times and peer into the garage but do not find him. He must have disappeared, perhaps driven away by fear of the dog. Lucky is supine on one of the terraces, panting contentedly. Little Ella dozing, her head resting against her companion's stomach. I return to my writing, mightily relieved. The incident has been settled with far less consequence than I had dreaded.

MICHEL IS IN PARIS, and I have been trying unsuccessfully to reach him by phone. Given the extreme nature of our crisis and my natural propensity to worry, I am concerned that something could be wrong. I telephone his office and ask his assistant where he is. She has no idea.

"When did you last see him?" I beg, eager to keep the alarm out of my voice and not panic his team.

"Yesterday morning" is her response.

"What, he hasn't been at the office since . . . is everything all right?"

Isobel, a stable and well-balanced woman, cannot see what I am so concerned about. "He's probably working from his studio," she offers as an explanation. I have been ringing there; no reply. Michel has never installed an answering machine at the little studio where he sleeps when he is in Paris because he guards it as a private space. Endless hours of his days are spent on phones, and he has always claimed to need this oasis of peace. We speak so frequently during the course of the day that this has never been a problem before. However, I am unsettled and ring Isobel again to ask him to call me when he comes in. By evening, I have heard nothing and try his studio once more. Still no reply, and the office have not seen him all day. He has probably been at meetings elsewhere is Isobel's latest explanation.

"You don't think you should go to the studio and break the door down?" I suggest. Clearly, she considers me preposterous. "I work for him," she replies tartly. "I am not in the habit of beating down my boss's door."

"No, no, of course not. Sorry to have troubled you." I replace the receiver, but I know that if all were well, I would have heard from Michel. Something must have happened. If he had been obliged to go away on short notice, he would definitely have telephoned. So what is the problem, and how am I going to reach him?

I am sitting on the terrace, tormented by worry, trying to take heart from the wintry sunset, when unexpectedly René appears. I am overwhelmingly grateful to see him. As is frequently the case, he has come with a little offering, a jar of fig jam, brown and slippery as a seal, made from our own freshly picked figs. From the eight trees on the property, Quashia and I gathered more than a thousand kilos of fruit during late September and early October before he left.

I thank my silver-haired friend and offer him a glass of beer, trying to disguise my present level of anguish. I am in a fix. Quashia has gone, I have no one to look after the dogs and I am thinking, broke or not, that I must go to Paris.

"Wine or beer, whichever is easiest," he says, and settles himself contentedly at the garden table on the upper terrace to enjoy a drink. He likes to do this, René. He has a key to the gate and will occasionally drop by to while away an hour, discourse a little, recount a tale or two and take pleasure from the burnt-orange sunset.

I head down to the fridge in the garage to collect us a beer and a bottle of rosé. To my amazement, the fridge is bare but for a bottle or two of wine; certainly, empty of all beer. Puzzled, I pull out the sole remaining bottle of rosé. I know I am stressed, but I definitely remember buying a case of beer at a local supermarket the previous evening after leaving the *épicerie*, which was out of stock. Given my present stress level, it is possible I have forgotten it somewhere. I try to recollect. The trunk of the car, perhaps? And then my thoughts fall to Manuel, who, with all my concerns about Michel's unexplained disappearance, had gone completely out of mind. The blighter must have made off with all the Stella Artois! I return apologetically to René with wine and a dish of our own olives.

"You look tired," he remarks. "Did you remember to send in that form?"

"What form?"

"For the olives."

Ah, yes, that form. Yes, I reassure him I filled it in, signed it and posted it on to Michel for signing and forwarding to Brussels. It is dealt with.

We raise our glasses and offer the usual French "*à la tienne,*" and sip our drinks.

I am about to ask for his help, to feed the dogs and hold the fort for a few days while I fly to Paris, when a strident trumpeting interrupts me. Amazed, we both turn toward the second plot from where the sound has emanated. "It's a wild boar," I croak.

René shakes his head. "I don't think so."

"What could it be, then?"

"We better take a look."

Leaving our drinks on the table, we set off into a wilderness of grass, brambles and weeds. Due to lack of resources, the second plot has, during the autumn and the earlier torrential rains, transformed back into a gentler version of the wilderness it was when we first discovered the place.

It is a sad spectacle. Lucky and Ella trot at our heels. Lucky is barking wildly, but the peculiar bleating or calling has stopped, and we cannot trace it. René suggests that it may be a distressed animal, trapped.

"In what?" I ask a mite defensively. I am totally opposed to hunting, and when this portion of land was first cut back, I personally saw to it that every hunting trap still buried beneath herbage was ripped out and burned or, if fabricated out of some lethal metal, slung in the trash cans.

It is not too long before we come upon the source of the bellowing. Manuel, though not a single drop of Latin blood runs through his knavish veins, is spread-eagled on the ground, dead to the world beneath our spreading bay tree. Head pillowed on his satchel, he is snoring contentedly. All around him like a spray of stars are our emptied beer bottles.

"*Diable.*" René grins. "Who is he?"

"He was meant to be your assistant for the olive harvest." I laugh and swiftly recount the story of Manuel.

We lift him between us and haul him, dragging him by his heels through the grassy earth, the entire length of the garden to René's Renault shooting brake, where we dump him in the open trunk. His breath is like dragon's fire.

"Let's finish that bottle," suggests René, giggling. "We've earned it, and then we'll return him to his woodshed." This is exactly what we do. During the entire exercise, Manuel never once so much as stirs.

During our little excursion to the *épicerie*, René agrees to hold the fort for me as of the morrow, assuring me that I am not to worry. He delivers me back to the gate. I thank him and begin my climb up the hill. As I do, he calls after me, "Do you want me to look for someone to help with the olives?"

"I'll let you know tomorrow," I answer, too whacked to think about it now.

Up at the house, the telephone is ringing. It is Isobel to say that Michel has been taken ill. I knew it. The dogs have been fed for this evening. I phone René, who is walking in his door, to let him know that I am leaving for the airport and intend to catch the last plane to Paris. I promise to be back as soon as I can.

PARIS IS DAMP AND WINTRY. Streetlights refract and rainbow in the rain. By the time I arrive at the studio, it is after eleven and Michel is in bed, doubled up in pain.

I am shocked by the sight of him but fight back my desire to quiz him about his sickness. I learn that he was taken ill the morning before, during a meeting with his lawyer. His lawyer called in a doctor, friend and specialist, who has taken some tests, sent him home to rest and promised to call again in a day or two, as soon as he has news.

"Why didn't you phone me?" I manage.

"I didn't want to worry you."

I refrain from mentioning that the silence over the past forty hours has nearly driven me around the bend. Instead, I slip into bed beside him, wrap my arms around him and we try to sleep.

The specialist phones at what seems first light. In fact, it's the lowering gray skies. He wants Michel at his clinic before the end of the morning. I feel everything within me tighten.

"Did he say why?"

Michel shakes his head. I insist on going with him, which at first he refuses, but I am adamant. Michel is not a man to ease up on his workload. On the few occasions I have seen him ailing with a common cold or minor health problem, he has ignored it. He refuses to accept or even acknowledge any form of physical incapacity. This is not going to be easy for him. Nor is it for me: I hate hospitals, I am the world's greatest coward when it comes to blood and I can barely stomach the sulphurous and alkaline aromas of unguents, tinctures and disinfectants. Those long, narrow corridors give me the shakes. Supine bodies on trolleys bring nausea and fear to my senses. But I want to be there. I refuse to sit around at the studio all day, chewing my nails.

Even though Michel is insisting on taking the Métro because a taxi is beyond our means, we take a taxi because I insist more vociferously and he is too weak to argue.

The doctor is a youngish, handsome man with a warm reassuring manner. He leads us through to his office and informs Michel that he wants to begin a series of tests right away. Michel is in so much pain—stomach cramps—that he can barely speak. There are many French words, medical terms, that pass me by. I have a dozen questions I want answered but say almost nothing. Michel is led away, and I am left alone in the office.

It is not even six months since I sat at my father's bedside. The images return and I try to drive them away, for they are too terrifying. I stand up and begin to pace, incapable of staying still. I open the door and peer out along a narrow corridor where figures in white flit in and out of opening and closing doors. Many are wearing face masks, carrying clipboards. I have no idea where Michel has been taken. Suddenly, the foreignness of everything hits me, and I begin to shake.

I love this man with every fiber of my being. I could not bear to lose him. Suddenly, I am tormented by pictures of my father, his deathbed and the funeral service. My fear is getting a grip. I must hold this together, I am thinking. And then the doctor returns. To give me an update, put me in the picture.

"I am zo zorree zat I kennot zpeek Engleesh." He smiles. I nod without regarding him because I am ashamed of my desire to weep, because I am terribly afraid and because I feel I am about the most useless partner. If this were a film, if I were playing a role, I would be bearing up: a mountain of controlled energy, stalwart, docile; the rock upon which our relationship is built. Or at the other extreme, roles I am frequently offered these days, the alcoholic who can't hold anything together. As it is, I am neither. Just ordinary and insignificant, lost in the labyrinthine world of another language and a situation over which I have no control and can see no signposts to guide me forward.

The doctor begins to explain to me what they are testing Michel for, but the words are long and incomprehensible and I cannot follow until I recognize one and lock on to it as though I have been slugged—*cancer*.

Have I understood correctly? These days, most of the time, I move between French and English almost as easily as changing my clothes, but there are occasions like now when I panic and the language becomes scrambled. It is as though I am on the outside looking in, a moth fluttering beyond glass intent on reaching the light. Desperate to be sure, I repeat the word once, and then again.

"This is difficult for you, *n'est-ce pas?*"

I nod.

"What I am trying to tell you is that we do not think there is a cancer but we must test, *non?* Come with me."

He leads me down one corridor after another to a vending machine where coffees, teas and various other beverages are on offer. Pulling out a five-franc coin, he asks me how I take my coffee. I cannot remember! So he orders me an *express*. At that very same moment, an aluminum trolley rolling on big black wheels appears from behind a swing door followed by a young, bleached-blonde girl, thin as a wisp, who offers me a choice of croissants, *chocolat au pain* or baguette sandwiches: *jambon* or *fromage*. The doctor sits with me, and we eat breakfast together. And then he leads me to a quiet corner, rests a kind hand on my shoulder and hurries off to work.

The day passes long and slow.

When I am too drained to pray any more, I cheer myself with lists of heavenly moments to keep me company:

Late warm evenings, returning home in evening dress, after film and dinner at the Cannes Festival, to the song of nightingales lyrical beneath a blanket of stars. Dancing to their music on the terrace, arms wrapped tightly around each other, my head on Michel's white silk jacket.

Summer Sundays on our own, floating together naked in the pool, in the world's largest azure-blue rubber ring—a birthday present from me to

Michel—water trickling through our fingers and toes. Heat baking our backs, circling on a cushion of bliss. The taste of chlorine on our lips. White flesh where watches and rings have hidden it from the sun.

Cool white linen sheets bearing the weight of sunburned flesh.

The notes we have secreted in each other's luggage when we were separating, if only for a few days.

Lines from songs we have sung to each other:

> *"You taste so sweet, I could drink a case of you."*

and

> *". . . when you need someone to love*
>
> *Don't go to strangers*
>
> *Lover come to me."*

Airport good-byes and then crushing kisses at the week's end which say how much we missed each other.

How Michel paints every mundane article in striking colors, even the hose rollers—all of them inspired contrasts. Picasso, when he lived close by our farm, was unhappy about an electricity pylon that blighted the view. (We have one, too!) The EDF refused to remove it, so he painted it a rainbow of colors.

A DOOR OPENS. BY NOW it is early evening. The doctor returns. I leap to my feet, piercing his expression in the hope of gleaning news. He does not speak directly, and I fear the worst. My stomach is churning.

"How is he? Where is he?"

"He's five minutes behind me, getting dressed."

All has been discovered. Michel is suffering from a mild form, early stages of, diverticulitis, probably caused and certainly aggravated by stress. The doctor is confident that it can be treated with plenty of rest, no work, an extremely strict diet, no wine and nothing that will aggravate Michel's nervous system. If, after all that has been tried, the condition has not been resolved, then an operation may be required. The best of the news is that Michel does not have to be kept; he can come home now.

During our return journey to the studio, he does not even question the choice of a taxi. He is silent, exhausted by tubes and machines.

Over dinner—a chicken bouillon and Evian—we discuss our predicament. With his usual brand of tenacity, which in this particular situation I would describe as stubbornness, Michel suggests that he will rest over the weekend and go back to work on Monday. I will not hear of it, and we begin to bicker until a stomach cramp reminds us both that he must be kept calm.

The positive news, he tells me, is that the series is out on offer all over the world. With a few healthy sales, we can release the farm. I smile encouragingly, but the battle to keep hold of Appassionata has paled for me now. After all, magical as the place is, we could always find another farm, another property, and begin again. It's the journey together that counts, not the points of departure.

Once upon a time, oh, it seems a long while ago now, I dreamed of a natural haven, of paradise winking down upon a tranquil blue sea. I had pictured friends and family at ease in my Garden of Eden, sharing and at peace, a place where artists worked and lovers loved. But it had been a vague sketch, a dream without lines between the dots, until I met Michel. Then it began to gain wattage, to take on a shape, develop light and shade, rhythm, sinew. Together we have breathed life into those blurred images. Together we have discovered how to live a new life.

Even more, what has blossomed out of those dreams surpasses any bricks or mortar, or even the loveliest of pearly terraced olive groves. Our paradise lies in the depth of our love. What geographical points our traveling takes us no longer matter.

You see, whatever Michel and his dogged determination believe, I suspect that our chances of hanging on to Appassionata are slim. Painful as it is, I am ready for the loss now. Prepared to watch our quirkily dilapidated farm be seized by bankers who cannot begin to calculate the wealth in every silvery leaf, each golden orange, the glittering of early-morning dew drooping in clusters from foliage and richly colored petals. We began this enterprise on a shoestring. Love and tenacity have held it together. We can do it again if we have to. And in the discovery of all this, I have shed skins—driving ambition, materialism, a need to control my life. I am learning to let go and am empowered. My heart has found heart.

CHAPTER THIRTEEN

RETURN

The airport at Nice is closed. I cannot get back. Each day I telephone Charles de Gaulle and am told that the situation has not changed. René is holding the fort, but the olive season is commencing and he has over seven hundred trees to tend. I must return. Michel's health is improving. He works from his little studio in the mornings, then we meander for an hour or so up and down the crooked, cobbled lanes of the Latin Quarter, pausing in the small garden facing Notre-Dame Cathedral before poking about in the musty corners of the English-language bookshop, Shakespeare and Company, until it is time for him to return and put up his feet for the remainder of the day. The pains have subsided. Our last visit to the doctor was very reassuring. If Michel's health continues to improve at this rate, there will be no need for the operation, and before too long, he will be able to return to a more civilized diet. I feel a little quieter about leaving him. In an ideal world, I would stay, but there is work to be done, and in a few more days, he will join me at the farm for a quiet and simple Christmas.

Curiously, frustratingly, the airport remains closed. What is going on? When I finally get through on the telephone, I am informed by a member of the Air France ground staff that the problem is the weather. Yes, but for five days now I have been trying to get a flight. What weather could possibly close an airport in a climate as temperate as ours for such a period of time? She does not know.

I check the weather pages in both *Le Monde* and *Libération*. In both papers, alongside Nice, is a miniature drawing of the sun, beaming at me beatifically. I am baffled. Eventually, I hire a little car and set off with everything we will need for the holidays. Just before my departure, Michel receives a fax to say that the first sale on the series has been made, to Greece. We are over the moon. And how fitting it seems to us both that Greece, mythological land of the olive tree, will allow us to make our first reimbursement to the bank. It buoys me, for the thought of separation never gets easier. These days together have been harmonious and dulcet. Parting, particularly under these conditions, hurts.

I LOVE TO DRIVE LONG distances. The solitude and the passing landscape clear my thoughts. Whenever I am blocked with my writing or have a problem to unravel, I will get in the car and go for a spin. This trip offers me the perfect opportunity to mentally catch up on the time I have been falling behind with my work. I stop for a quick lunch and, to stretch my legs, stroll around the medieval town of Beaune, gazing in the windows of antique shops, before continuing my journey. It is a pleasing drive. The weather throughout the day is crisp and topaz bright. The passing coun-
,tryside is naked but for row upon row of twisted vines, smoking hillsides, frozen runnels of dark earth and occasional sightings of farmers or country folk clad in gloves and scarves and overcoats.

It is somewhere around Montelimar that night falls; early, because we are approaching the shortest days of the year. The sky is clear, a deep wisteria blue, and the stars resplendent. At first I mistake the glaringly bright

light behind me for a car approaching on high beams and feel irritated by
the selfishness of certain drivers. Then I glance in my side mirror again and
look harder. There is no traffic. The great globe of light is the moon. I
slow, move over into the truck lane and, because the road is deserted, pull
up on the hard shoulder.

Everything on earth seems to be illuminated by the lunar glow. I have
never seen the moon this bright, waves of flaxen light on the silent, distant
hillsides. I step out of the car and tilt my head to gaze heavenward. It
seems so close I could caress it or draw it down, cradle it in my arms.
A platinum balloon, a great round scoop of Montelimar nougat. Its proximity is eery, awesome, but it lights my path all the way home.

Journey's end. I cross the bridge and turn into the lane. The familiar-
ity of the approach is gratifying. Here are sweet-scented orange groves and
agave cacti to welcome me. Here, silhouettes of lofty coned cypresses. Here
there is peace. I draw up outside the gates to search for my keys. The
cottage, meant for a caretaker and sadly empty since the departure of
Quashia, is lit up. For a fleeting moment, I think that someone is in there,
and then I see that it is this same extraordinary moon casting beacons of
light across the desolate garden, knee-high in weeds, illuminating it as
though with electricity.

The dogs plunge down the drive to meet me. *Three* of them. Ella,
Lucky and who? No Name? No, the third animal is too small to be No
Name. They yap and bark, panting and frolicking with excitement, following the unknown car the full reach of my ascent. Flanking us are the
olive groves and, at the foot of each tree, our circular sprays of netting.
Ah, it is a joy to be back. I wind down the window and breathe in the
perfumed air. An owl screeches from somewhere in the forest high
above. I step from the car and am instantly bowled over by three pairs
of paws landing against my hips. There is much licking and tail-
wagging happiness. The third fellow is a black and white hound with
long, droopy ears and an even longer piebald body. He is compact and

muscular with legs like a soccer player's. "Who are you, where did you come from?" I ask him, but he backs off shyly and begins to yowl like a country and western singer, which makes me laugh. Before going inside, I walk the terraces for a few minutes, stretching my legs. Twisted galaxies of stars dazzle like tinsel in the moonshine. The world is as clear as broken daylight.

Dare I take it as a sign that our days of darkness are coming to an end? That life will soon be reconciled and polychromed once more?

I AM DEAD TO THE WORLD the following morning, coming to consciousness only when I hear the diesel spit of René's sturdy Renault climbing the drive. His arrival is followed by a chorus of barking dogs. I turn over and glance at the clock. Seven-thirty. Downstairs, I hear the clatter of aluminum dog bowls scraping the ground as they slurp and guzzle greedily. I grab a robe and head out onto the terrace in bare feet, calling as I go. The tiles are cold beneath me. The air is brisk. The day is clear and ominously still. René looks up and waves. "*Bonjour! Tu vas bien?*" I nod, yawn, stretching my sleepy, bed-warm body as I glance out across the sweeping valley to the sea, where white horses are discernible on choppy waves. A sign of wind. Bad weather coming in. "*Tu veux un café?*" I ask him.

He tells me yes and heads to the trunk of his car, drawing out a chainsaw. One of ours. Needed sharpening, he explains.

"By the way," I call as I head back into the house. "Whose dog is that?"

"The hound? He turned up about a week ago, following behind your shepherd. Never leaves her side. I tried to shoo him off, but he's not budged. He's only a puppy."

Coffee mugs in hand, on the terrace by the pool, we study the olive groves. Birds trill and echo in winter song. Overhead, a buzzard tracks and circles.

"Have you looked at the trees?" he asks.

"Briefly, last night. What is it? The *paon*?"

"No, no. I said it would be a bumper crop, but even I underestimated. We'll need help. When's Michel back?"

I explain the news, and he nods thoughtful concern, then asks me to take a walk with him. We leave our cups on one of the garden tables and set off to tour the terraces. The trio of dogs canter at our heels until our new arrival lets out a curious and rather comical baying, then takes off like a streak of lightning and the other two follow.

"He's a proper little hunter, that fellow."

"I wonder where he's come from. I'll have to call the vet and the *refuge*, find out if he's been reported missing."

"Runt of the litter, I'd say. You might be stuck with him."

I laugh, wondering what it is that makes our home such a popular hostel for stray dogs. In spite of our renovations, is it possible that they can sniff the old kennels here? Do scents linger as long as memories?

During my absence, the olives have grown plumper, slightly softer, but remain purply-green. The weight of such a crop is dragging the branches low. A few are brushing the nets. René drops onto his haunches and scans my famous green netting. There is barely an olive in sight. "They are clinging fast to the trees. Not ripening. It's the same everywhere. I don't want the branches to start snapping."

"What's the forecast?" I ask. "It doesn't look too good out at sea."

"I didn't hear. We should harvest some of this fruit. Of course it won't yield the same quantity of oil, being so green, but I have—I don't know, a feeling in my bones."

"What about?"

"Not sure. Never in all my years of *oléiculture* have I known the fruit refuse to ripen like this."

"Could it be the *paon*?"

"It's not only your farm, it's all over."

The hound returns, tail wagging, a dead rabbit hanging limply from his jaws. His front legs are bloodied. I am appalled and want to chide him but what's the use, the little fellow is a hunter. He pants, pleased as Punch with himself. I confiscate the still-warm corpse and carry it to the dustbin while three disappointed mutts stare at me miserably, watching their postbreakfast treat disappear before their eyes. I pretend to be cross with the little fellow, but I cannot help grinning, for what a splendid threesome they make: retriever, shepherd and hound, tails awagging.

René and I agree that he will make a start within a day or two. Ideally, if I can find someone to lend a hand, it would save him some time; or he can try to rope in some of his own cronies, but the problem is they are harvesting elsewhere. I promise to do my best, but thoughts of Manuel stunt my expectations. As René settles in his car, he asks, "You better collect your oranges. My wife makes excellent marmalade, and I'll make you the finest *vin d'orange* you've ever tasted. By the way, did you see on the television that this region is going to be granted an AOC next year? It won't be for the likes of you and me, but it should improve the local oil prices on the national market, and that can't be a bad thing, can it?"

I smile. I have never tasted *vin d'orange*.

"*Diable!* I'll make you bottles of the stuff. You won't forget it!"

An *Appellation d'Origine Contrôlée* for the finest of the olive oils from this region. One or two areas of northern Provence have already been granted this coveted mark of respectability, and certain connoisseurs believe the olives from our coastal strip—particularly the modest *cailletier*, which is the variety we farm—to be the one that produces the most delicious of all oils. I think it would be a rather splendid tag.

AFTER COMBING THE EMPLOYMENT pages of the *Nice Matin*, our local rag, phoning one or two possible candidates, even interviewing one rather pompous ex-military chappie who arrives with a list of rules of what he will and won't do and then, due to his overaggressive demeanor, gets bitten by Lucky (I spend the rest of our farcical interview bandaging his hand

and generally pampering him for fear he will report both us and dog), I give up and put through a call to Quashia in Africa. It takes me several attempts, each time trying to make myself understood in either French or English while at the other end a male voice—*le patron* of *le café*?—replies in Arabic and replaces the receiver.

"How are you?" I ask several hours later, when I eventually touch base with him.

"What's happened?"

"Any chance you could get back? René is inundated with work and—"

"And the olives need harvesting. Yes, I've been thinking about it. I gave you my word. If you need me, I'll come."

"What about your family?"

"I'll be there. Don't you worry about them. Is it urgent?"

"Pretty much. When could you be here?"

"I'll find out about flights tomorrow, or I'll organize a boat ticket. It shouldn't be too hard. All the traffic is going the other way, men returning to their families for Ramadan. Call me Saturday."

We settle on that and linger a while longer, chatting about his life at home in Constantin, news of his ever expanding family. I can hear the background hubbub of the Arab café, that world, so alien to mine, surrounding him. I picture him—where?—leaning up against a counter, occupying the proprietor's one crackly phone line. In the background, well-worn plastic tables and chairs crowded with crease-faced elders, sticks at the ready, drinking minuscule shots of pitch-black coffee, putting the world to rights. Who else, aside from us, I am asking myself, telephones a bar in northern Algeria to book the gardener? I smile; the image amuses me.

"Saturday, then," we agree, and say our good-byes.

"If there are any problems, I'll ring you tomorrow," he shouts as a parting afterthought.

The next day, around one, I am working and hear the phone. As a rule, I would let it ring or let the answering machine get it, but I have a hunch it might be Quashia, which indeed it is.

"*Bonjour.*" My ears are keen to the fact that he is not calling from his local café. The background is silent, a truck or two roaring by, nothing more. Is he in a phone booth in some dusty Arab side street? I fear the worst but try hard not to reveal how desperately I need him to return. "What's the news?"

"I am in Marseille. My train gets me to Cannes at three-seventeen."

"When? Today?" I am speechless. "But how did you . . . ?"

"I took the boat, traveled overnight. I'll see you later."

We say nothing about me meeting him off the train in Cannes. I have no idea if that is what he has in mind, but by quarter to three I am down at the station, sitting in front of an *express* at a café across the street. From a well-chosen seat, in case his train should arrive early, I can keep an eye on all the comings and going of passengers. His TGV is on time, and then I sight him, black Persian wool hat on his head, carrying not even so much as an overnight bag. One split shopping bag with Arabic lettering printed on its side is his sole piece of luggage. He looks exhausted and unshaven. I wave and shout and run to greet him. His warm eyes dance merrily, and he grins his tobacco-toothed grin and we embrace like long-lost family. People look on, some with disapprobation. After all, this is Le Pen country and here am I embracing an Arab workman.

"Here, I brought this for you." He hands me the shopping bag. Inside are swags of fresh, sticky, honey-colored dates clinging fast to skeletal fronds. There must be a thousand of them. I thank him and picture the little pencil box of dried dates my mother used to buy us as a treat at Christmastime. On its lid were colored illustrations of camels trekking a desert. How exotic they seemed to me then.

"My grandson picked them from the garden before we left for the port. He said that next time you and Michel are to come and pick them yourselves."

"We will," I promise.

"My family wants to meet you. We'll go to the desert, take off on a trek."

Arm in arm, we thread our way through the tangle of vehicles, impatient scooters and pedestrians to Michel's car, which is barely more roadworthy than mine was and twice as unmangeable because it is extremely ancient and has no power steering.

"Where's the Quatre L?" he asks. It is pronounced "Katrelle" and is the nickname the French use to fondly describe that most typical of all workman's cars, my sadly missed Renault 4.

I sigh. "It drowned."

"Drowned?'

"A storm in Nice swelled the banks of the river alongside the airport. The place was closed for days. I couldn't get back, and when I went to collect the car, I found the lot had been flooded and all the cars had drowned. How forlorn it looked, the little Quatre L. Swimming in silty mud, dilapidated, tires sinking . . ." I recount, smiling. "The attendant said to me, 'No charge for the parking!'"

Quashia roars with infectious laughter. Climbing the hills, blue smoke billowing from the exhaust, I listen to his tales, at ease in his company. First his journey: at such short notice, there were no bunks to be had. He traveled across the sea sitting on the upper deck, perched against a lifeboat, watching the stars.

"You must be dead."

He grins, and a solitary gold tooth glints his happiness. "Yes, but it's how I like to travel. Not a soul around. Constellations of stars and a full moon to guide us, and the roll of the sea beneath me, wending my way back." I glance toward him. His wrinkled, baked-brown features are animated with the recollection of it, and any guilt I may have felt about having dragged him out of his early retirement disappears instantly, for I understand him well enough to know that he is positively delighted to be back. Quashia is not a man made for retirement. And this corner of France is for him, as it is for us, a spiritual home.

THE FOLLOWING BRIGHT winter's morning, while gathering our first crop of oranges, Quashia begins to talk of his past. He was twelve years old when his father died, leaving behind a wife, three sons and two daughters, but not a penny. Their sole possessions were two barns. It was during the Algerian war with France; the soldiers came, the family fled and the soldiers burned the two barns. Quashia went up into the mountains and began to cut wood which he sold to buy food for his family. His eldest brother left for France, where he found work and each month sent money back to Algeria. With the modest income Quashia acquired from his wood sales, he constructed a small homestead for his family which, even today, he assures me—and will show us when Michel and I go there to visit his family—is still standing, although now abandoned. He had never placed one stone on top of another before, but he built the little house by watching others at their work. Reassured that his family was safely esconced in a home, a roof over their heads at last, he left by boat for Marseille to join his eldest brother here on the coast and to learn the masonry trade in earnest. He had been in France only a week when his brother was run over and killed instantly by an American army jeep, Marines on shore leave driving along the seafront in Cannes. There was no inquest. Quashia returned to *la mairie,* the town hall, day after day begging for justice, but his French was minimal, he was a lad of fifteen and no one listened. The Americans were the liberators here, the Arabs had been the enemy and those living in France were—still are—nothing but a secondary labor force. The matter was never investigated. A couple of years later, his mother received a check for the equivalent of five thousand French francs: a settlement for the death of her eldest son. Strangely, Quashia bears no grudges. He tells the tale of fifty years ago as though recounting the history of another man's life. It is the way of Allah, he says, shrugging. And the healing of time, I am thinking.

THE WEATHER IS STRANGE, unpredictable. Yes, clear and warm, typical for this pre-Christmas season, but unnaturally still. Every now and again, the vegetation shivers a warning. Out at sea, the whitecaps are still on the waves, but no wind comes in. René arrives, and we begin to gather olives. "If they don't fall at the touch, don't force them," he commands. Quashia cuts himself a long sturdy stick to beat the upper branches, but René forbids him.

I leave them to their debate and drive to the airport to collect Michel. First, though, I make a stop at the fruit and vegetable market to buy the fresh food essential to his diet. There I find kiwi fruit on sale, twenty for ten francs. Delicious for breakfast along with mandarins, bananas, grapes and two succulently ripe mangoes flown in overnight from the Dom Tom—*Départements et Territoires d'outre-mer*—islands belonging to the Republic of France; in this instance, the island of Martinique. Michel prepares the best fruit salads known to man. They are a feast not only for the taste buds but also for the eyes. He serves them sliced and arranged in a rainbow of colors and shapes which would rival any decorative plate designed by Picasso in the nearby village of Vallauris. I arrive at the airport to greet him, merrily swinging my shopping bag of exotic fruit and crisp verdant salads, which has cost me in total the princely sum of fifty-seven francs, ninety centimes.

He is looking far more relaxed but has lost a great deal of weight. At first this scares me, and then I remind myself that anyone who has spent a month or more living on chicken broth, mineral water and herb teas would have lost weight. Our Christmas diet will be regulated but not untenable. We hurry to the car park holding hands. It seems an age since he was home, and I want nothing more than to cherish and feed him.

Back at the house, we find a message from René. He delivered our olives to the mill this afternoon, where they were pressed immediately. Six and a half kilos of fruit required for every liter of oil. He sounds very depressed. If the fruit does not ripen and the yield is no greater—a third more fruit for each liter of oil—the season will be a catastrophe for the local farmers.

I understand his deep concern in a way that I might not have a year or more ago. We are not dependent on our farm for our livelihood, but we have known the icy winds of scarcity this autumn, and we are still battling very unfavorable odds. All the hard work and determination in the world cannot change the tides of fate, it seems, whether it's a shortfall in a film budget or a poor harvest. The point is, somehow or other, to outride it. "*Gardez le cap.*"

FUNNY VALENTINE. WITH Chet Baker on the CD player, we stoke up the fire, ditch the dishes from our *pâte à langoustines* in the kitchen and prepare for an early night. From the terrace, while shutting up the shutters, I notice the waves rippling fast across the water. They glint in the soft shadows of night like chain mail, while high up on the hill behind us, an owl screeches raucously and I hear creaking and moaning in the treetops. The weather is spooky tonight, unsettling. It is as though nature were on the move, shifting, readjusting, reclaiming its territory. I think of *Macbeth*, I don't know why. That forest, or wood, rather, creeping closer.

"Stones have been known to move, and trees to speak—"

We curl up in bed together, and I feel grateful not to be alone in the old house tonight.

It is the crashing of pottery on the flat roof right above my head that wakes me, jolting me back to consciousness. Outside, beyond the solid stone walls which encircle us, a storm has whipped up. I lie still, listening. There have been storms here before, many of them, but this is furious. At my side, Michel sleeps on. I creep from the bed and tiptoe across cold tiles to peer from the windows. Beyond, everything is pitch black, which means that the electricity has been cut. Not only ours—whenever there's a storm, our trip switch in the garage cuts off the current as a safety precaution—but way across the hills and valleys. I can make out nothing but black shapes that look like hunched goblins. Out at sea, the horizon is murky with cloud or spumy spray. In the foreground, the tall, pointed cypress trees are bending and swaying, wraithlike beings lost in a frenzied voodoo dance.

I pad back to bed and close my eyes. I want to sleep, but the storm grows. Its force escalates from one minute to the next. It blows relentlessly, screaming, howling like a banshee—the Irish fetcher of the dead. This image terrifies me, and I rise up from the bed again. My heart is beating too fast. I want to wake Michel but decide not to. He needs to rest. The shutters everywhere in the house are slapping against their locks. I fear this wind will rip them from their hinges. I light a candle, which gutters furiously and then dies. I return to the window. I consider the dogs in their stable. They must be petrified. I am. I would go out and fetch them but if I opened the door, it would be whipped from its hinges and carried off. Garden chairs are flying everywhere. A table sinks to the depths of the pool. Things—Lord knows what—are crashing and shattering.

Nothing stands in the way of this untamed wind. Its raging has risen to tempest, even hurricane, force. I press my trembling body against the glass, recalling lines from Eliot's *The Waste Land*:

> *There is not even silence in the mountains*
> *But dry sterile thunder without rain.*

Every tree is bowed over, mastered by the gale. And then a groaning, a destruction, which is akin to a werewolf's howl: a tearing of life to shreds. Freaked, I retreat to bed and curl up like a squirrel. Michel, from somewhere within his slumbering subconscious, must hear my wakenings, because he stirs. "Be still, *chérie*," he whispers and wraps his arms about me, drawing me to him, and I fall in with his breathing, breath for breath, heartbeat for heartbeat, and drift off to sleep, dug into the crook of him, from midnight to dawn.

MORNING COMES. EVENTUALLY. The wind has not abated. We are woken around six by furious thumping: the wind beating at our door. We leap from the bed and rush to shove furniture in front of it. A wooden chest, two chairs and a bookcase which totters in the panic and causes my precious, well-thumbed orange Penguins to slap to the floor. It takes all this to hold the door in place. Peering from the one unshuttered window in my workspace, we see that the landscape has been flattened. The views are wider where trees have been ripped from the ground, crashing everywhere like tin soldiers. But it is not over.

"How will we get to the dogs?" I ask.

"I'll go out by the front door. As soon as I'm out, push the furniture back in place." We haul our wooden pieces into the corridor, and the door begins thumping again. Michel turns the key and opens the door less than an inch. A blast of wind and the pungent scent of pine engulfs us. Felled like a monster, an underwater sea beast with tendrils, is our beautiful blue pine tree. It has swamped the entire length of the upper terrace. There is no exit.

"My God, that must've been what I heard crashing. It must've taken part of our renovated wall and some of the balustrades with it."

We cannot make coffee, as we have no electricity. There is nothing to be done but to wait it out. I return to the window, staring out at this raging, chaotic world. This pertubation of nature. We could go stir-crazy on this windswept hilltop, and what of those poor three dogs? Have they fled in fear? And then I light on a vision that warms my heart.

"Michel, look!" He comes to join me, and together we regard Quashia, hand pressed against his wool hat, mounting the drive, tacking in wide zigzags, blown from one step to the next in a slow, heavy slog as he battles against the weather. When he reaches the summit alongside the pool, in front of the garage, he pauses and stares about, horrified. We cannot see what he sees, but the devastation must be shocking. I beat on the window, but he cannot hear me. And then, as a reflex, he looks up, sees us and beckons. Michel signals our dilemma.

Once the blue pine has been dragged away from the door, we are free to go out. I consider Noah and how it must have been to step from that ark, and I smile, remembering the dove carrying an olive branch that told him the floods were ended. But our wind has not abated. It is calming but is far from done.

Michel lets out the dogs, and then we check out the wreckage. As far as we can tell, we have lost about fourteen trees. All pines, our glorious blue among them, and possibly one oak farther up the hill. At the foot of our recently discovered Italian staircase, a very tall pine has been ripped from the ground. Its roots have dismembered the lower part of the ancient wall, while the massive trunk has smashed and sundered into thick chunks a romantically sequestered stone table and banquette I had placed there. A cypress, one of a dozen that encircles the driveway, has been uprooted and taken with it a dry stone wall and a *opuntia ficus-indica,* a giant prickly-pear cactus. We should be grateful that it has fallen toward the vegetable gardens—mercifully missing them—and not the driveway or our sole means of transport, Michel's decrepit thirty-year-old Mercedes, which would have been flattened in its wake. I am heartbroken to discover that four of my antique Moroccan Barbary pots, a birthday present from Michel, have been smashed to smithereens.

We set to clearing up the devastation of this first night, dragging entire branches of wood pregnant with clusters of pine balls. Small yolk-yellow flowers gild the dusty blue boughs of our favorite pine—the only one of its kind on the estate—while the potent perfume from its seeping, sticky gum pervades the clear, crisp morning. It is as though the dying tree is bleeding, or weeping.

The wind is bitter. It has an arctic bite to it and stings our sweating flesh. As we work, Quashia talks of his youth again, of the long, cold winter after the death of his father, recounting endless journeys marching alone over several days into the mountains, in search of wood for his mother and her brood. There, in the snowy mountains, he gathered and stacked until he had all that he could carry. Then he began the slow march back, like a donkey, his body weighed down with strips of wood, to the humble dwelling where he and his grieving family were hibernating. In my mind's eye, I picture that small dark-skinned Arab youth, his loss and his determination, and I feel honored that through the sharing of his memories he has taken us with him, back half a century to an Arab world that we might never have entered without him.

It reminds me that the Australian aborigines have no words in their language for yesterday or tomorrow.

In return, Michel talks of his childhood in northern Germany not far from the Belgian border, of a countryside ravaged by war, of a father who, before Michel was born, spent several of those war years in a prison camp, though he was an army cook and not a soldier. I am moved when I hear that Anni, Michel's mother, walked from their village all the way to the camp, a trek that took her several days, carrying her firstborn son with her to introduce the boy to his father. And then it is my turn. I spin tales of my English and Irish past. I paint the rolling verdant landscape, the incessant soft rain, salmon fishing down at the coursing, bouldered river with my uncle, the lingering smell of potatoes boiling on the wood stove, losing my sister in a corn field, a maze of gold taller than the both of us, the warm cackling voices of my grandparents' neighbors, as well as illicit friendships with "those Protestant kids" huddled in packs behind the village post office. And I recall the scenes of violence I witnessed. The bloodshed. Family member against family member. Hesitantly, I touch upon those.

And so we pass our day. At sunset, we settle around our big table and drink hot mint tea sweetened with lavender honey, and Michel reminds me that we should be thinking about acquiring our own hives and planting vines. I invite Quashia to stay and eat with us, but he waves his hand and smiles. He has a pot prepared, he says, and bids us good night, wending his way down the drive to the cottage where, because it is situated in a sheltered nook, there has been no damage whatsoever.

I wonder at his solitary existence, but it seems to suit him. Months in Algeria and then other months here with us: his two families.

And now the wind is rising again, but according to the news on the radio—for we have electricity again—it will be less forceful tonight. We are worn out from the physical work of the day but also deeply grateful, because in one of the neighboring villages, the toll this morning was eight dead. At its peak, the wind on this Alpes Maritimes coast reached one hundred and fifty kilometers an hour. The roads are closed, even our little lane. We cannot get our car out to buy food. If we need supplies, we must walk the towpath by the stream to the village. We learn that three million families in France are without electricity and half as many again without telephone. Thousands are without homes, and the death toll is rising.

THE FOLLOWING MORNING, this holocaust of nature is at an end. We step from shuttered darkness out into blindingly bright sunlight and a sky as clear as cut glass. The air still has a frisson of danger; every now and then a branch stirs and shivers a reminder. Bushes and trees have been twisted and split out of all recognition. They will forever bear the imprint of this tempest's passage.

There is so much work to be done.

The hillsides are alive with the whir of chainsaws. I find it a reassuring sound, like the summer song of the cicadas. On neighboring peaks, folk are beginning the work of cutting and stacking the trees torn from the earth and riven. Sawdust floats like snow in the bright clean air. Nature's quiesence today feels almost as alarming as the roaring winds of the past two nights, its quiddity disturbingly manifold.

Michel and I repot the yucca plants lifted from the smashed pots. When we are less up against it, I will need to buy more. We shovel debris, wheeling the barrow backward and forward to the compost and to dozens of small hillocks piled high with stripped branches, ready for burning. I lift the plastic cover off one of the pool skimmer baskets and put my hand in to dig out the fallen leaves and there, to my horror, coiled like a spring, is a snake. My shrieks bring gales of laughter and the perfect opportunity to pause for refreshment. In the devastation, early cyclamen are flowering rich reds and luscious pinks. I come across an uprooted palm, one of a dozen baby ones we had planted which had grown tall, furnished with long prickly fronds. It will not survive.

All day we labor in a garden bathed in seductively warm Christmas sunshine. High above us in a perfect blue sky, the birds are returning. Gulls wheel and pipe lazily, on the lookout for food. In the treetops, tiny, busy birds are chirruping insanely. Their chatter seems so urgent and engaged. What fun to be able to understand, eavesdrop or even partici-pate. And three, no four, even five, cooing turtledoves, settle in the *Magnolia Grandiflora. Les tourterelles*; welcome, timely visitors.

René arrives. He is depressed. Damage to his olive farms everywhere. Trees destroyed. Magnificent, centuries-old *oliviers* split, amputated, fallen. The moon's proximity to the earth, they say, is the cause. Once in a century, it draws so perilously close. What of his crops? Tons of fruits lying on the ground, scattered everywhere. Now the olives will never ripen. We take a tour of our own groves and discover that a pair of our trees, growing along-side each other, have been severed in two by the storms. It is as though a colossus came by with an ax and sliced right through the heart of the trunks, sheer, like a knife through butter. In each case, one half of the tree remains upright, bearing its semiripened fruit, while its twin lies on the ground like a smashed bird, wings limp and broken. Its fruit is still intact but drying up fast, wrinkling toward death. It is a tragedy. We must begin collecting the fallen fruit without delay. Our windblown nets are all over the garden, curled like sleeping caterpillars. Inside, they bear the fruit that had fallen to the ground before the storms.

Elsewhere, the fruit has been blown hither and thither and needs to be collected by hand from the earth. The four of us, baskets at our sides, pass the sunny afternoon on our hands and knees. Gathering the wind-blown fruit is a slow and painstaking task. All my nails crack and break as my fingers root between the grass shoots and dig into the earth to lift out the buried olives. Every drupe is collected individually. Many of them have already begun to wrinkle or, worse, rot.

Later, we relax with several glasses of rich, ruby-red *vino* from Chianti—not for Quashia, who accepts only water *citronné* with sliced lemon off our own tree. As the sun sets behind distant hills, the view is as clear as shined windows, and dusk falls. All at once, the sky grows gentian with bold, untidy streaks of orange, brilliant as a ripe Jaffa from Seville. It must have been raining somewhere along the coast, for a rainbow appears and straddles the calm sea. This earth made out of chaos is settling back into peace.

THE FOLLOWING AFTERNOON, Manuel turns up. He happened to be passing, he says, though there is no reason on God's earth to ever pass this way. He staggers the length of the hilly drive, spluttering and perspiring, shakes our hands enthusiastically and asks after a spot of work. "A bit of tidying after the wind?" Our answer is a most emphatic *no!* to which he shrugs amicably and, as he turns to go, remarks on how very much he enjoyed his time working for us!

THE NEW YEAR COMES and passes tranquilly. The olives are ripening at last; each day we watch the shift in colors as they turn from green toward violet, then a luscious grape purple and onward to deep succulent black. They are plump, fleshed out with oil, and and there is a packet of them, or as the French would say, *un vrai pacquet!* Christophe greets us at the mill with a dramatically sullen expression. This year is a tragedy, he repeats over and over while shaking his shaggy hangdog head. He peers into one of our brimming baskets, picks up a fruit or two and pulls that Provençal face which could mean one of many things. In this case, *Pas mal, pas mal.* Michel needs to make some phone calls, so he and I take off for a coffee and leave René to oversee the pressing. When we return, the pair of them are as gleeful as children. René grabs Michel by the arm and asks anxiously, "You did mail that form, didn't you?"

Michel is confused. "Which form?"

Christophes pushes forward impatiently. "I gave René a form for you to register yourselves as *oléiculteurs.* Did you or did you not fill it in and send it to Brussels?" He is bawling like a madman while Michel responds with a composed "*Mais oui, pourquoi?*"

Christophe sighs a dramatic sigh of relief. We are puzzled by the intensity of his concern. "Your farm is the first this year," he goes on to explain in a more reasonable manner, "to produce oil at less than four kilos a liter. And what is more, the quality is exceptional." And with that he yells for wine. His young son, the miller, obliges. René is pouring glasses. Their ebullient mood is contagious. The wife is called down to the mill floor, as well as the brawny chap who shovels the olives into the chute and whom I have never seen without a cigarette clued to his lips; also the youngest son, who is responsible for the quality of the *tapénade;* even a customer or two is roped in to celebrate what they are all but claiming is the future of the local olive industry.

Everyone congregates in a grand circle while, in the background, noisy machines belch and deliver. More glasses are poured, cookies flavored with essence of orange are offered. This is a real fête, and all in our honor, it seems.

"Any week now," Christophe bellows, "the inspectors from the AOC will be arriving. How could I admit that not a single farm in the vicinity is producing oil at anything less than six kilos a liter? And even that is of average quality. I would be disgraced. All my new equipment, transported from Italy to comply with Brussels, bah, it would count for nothing. *Rien! Rien du tout!* We, this region, would be a laughingstock. Dismissed! *Nul! Zero!*" By now he is roaring at the top of his very forceful voice. It must be because he spends his life battling against this thundersome machinery, I am thinking. His red cheeks are shiny with exertion and proclamation while his long-faced audience hangs on his every word. This could be a rally. "*Mais, vous, mes chers amis*"—Here, wineglass in hand, he points at us, while René, flushed and proud, smiles on benignly as though we were his children—"have proved that this area is worthy of the honor. *A la vôtre!*" And all glasses are raised to us!

Back at the house, a fax awaits us from Michel's production office in Paris. It tells us that the Greek money has arrived, and with it details, pages of news of a dozen or more other sales. Dollars are finally en route to the bank.

We should whoop and dance, open bottles of champagne, pour them over ourselves, yell and jump for joy. That is how I have imagined this moment over and over in my mind, and prayed for it. But we don't. We stand quietly, reams of floppy fax paper in Michel's hands, and smile at each other.

"Looks as though we're going to make it," he whispers.

"Looks like it." I smile.

And so we can be confident that, in the fullness of time, the debt will be cleared entirely. We will not lose our farm. Not this time. Our crazy little ramshackle farm, which boasts herb and vegetable gardens but still no kitchen, where the walls continue to flake and chunks of plaster still occasionally fall on our heads, which now, thanks to Christophe and René and the work of dear, loyal Quashia, looks set to be awarded an AOC status for the quality of its olive oil. How did this all happen? We never intended to be farmers!

The girls, *les belles filles,* are arriving later this evening. Tomorrow we will party. We are taking them to Menton, where a street festival in celebration of the lemon is to take place, *La fête des citronniers*. Menton, the Franco-Italian border town where every garden is gilt with sweetly scented citrus fruit, and where every hot-blooded Latin lover will be ogling our two teenage beauties and not giving a damn for the tons of lemons and oranges adorning the floats—which, by the way, have been imported from Spain!

SPRING IS RETURNING. Baby geckos scuttle out from behind the shutters. A red fox sits in the sun on one of the upper terraces, among the wild irises which deck the dry stone walls. A beetlelike insect trundles over a rose-pink wild garlic flower. Today his carapace is a deep, iridiscent bottle green. In a month or two, he will be bracken brown. The almonds are in palest bloom once more. The lizards who spent the winter holed up in a million fissures in the walls are zipping to and fro, shy as ever. Shiny lime-green leaves are breaking out everywhere. Orange blossom scents the air. I pause and gaze upon our ruin, bathed in flaxen stalks of dappled sunlight. Budding Judas trees, peaches and figs encircle it, and I know I woke up in a poem. Soon, there will be heavenly purple and white lilacs, pear and cherry blossom, and apple blossom on the trees in the little orchard I am creating in memory of my dear much-missed father.

Yet another year is unfolding, flush with romance and exploration. And while I am musing on where to place a sundial, Michel comes running toward me, smiling and healthy. News of another sale has just come in. An important market, rich in dollars, a small percentage of which can go to the bank.

"Yes!" I whoop. "Yes! I was considering a sundial. I have always fancied a garden with an antique stone sundial."

"You are such a romantic, *chérie*."

We chatter on about the projects we might begin when we return from our travels, of the baby olive trees we want to plant. Michel sees beehives and vine on the hillsides. I picture myself atop a tractor trundling up and down the terraces, mounds of *fumier de mouton* behind me to feed our sapling trees.

Arm in arm, we hike the terraces, three loyal dogs at our heels—including our comical hound who answers to the name Bassett. We are searching out the first spiky tulip shoots when unexpectedly, from the radio on our balustraded balcony, I hear, "I'll be with you in apple blossom time," and I am reminded that love is timeless and regenerative. There is no beginning or end. All things are changing; nothing dies. And like the wind, love leaves its imprints everywhere.